INDO-NEPAL TRADE RELATIONS

INDO-NEPAL TRADE RELATIONS 1846 TO 1947

Vijay Kumar Tiwary

GYAN

Indo-Nepal Trade Relations : 1846 to 1947

ISBN: 978-81-212-1134-5

Published in 2013 in India by
Gyan Publishing House
23, Main Ansari Road, Darya Ganj
New Delhi-110002
Phones : 23282060, 23261060
Fax : 011-23285914
E-mail: books@gyanbooks.com
Website: www.gyanbooks.com

Laser Type Setting by: Rudra Computer Graphics, Delhi
Printed at : Chawla Offset Printers, Delhi

Contents

Foreword

Among the South Asian countries, Nepal, a landlocked country, presents fascinating case study of a small underdeveloped country, which is largely dependent on India for its trade and transit facilities. The impact of the trade relations between India and Nepal during 1846–1947 is an important aspect to study the developments during the period of a century. Such a study will help us to understand the problems and prospects of Indo–Nepal trade relations in a better way. Needless to say, there are a few good studies and published works on the subject.

The present book on the **"Indo-Nepal Trade Relations 1846 to 1947"** is based on the doctoral dissertation submitted by Mr Vijay Kumar Tiwary, to the Department of History, Ranchi University, Ranchi. The work is based on the archival records and a number of primary works, offering a fresh analysis of some of these records for the first time. It has also been pointed out in this book that how the Nepali Regime was always suspicious of the intentions of the British policies and measures, which is clear from this Nepali proverb– "The tradesman brings the Bible, the Bible brings the bayonet". This can also be said about the British, who too suspected the intentions of the Nepali Regime.

Trade led to the growth of a number of towns and markets in Nepal, like Nepalganj, Birganj, Biratnagar etc. Newar merchants from Kathmandu and merchants from India flocked to the places. Rivers and rivulets flowing from Nepal into the bordering districts of Purnea, Bhagalpur, Darbhanga, Muzaffarpur, Champaran, Gorakhpur, Basti, Pilibhit, etc. also served as important channels for trade between the two countries.

Dr Tiwary discusses the impact of the trade relations between the two countries on the social and political life, which also had an impact on the political and cultural relations between the two countries. There were fluctuations in the trade relations between the two countries on account of the changing politics and attitude of the two governments, which were often dictated by the motives of personal gains and occasionally by their whims and caprices.

This book by Dr Tiwary should be of interest to both Indian and Nepalese readers. It will be apparent that the interests of both the countries are inextricably the same. Geography and history have destined India and Nepal to work together for their common development and welfare.

31st December 2011
Delhi-110007

Prof S.Z.H. Jafri
Department of History
University of Delhi

Preface

Foreign trade plays an important role in a country's economic development. All the South Asian countries are developing countries. Among them, Nepal presents fascinating case study of a small underdeveloped country. It is entirely dependent on India for its trade and transit facilities because it is a landlocked country surrounded by India from three sides and inaccessible mountains on northern frontier with Tibet.

Since ancient time, trade and commerce has been proved as the twin pillars of human civilization. Commerce not only radiates cultures but also fulfils the needs of human civilization; where trade works as a facilitator. Indo-Nepal trade relation is as old as history. The book Indo-Nepal Trade Relations: 1846 to 1947 is essentially based on my Ph.D Thesis, submitted to the Department of History, Ranchi University, Ranchi.

Perhaps there is no other example in the world in the sense that the border inhabitants of any two countries are as much tied together as of India and Nepal. Inhabitants of the both sides of the border speak similar languages like Maithily, Bhojpuri, Awadhi or Hindi. The ways of living, culture, and appearances of these inhabitants are almost identical. Another factor for this is that the long border between these two countries has remained open. There is no requirement for passport or any other legal document for entering into each other's territory. Therefore, thousands of people of each country cross the border every day and enter into the territory of the other country for social, economic, cultural and other interactive activities. Nature binds India and Nepal together. The bond that unites the people of the two countries is ancient. It is estimated that the trade relation Between India and Nepal had existed more than five hundred years before the Christian era.

Numerous books have been written on Indo–Nepal relations. However they are insufficient in the sense that they have simply recorded the history of Indo–Nepalese relations pertaining to politics, cultures, traditions and values, but trade and economic relation have not received adequate attention from historians. The present book is an analytical exercise in this regard and is perhaps for the first time that an advanced research study of this type covers the whole period of Rana regime, has been undertaken. During this period, the pattern of Nepal's trade relation with British India underwent a significant change. I have tried to incorporate all these changes and carefully analysed the circumstances under which it all took place.

The British occupation of India was a classical example of imperialism gradually spreading its tentacles over the entire life of an ancient, culture. Beginning as a trading company in the era of mercantilism, the British dragged India through the period of industrial capitalism and ultimately converted it into the exporter of raw materials and importer of finished goods in the age of finance capitalism.

It was this colonial India whose trade relations with Nepal (1858–1947) which is examined in this book. Secure in their mountainous vastness and extremely proud of their freedom in their land-locked country, the Nepalese were very suspicious of the motives of the British. They had already had a foretaste of British diplomacy arid armed might in 1816. They had also perceived how India had been pulverised in course of the preceding hundred years morally as well as materially. They had seen the Nepalese proverb– "The tradesman brings the Bible, the Bible brings the bayonet".

I also throw light on the nature of Indo–Nepalese trade. Nepal had a very favourable balance of trade. Her exports were forest products, food grains (particularly rice) etc. The imports to Nepal were salt, sugar, tobacco, cloth and luxury goods for the use of the Rana family and the elite groups.

An important feature of the Indo–Nepalese trade was slave traffic. Slavery had been abolished in colonial India long back but it was still legal in Nepal. Poor people from North India sold their children in Nepal to officials and the gentry. The author has also discussed the impact of Nepal's trade relation with colonial India on the social and political life of the country.

Nepal encouraged trade and commerce and observed a growth of towns and markets on the Nepalese side as well, for example, Nepalganj, Birganj, Biratnagar etc. Newar merchants from Kathmandu and Muslim merchants from India flocked to the places. Rivers and rivulets flowing from Nepal into the bordering districts of Purnea, Bhagalpur, Darbhanga, Muzaffarpur, Champaran, Gorakhpur, Basti, Pilibhit, etc. also served as waterways and encouraged trade between the two countries. But the Nepalese were not enthusiastic in developing the roads which would break the hills. The Nepalese were opposed to it as they regarded the hills as their natural fortifications. But this did not seriously hamper the Indo-Nepalese Trade.

I have made an in-depth study of the commercial transactions between Nepal and British India around which political and cultural relations between the two countries revolved. There were fluctuations in trade relations between the two countries, but these ups and downs were not always due to economic and commercial causes and often non-commercial factors interceded to alter its pattern and the commodities involved in transactions between the two countries.

The methodology used in the present book is historical and analytical. The data for this study have been collected from various sources. Apart from the published data, some primary data have also been used. These data were collected during the field work in Nepal as well as in India.

The Indo -Nepal trade relations entered into a critical phase with the opening of the Indian railways in the districts bordering Nepal. The railways had great impact upon the markets and trade centres in the border districts of Nepal and India. The branch lines of the railways were entered to the convenient points at the frontier with view to encourage and to facilitate trade with Nepal. Several new lines pushed up the growth of trade or affected its traditional passage.

The Indo-Nepal trade witnessed significant expansion and ramifications and it served as a pivot around which political, cultural and other relations between Nepal and the British India revolved. The British Government in India adopted free trade policy with Nepal.

To sum up it can be said that Indo-Nepal trade relations had a continuous and steady progress throughout the entire period. The period between 1858 to 1950 may be regarded as the Golden age in Nepal's commercial annals because trade flourished throughout the entire Rana period. Since Nepal's trade with India has a significant impact on her economic development, I have highlighted all the important aspects of Indo-Nepal trade and have given some concrete suggestions and an action plan to promote and strengthen trade relations between these two countries.

For the sake of convenience this book has been divided into seven chapters. The first chapter of this book deals with historical background of Indo- Nepal trade relations starting from ancient times to the end of East India Company's rule in 1857. Indo–Nepal trade relations are as old as history. Nature binds India and Nepal together. The bond that unites the people of these two countries are ancient and varied chronicles are replete with miscellany of events that determined the ebb and tide of Indo–Nepalese trade relations through the ages. It has been estimated that the trade relation between India and Nepal had existed more than five hundred years before the Christian era.

In the regime of Jang Bahadur Rana, the Nepalese adopted the policy of cooperation with the British. But he was also extremely sincere in developing commercial intercourse with British merchants for engaging with Tibet. The Government of Nepal felt that if Tibetans and Englishmen meet and trade with each other, our traders could lose their employment and the result would not be good. The traders were prohibited to deal directly with the English. But the Indo-Nepal trade continued to grow rapidly with the passage of time.

The second chapter of this book presents a detailed account of trade routes between India and Nepal (Road transport, Railways, water ways and other means of communication) which helped in carrying on bilateral trade. Under this chapter various means of conveyance such as ponies, pack animals and coolies have also been dealt with. This chapter also covers items of trade through various concerned routes as well as particular means of conveyance used. Government trade policies of British India and Nepal have also been discussed.

The chapter third discusses the changes in commercial policy, commercial taxes levied in India and Nepal, and its impact on Indo-Nepal trade during the period under review. Before 1848, Nepal was hesitant to the British in India but in the latter period, Ranas had followed the policy of cooperation with British India. During the period of Jang Bahadur, Nepal's relations with British India became friendly and Gorkha troops were offered services in the British Army.

The restricted commercial relations between India and Nepal thus gradually became intense as the Ranas earned a lot due to the monopoly trade with British India. The Rana rulers never accepted to introduce British proposal for unrestricted or less restricted trade.Commercial policy adopted by different Rana rulers has been discussed in detail in the third chapter.

The Chapter fourth is intended to discuss about value and volume of Indo-Nepal Trade, changes in composition of export and import along with entreport trade during the period under review and important trade registration centres. This chapter also focuses on illicit trade such as smuggling, slave trade, and so on. The volume of trade between India and Nepal was always on a larger scale due to easily accessible trade routes. Major imports of Nepal from India constituted of cotton piece goods, sugar, salt and provisions-grains, some forest products like timber, ginger, *tejpat,* ghee, honey, fruits, hides and elephants and a few manufactures like cutlery and war like instruments, metal utensils and a superior quality indigenous paper.

Nepalese import from and export to India fluctuated over the years in all the commodities. According to the then collector of Bhagalpur, the difference in the rates of duty had very little impact on the fluctuation of volume of trade. The volume of trade was dependent more on the demand for different commodities in different places. Major trends regarding volume of trade observed in the period has been studied in the fourth chapter.

The fifth chapter critically examines the currency system viz. evolution of currency, barter system, real currency system, and so on. It also focuses on credit and payment of debt along with prices of commodities. It was in the fifth century A.D. that the first Nepalese coins were found. Since then several kings issued coins. Most of these coins bear images of animals and other religious symbols like those of Indian coins. However, the denomination and dates of these coins are not known.

Barter was common along the Indo-Nepal border. It was mostly restricted to the exchange of local products such as dried fish, coarse sugar, earthen vessels and more rarely tobacco, cotton and salt for vegetables, rice and ghee.

There was ample evidence to suggest that credit transactions were made to a limited extent, and in such cases the rate of interest was usually 2 anna (per rupee). Thus, lower transactions could fetch only low rate of interest. The Deputy Commissioner of Gonda informed that on credit transactions to very limited extent, interest charged was also few bucks. The Deputy Commissioner did not find any evidence in which Nepalese traders appeared in the Indian Courts regarding the enforcement of the payment of debt in the British and Nepalese courts. It means the enforcement was very simple and people were very helpful and straight forward without fear. They obeyed their promises and took the obligatory route.

If we look at the rise in the prices during the reign of Jang Bahadur (1846-77), it rose to 200 per cent. The price rose rapidly and it doubled in every ten years. After the death of Jang Bahadur, the price index increased by 381 per cent within 15 years. The prices of all the articles rose rapidly but in the case of rice and paddy it was more rapid.

The sixth chapter provides information regarding different trading centers, markets and centres of production etc. It also deals with various major trading regions in India and Nepal. Various big and small trade centres were developed along the long open border provinces of Bengal, Tirhut, Bihar, North-Western Provinces and Oudh through which trade traffic passed. The most important among them were Birganj, Raxaul, Sitamarhi, Purnea, Madhubani, Nepalganj, Bhutwal, Hanumannagar and Dhulabari. These markets were of two types: permanent and temporary. *Mandi* or *Golas* constituted permanent markets and *Hat-Bazars* were temporary markets.

Finally, the seventh Chapter analyses the impact of Indo – Nepal trade and concluding remarks. Among all the countries with which India carried overland trade, Nepal occupied a leading position. Nepal's share in Bengal's total foreign overland trade was about 92 per cent. Unlike trade with other neighbouring South – East Asian countries, India's trade relations with Nepal were confined to the movement of goods only and did not involve the movement of other factors sof production like labour, capital and enterprise. This chapter provides suggestions to strengthen trade relations between these two countries and gives an action plan to promote bilateral trade.

This book will certainly prove to be a landmark in the field of interdisciplinary research in the areas of history, political science, commerce and economics. I wish this book will have a wide circulation and lend a hand in understanding the trade relations between the two countries in the light of facts presented by me.

Dr. Vijay Kumar Tiwary

Acknowledgements

This book has been made possible as a result of the whole hearted support and generous cooperation from many persons. In this regard, I am sincerely grateful to Prof. S.Z.H. Jafri, Department of History, University of Delhi, who in spite of innumerable engagements was my constant mentor. It was only his able guidence and supervision that it has become possible for me to complete this work.

I would like to express my deep sense of gratitude to Dr. P.K. Shukla, former Member Secretary, the Indian Council of Historical Research, New Delhi, Prof. Ratneshwar Mishra, former HOD, L.N. Mithila University, Darbhanga, Dr. S.M. Mishra, Deputy Director (Research) ICHR, Prof. H. S. Pandey, Former HOD, Deptt. of History, Ranchi University, Ranchi. I had the privilege of having long and useful rounds of discussions with them on various aspects of the present book. In spite of their busy schedule they were kind enough to extend all possible help to me throughout the entire period of this endeavour.

I also acknowledge with thanks the help and support extended to me during my work by D.N. Tripathi, former Chairman, the Indian Council of Historical Research, New Delhi, Prof K.K. Nag, former Vice-Chancellor, Ranchi University, Ranchi, Prof D.N. Jha, former HOD, Deptt. of History, University of Delhi, Prof Panchanand Mishra, former HOD, TM Bhagalpur University, Bhagalpur. Prof G.D. Jha, Retired Prof. IIPA, New Delhi, Prof Bimla prasad, Retired Prof, Centre of Historical Studies, JNU, Prof Iswari Prasad, Retired Prof JNU. Prof I.K. Choudhary, HOD, History Deptt, Ranchi University, Ranchi, Dr Madhukar Shayam, Editor, Anusandhanika, Research Journal of Social Sciences and Humanities, Dr Ajit Kumar Mahto, Reader, Ranchi University, Ranchi.

I also thank various teachers of University of Delhi, Ranchi and other University, who have helped me with encouragement, inspiration and comments. They have all along been a great source of inspiration to me in my endeavour to explore this work.

The inspiration and friendly attitude of Dr. Anil Kumar, Lecturer, Deptt. of History, Ranchi College, Ranchi, at every stage of this work is duly appreciated. It is indeed a great pleasure to be associated with him. I thank him for his support and useful discussion throughout the project work. I also owe a great deal to my friends, Dr. Maheshwar Dwivedi, Ahmed Hasan, Assistant Professor, Hindu College, University of Delhi, Dr. Amarnath Jha, Assistant Professor, Sharadhanand College, University of Delhi, Delhi, Sudhir Kumar, Arisudan Tiwari, Scientist, DRDO, Devesh Nath Tripathi, Scientist, DRDO, Bhaskar Priydarshy, Mr. Rajeev Nayan, Sumit Kumar and many others for helping me in several ways in the completion of this work. I would also like to thank my brothers Mr. Manoj Kumar Tiwary, Mr. Anil Kumar Tiwary, Sanjay Kumar Tiwary and Vinod Kumar Tiwary who have assisted me at all moments of need.

I would also like to thank Gyan Publishing House, New Delhi, its editorial and production team for their careful processing of the manuscript.

I would also like to record my gratitude to the authorities and official personnel of Nepalese embassy, Delhi for their kind co-operation and extension of support in the collection of relevant data and information. I would like to express my deep sense of appreciation and gratitude to the then Ambassadar of Nepal to India, Delhi, H.E Sri Karan Dwaja Adhikari, for his kind help.

During the course of the work I also visited several ministries and institutions in India as well as in Nepal, like the National Archives of India, New Delhi, the ministry of commerce, ministry of finance, His Majesty's Government of Nepal, etc. I am grateful to the officials of these institutions.

I had free access to almost all the libraries in Delhi. Special mention may be made to the Ratan Tata Library, Central Library, University of Delhi, Library of the Indian Council of World Affairs, Sapru House, New Delhi, The British Council Library, New Delhi, Library of Indian Council of Historical Research, New Delhi, ICSSR. Library, New Delhi; IIPA. Library, New Delhi; JNU. Library, New Delhi; Nehru Memorial Museum and Library, New Delhi etc. I am grateful to the respective officials for allowing me to consult the relevant material available.

I express my profound gratitude to my parents for their sacrifice, constant support, understanding and encouragement extended.

Last but not the least, I am highly indebted to my wife, Sudha, for her moral support. I am extremely thankful to my beloved daughter Smriti and son Prateek for their co-operation, which I got from them in the completion of my book.

Finally, I thank all individuals who were directly or indirectly involved in the successful completion of the book. This book is the product of collective efforts of many people who gave me valuable information, inputs, comments and suggestions. However, I remain solely responsible for any errors and shortcomings. Constructive comments and suggestions from the readers will be highly appreciated.

January 28, 2012 **Vijay Kumar Tiwary**

Abbreviations

Admn	:	Administration
Ag	:	Agriculture
App	:	Appendix
Dist	:	District
Ed	:	Editor
Edn	:	Edition
EIC	:	East India Company
Enclo	:	Enclosures
FASC	:	Fascicale
FN	:	Foot Note
Gaz	:	Gazetteers
Govt	:	Government
Ibid	:	Ibidem (in the same place)
i.e.	:	id est (that is)
ICHR	:	Indian Council of Historical Research
J.A.S.B.	:	Journal of Asiatic Society of Bengal
J.B.R.S.	:	Journal of Bihar Research Society
J.H.R.	:	Journal of Historical Research (Ranchi) University)
J.R.A.S.	:	Journal of the Royal Asiatic Society
J.B.O.R.S	:	Journal of Bihar and Orissa Research Society
L	:	50 (in Roman numerals)
L.R.	:	Land Revenue
MSS	:	Manuscripts or Handwritten
N.A.I.	:	National Archives of India, New Delhi
n.d.	:	Not date
Offg	:	Officiating
Op.cit.	:	Opero citato (in the work cited)
P	:	Page

Proceed	:	Proceedings
Pt	:	Part
Pub	:	Published
Reg. No.	:	Register Number
Rev	:	Reverend
Rep	:	Report
S.C.R.O	:	State Central Record Office, Bihar, Patna
U.P.	:	Uttar Pradesh
Vol	:	Volume
V.S.	:	Vikram Samvat
W.B.S.A	:	West Bengal State Archives, Calcutta

1

Introduction and General Background

1.1 Introduction

The people of Nepal belong to one of the oriental races and have close resemblance with Indian race. Neither Nepalese nor Indian are a pure race because of the continuous migration process. The main reason for the intermingling of Indian and Nepalese people was the growth of trade and commerce between the two countries. The trade proved to be the major vehicle through which the people interacted amongst each other. The language dialect, cultural intermixing, all had prompted to forge a closer link between the people of these two separate entities. But the Nepalese were very conscious of their purity of thought, action and interaction with other people. They watched the changes in the Indian sub continent.

Except occasional strains, India's relations with Nepal are rooted in antiquity. Even today Nepal is heavily dependent on India for almost all its requirements. In 1975, 93 per cent of Nepal's total trade was confined to India.[1] Regarding geo- political importance of Nepal, Landon writes, " it is not surprising that Nepal may be called upon to control the destinies of India itself.[2] Jawaharlal Nehru, the first Prime Minister of India once said, "our interest in the internal condition of Nepal has become still more acute and personal in view of the developments across our borders in China and Tibet."[3]

When Britishers defeated the last Indian combined forces in 1757 and captured Indian territory, the Nepalese became suspicious and the British trade policy was then on looked upon with suspicion in Nepal. There is a Nepalese proverb "The tradesman brings the Bible, the Bible brings the bayonet" which is highly critical of the English culture. Even the Malla Kings of the Kathmandu Valley did not have healthy opinion about the British. But war against the Gorkha by the Malla king, compelled Jaya Prakash, the last

Malla king, to seek for British help[4]. Both the rulers fought for controlling the revenue derived from the Tibetan trade[5]. The Gorkha soldiers under the leadership of Prithvi Narayan Shah blocked the Kathmandu valley. The impact of the blockage was felt by both the Kathmandu valley and the East India Company. The British reacted to this loss by military intervention favouring Jaya Prakash.[6]

The well organised Prithvi Nayayan Shah defeated the East India Company soldiers under the command of Captain Kinlock at Sindhuli in 1767.[7] Then onwards until the mid-nineteeth century, relationship between Nepal and the company remained unsettled and got entangled with misunderstanding, hostilities and enmity.[8] Prithvi Narayan Shah was very clever in assessing the British motive and never engaged with them with an intention of friendship.

But British lost no time in altering their motive and changed their policy suitable to Nepalese. A mission led by James Logan was sent to strengthen the tie up to improve the trade relations[9] with Nepal. He had two letters with him for Prithvi Narayan Shah where the Governor Verelst was apologetic for the act of supporting Jaya Prakash Malla against Gorkha. But Prithvi Narayan Shah paid no heed. The Logan Mission thus failed to achieve its purpose.[10]

The Nepalese were totally against the British in spite of several policies of reconciliation. However, the Britishers sent envoys and residents and proposed treaties and agreements, but Nepal remained firm in its approach towards the British. Soon thereafter the British also closed the markets of Nepal completely. They were not allowed due to these acts of British the lucrative markets of Tibet as well.[11]

But the Nepalese responded to this activity by adopting a direct confrontation with the British in 1814.[12] Nepal was badly defeated in the war and had to lose a vast area of its territory. Altogether some forty thousand square miles were given up[13]. As per peace agreement, a permanent resident was kept in the Nepal Durbar but the Nepalese remained suspicious of the Resident's presence. This was an opportunity for the British people to garner the Nepalese support for commercial interaction between the two countries.[14] Thus, after the war of 1814-16, Nepal not only remained a mere centre for their commercial transaction, but also acquired an important position in their strategic calculations[15]. For the first time, the British realised that peace with Nepal should be maintained at any cost and any hostility might cause a heavy loss for them.[16]

Jang Bahadur Rana came to power in 1846 which heralded a new phase in Indo-Nepal relations. The British got a stable, friendly and co-operative Government. Jang Bahadur mobilized his army to protect the British during the dark days of the great mutiny in Nepal, in 1857[17]. Nepal was rewarded with the entire area of lowlands between the river Kali and Rapti and the lowlands, between the river Rapti and the district of Gorakhpur. These areas were in possession of Nepal prior to the year 1815, and were ceded to the British government by Article III of the treaty concluded at Sugauli on 2 Dec. in that year.[18]

The policy of Jang Bahadur towards British was friendly and co-operative but not very warm and intimate. He dealt with Britishers cleverly and never allowed them to interact commercially, socially or politically.[19] But sccurring more favour for enhanced trade and commerce was the main irritant between British and Nepalese Government. However, the Indo-Nepal trade showed a new high. This can be proved from the data then available of import and export. Annual value of trade which appropriately trebled in the fifty years from 1835 trebled again by the end of the century with the value of Nepalese exports being doubled to that of imports.[20] However, the World War I (1914 –18) impacted the Indo-Nepalese trade due to decline caused by the large scale violence and stoppage of the cargo world over and thus the volume of trade declined considerably as a result[21].

The British had a great respect for the fighting quality and determination of the Gorkha soldiers. One more factor was that Tibet and China were no danger to the security of the British Indian empire. Even the alien Government of India did not feel the necessity of controlling Nepal. On the other hand, the Rana rulers of Nepal supported the British cause in India from time to time until they left India in 1947.[22]

From 1945 to 1947 the British were an important factor in Nepal's relations with Tibet. They preserved peace between them and mediated in their frequent disputes. The British Government did not openly ask the Rana Government of Nepal to have no relations with the Chinese republic[23], although they made it amply clear that the relations had better not have any political content.[24]

The Indian leaders, from the very beginning,were critical of the 'forward policy 'of the British Government. Jawaharlal Nehru opposed the British policy and denied that India had any security problem. He further said that Security problems vis- a – vis China could be solved by having a friendly attitude towards that country.[25]

With the establishment of People's Republic of China in 1949 and the independence of India in 1947 the Ranas in Nepal who ruled the kingdom for 104 years found themselves under the weight of changing time. The Royal takeover of the country in 1950 with Indian assistance marked a new era in economic thinking. The above treaties reflected India's interest in her political and economic security.[26]

1.2 Factors Affecting Indo-Nepal Trade Relations

1.2.1 Geographical Factors:

The geographical situation has prompted Indian policy makers to accord important considerations to all the Himalayan Kingdoms in general and Nepal in particular, in formulating India's foreign policy. Geography is considered as the corner stone of international politics.

The Kingdom of Nepal lies in the middle sector of the Indo-Tibetan border, on the southern slopes of the mid-Himalayas. It is situated between the latitudes 26″20′ and 30° 10′N and the longitudes 80° 15′ and 88° 15′ E. In the north, Nepal's border lies along the Himalayan watershed and forms a natural border between the Tibetan region of China and Nepal. Its southern border lies more than five hundred miles along the Gangetic plains of India.[27] Nepal's international boundary touches Indian states of Sikkim, West Bengal, Bihar, Uttar Pradesh and Uttaranchal on east, south and west. There is a very long border approximately 1,753 km. between India and Nepal.

The security of India in the north depends on Nepal. If Nepal succumbs, India's security will be imperiled. The policy makers as well as the people of India at large, have been led to believe that the natural line of India's defence lies on the northern frontier of Nepal.[28]

The Terai region of Nepal which is contiguous to the Indian border was once considered as an important barrier between the two countries due to the prevalence of impenetrable forests and swamps. But with the clearance of these dense forests and the swamps, the situation has changed. Terai region can now be easily crossed. Thus, there are no natural barriers between the two and both the countries are easily accessible to each other.[29] The line of long and open border between India and Nepal, having all the "characteristics found along the US-Canada border", witnesses constant crisscross of people, goods, currencies and ideas.[30]

In the north of India, Nepal is a narrow strip of land. Except passing through the Indian territory, Nepal has no easy outlet to the outside world because it is blocked from three other sides by the Himalayans. Being a land-locked country (the nearest sea coast being over 1125 km from its border) also accounts for her close economic links with India.

The east–west communication is very difficult in Nepal because the mountain ranges run east-west and the rivers run from the north to the south. North -south communication is easier than the east-west communication. Many parts of Nepal are more easily accessible from India than from Kathmandu. "Most of the overland routes from Kathmandu to outlying districts in the east and the west go across the Indian border, through Indian territory, and back into Nepal.[31] As a consequence, it makes the political and administrative unification of Nepal difficult and "it has also made Nepal's economy dependent on that of India".[32]

Nepal is equally important for India as most of the rivers of the Gangetic plains have their origin in Nepal. Nepal is also a big market for Indian goods, both finished and unfinished. The Terai inhabitants in Nepal have close economic, social and cultural relations with the people across the border in India because it is almost similar to the region across the border is cropping and resettlement pattern.

India and Nepal are interdependent in many respects because, geographically, Nepal is a part of the Indian subcontinent. Co-operation between them is essential for mutual benefit. Thus, India's trade with Nepal is greatly influenced by the geographical factor. While the small size of Nepal compels her to resort to internatioanl trade, geographical position limits her options to trade with countries other than India.[33]

1.2.2 Historical Background

Nature binds India and Nepal together. The bonds that unite the people of the two countries are ancient and varied chronicles are replete with miscellany of events that determind the ebb and tide of Indo-Nepalese relations through the ages.[34] Sylvain Levi has drawn our attention to some references in *Mulasarvastivada Vinaya Samgraha* which point out that Gautam Buddha reached Nepal accompanied by, among others, a group of merchants from India [35]

Kautilya's *Arthashastra,* describes the popularity of Nepalese blanket called 'Bhingise,' and (Apasarak) in the Indian market[36]. Thus, it can be calculated that the commercial relations between Nepal and India had existed more than five hundred years before the Christian era.[37] According to Przyluski, since Mauryan age there was a northern route from Pataliputra to Nepal via Vaisali and Sravasti. The Greek accounts mention the Royal road running from North-west frontier to Pataliputra, about 1,300 miles in length, "the Grand Trunk Road of ancient India." There were offshoots from this main road like the Nepal route connecting India with China and Tibet and the Assam route leading to China and South-east Asia.[38]

According to *Tang Annual* the merchants were numerous and cultivators rare in Nepal. In the first half of the seventh century A.D., Nepal was the centre of transit trade between India and Tibet. That, trade was in most developed stage in those days.[39] The land in Nepal was of hilly nature and there was a little prospect of a large scale agricultural development. The Sharthabaha Ratnasangha, a prominent merchant community in the fifth century Nepal, guided the land for its trade with outside world. A famous merchant named Guhyamitra sent caravans to distant places within Nepal and to neighbouring countries.The caravan drivers were enterprising, courageous and resourceful. They controlled export and import of the country. They had contacts in Tibet and India through their agents.[40]

Famous Chinese pilgrim, Hieun Tsang who visited India and was present in north Bihar in 637 A.D., heard that trade was in very flourishing condition in Nepal.[41] He described that Nepal exported corn, fruits, copper and yak to Tibet and India. On the basis of Hieun Tsang's testimony, it has been concluded that red copper of Nepal "might have' crept into the workshops of Bihar through the Nepal-Vaisali-Pataliputra route."[42]

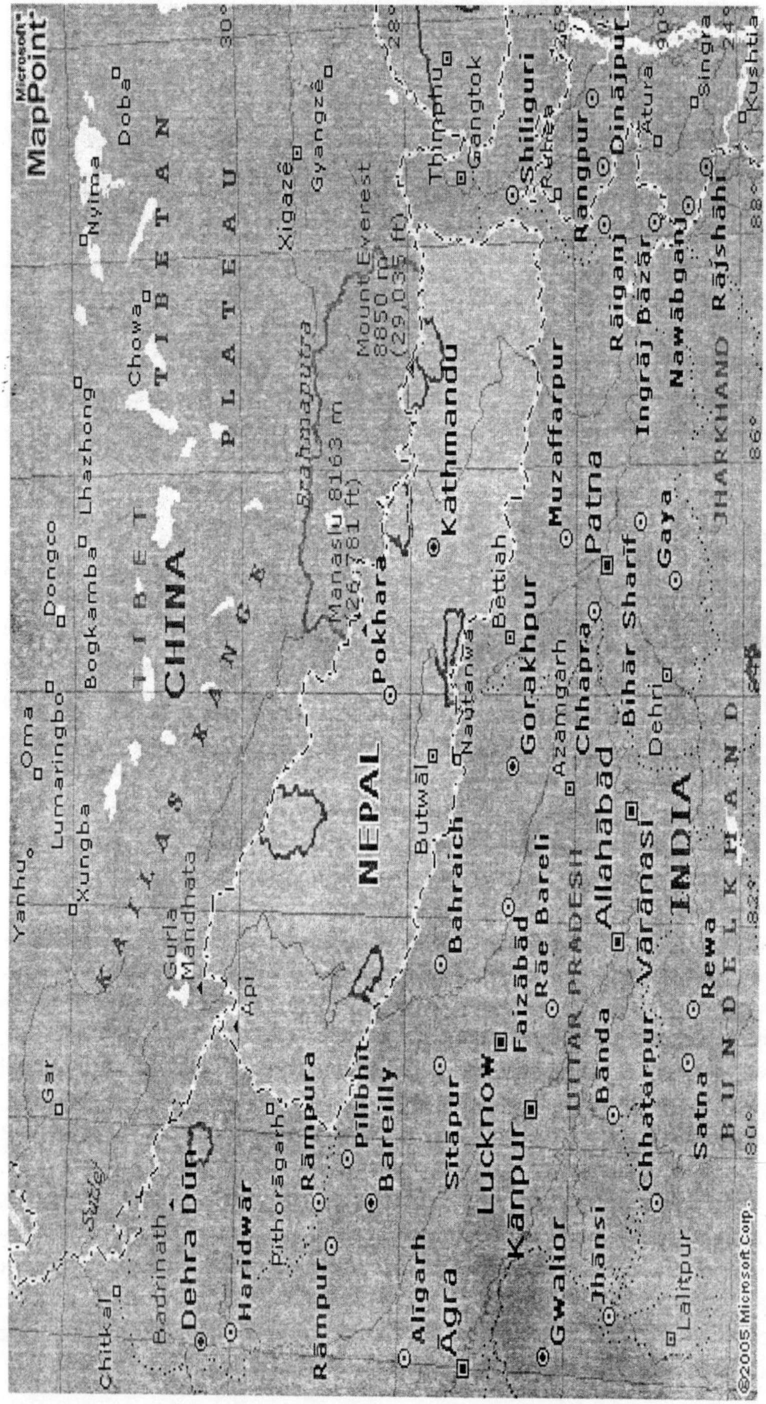

INDIA (Uttrakhand, UP, Bihar, West Bengal, Sikkim) and Nepal

Nepal got yak, from the areas bordering Tibet which formed an important article of commerce. The itinerary merchants always carried the merchandise and handed over to marketing organisations stationed in Tibet and India. These organisations did the disposal business amongst the consumers[43].

A famous ruler named, Amsuvarma inspired the people for the development of trade. He took steps for liberalisation of trade. He allowed exports of articles such as iron, fly whisk, musk and copper utensils. His liberalised policy started from the people of Tistung village. The merchants went without obstruction through the customs with these articles for sale and returned with other articles purchased in. They were exempted from paying customs duty.[44]

In the medieval period also there is a mention of the flourishing Indo-Nepal trade[45]. Some of the Indian texts[46] record the prosperity of this bilateral trade. The Christian missionaries and various travellers have also praised the growth of Nepalese trade. *Yukitkalpataru* of Bhoja mentioned that Nepal's reputation in sword-making industry was quite well-known in India.[47] *Rasaratnasamuchchaya* also testified the superior quality of copper brought to India from Nepal. *Dhatumanjari,* a part of the *Rudrayamalatantra,* probably a work composed not earlier than the fourteenth century, also mentioned the location of copper in Nepal.[48]

In 1583, a Christian traveller of England, Ralph Fitch, who visited India during Akbar's reign heard that there was regular commercial transaction between India and Tibet through the passes of Nepal and Bhutan.[49] An American merchant, named Hovhannes Joughayetsi, wrote in the closing decades of the seventeenth century that the merchants from India, who carried on trade with Nepal and Tibet used to derive net profits ranging from 70 to 130 per cent from their transaction[50]. Another merchant, named Father Horace Della Penna who visited Nepal in the early 18th century also mentioned some of the articles of export and import with Nepal. The flow of trade was free and unrestricted which was protected by the Newar Kings of Nepal.[51]

Father Ippolito Desideri who arrived in Kathmandu in December 1721 on his way back from Lhasa, wrote that there was much commerce in Nepal. Many merchants from India and Tibet used to come for trade there and merchants from Kashmir also had offices and shops in town[52]. The merchants of India and Nepal had good commercial contacts with each other. They had commercial depots in each other's country. In Patna and Benares there were depots made by the Nepalese dealers. In the trade marts of Kathmandu, Bhaktapur and Patan, some Muslim and Kashmiri merchants of India lived permanently. In pre-Plassey days, borax, procured from Patna, was one of the important items of Dutch commerce in Bengal.[53] Borax was brought from Nepal to Patna. It was estimated that from 800 to 1200 maunds of borax was imported annually.[54] Bengal was the market for Nepalese saffron [55] and Nepal was a market for Bengal salt.[56] According to a Christian missionary,

Padre Tranquille, Muslim merchants from Bettiah (Bihar) carried some articles like bangles for trade from Tanahu in the western Nepal.[57]

Nepal was a trade link between India and China till the eighteenth century. Herbs, salt, yak-tail, silver and gold, were imported to Nepal from Tibet. Nepal imported spices, salt, embroidery and silk clothes from India. India got herbs, hides, wooden frame and certain metal goods from Nepal.[58]

The Gorkha conquest of Kathmandu valley in 1769 diminished Indo-Nepal trade[59]. The East India Company tried to revive the trade relations after gaining control over Bengal. Representatives and trade missions were sent to Nepalese Darbars. Warren Hastings sent several missions to Tibet and Bhutan to explore the possibilities of Indo-Tibet trade through Nepal[60]. In 1784, the Foxcroft Mission, with letters to the King of Nepal was sent for opening the trade relations[61]. Prithvi Narayan Shah was not unfriendly towards the British.[62] But he always followed a policy to keep them at length[63]. He always understood the nature of foreign merchants and he also came to know the exploitative nature of the foreign rulers.

It was certain to cause impoverishment of the poor people of Nepal. He directed the people not to use foreign goods and prohibited the British clothes in Nepal and ordered the poor weavers to be trained to make clothes of the same nature as was from the British people. He ordered to provide samples of the same fabrics. His main intention was not to send the money outside the country. Every effort was directed for export of the articles from Nepal for gaining maximum foreign currency into Nepal.[64]

However, Nepal signed a commercial treaty with the East India Company on March 1792. The treaty provided unrestricted trade between the two countries subject only to a reciprocal collection of customs duties at 2.5% ad-valorem.[65] The main aim was to capture the Tibetan market[66] but it was silent on all trade matters with that country.[67] Nepal government did not allow the passage of goods from the Nepalese territory[68]. On the other hand, they followed the policy of furthering the exports to India and thus prevented all efforts of the British Government to put its articles to Tibet through its territory.

The permission for export of wax, timber and other indigenous commodities to India was granted often even on a tax free basis. Local officials who tried to prevent them from purchasing such commodities were scolded and ordered not to create trouble with the agents of English merchants on minor matters.[69]

The treaty of 1792 was never actually implemented. The urgency of British assistance against China in the Sino-Nepal War of 1790–92 led the Nepalese Government to sign the first trade treaty with India. The Chinese army withdrew from the actual position in November 1792[70] and thus the utility of the treaty ended here. The trade mission led by Captain Kirkpatrick returned from Nepal after failure of treaty with Nepal related to China. But the commercial contacts between Nepal and India were not entirely cut off. Sir

John Shore, the Governor General of India, sent another mission headed by Maulg Abdul Qadir to Nepal in 1795. He tried to show off the liberal British nature of sending an Indian Muslim rather than of a Firanghee.[71] Abdul Qadir only communicated some valuable information regarding their trade possibilities. It was emphasized that Nepalese remained the vital link between India and Tibet. He estimated the total annual exports from the company territories to Nepal at 4 or 5 lakhs.[72] He also suggested the linking up of the Tibetan and China trade through Nepal. As per information, the British interaction with Nepal was restricted to occasional friendly letters.[73]

In 1801, Nepal Government tried to revive the treaty of 1792, which became only insignificant. The Nepalese Government signed another treaty with East India Company. Captain W.O. Knox was sent to Nepal as the first British resident at Kathmandu.[74] He was given the task of providing information regarding the demand to European and Indian manufactures in the Nepal's market and possibilities of opening trade with Tibet and Bhutan either directly or through Nepal. But he soon realized the futility of his efforts and returned on 19 March 1803 without achieving his goal.[75]

Despite several efforts to secure the market of Tibet, the Nepalese Government lost faith in winning the Nepalese. Continuous efforts of Nepal Government to secure the Tibeten market upset the Nepalese people. Therefore they declared war against Nepal in 1814–16. This war ended the military activity of Gorkhali forever. A treaty named Treaty of Sugauli was signed in 1816. Gardiner, the British resident in Nepal, was directed to follow a policy of winning the Nepalese and not to create any trouble in the trade relations.[76]

In fact for twenty years there was no good relations between the two Governments.[77] The event took different turns when Bhimsen Thapa, who was called as the Iron man of Nepal,[78] was deposed from Prime Ministership in 1837[79]. Thus, the British Resident Brain Houghton Hodgson got a chance.

He exploited the situation of Nepal in his favour. But he wanted to tackle the situation tactfully. He argued, "I would reach the Government through the people, commerce should be my instrument[80]. He wrote a voluminous thesis in which he discussed the possibilities of improving Indo-Nepal trade. According to his report there were 52 natives and 34 Indian merchants in Kathmandu valley engaged in foreign commerce. The trading capital of natives was to be not less than Rs. 50,18,000 and of merchants not less than Rs. 2,305,000. In 1831 the total value of exports was lacs of rupees. Hodgson was a strong supporter of opening of Indo-Tibetan trade through Nepal.[81]

Dr. A. Cambwell, an officiating assistant to the resident from 1830 to 1838 also favoured the necessity for developing Indo-Nepal trade[82]. Hodgson presented a draft of proposed treaty with Nepal to the Governor General's consideration in march 1835 . Dr. Cambwell proposed the duty of 4 per cent Kuldar ad valorem for the products and manufactured goods of Nepal and Tibet. He also proposed a rate of 5 per cent Mahendera Malli rupees ad-valorem according to the market rate of exchange in Nepal. It was suggested that there should be 17 Customs Houses in India and 21 in Nepal[83]. Duty was to be levied once and at one of the specified places in India.[84] But this paltry rate of 4 per cent was not acceptable as it was very low compared to the normal rate of import duties levied by the British in India.[85]

The Govt. of India exempted all the Nepalese goods from certain duties in June 1836. It expressed the hope that the Nepalese Government should follow suit but it denied to do so.[86] The articles 4 and 5 of the engagement with British India signed on 6 November 1839 mentions British subjects shall hereafter be regarded as own subjects in regard to access to the courts of law and the causes of the former shall be heard and decided without denial or delay according to the usages of Nepal. The engagement further, reads that the Nepal government engages that an authentic statement of all the duties leviable in Nepal shall be delivered to the resident and that hereafter unauthorized imports not entered in this list shall not be loaded on British subject.[87]

During the regime of Jang Bahadur Rana, the Nepalese adopted the policy of co-operation with the British. But he was also extremely sincere in developing commercial intercourse with British merchants for engaging with Tibet. The Government of Nepal felt that if Tibetans and *firangi's* (Englishmen) meet and trade with each other, our *riots* and traders could lose their employment and the result will not be good[88]. The traders were prohibited to deal directly with the English. But in course of time the Indo-Nepal trade continued to grow rapidly with the passage of time.[89]

1.2.3 Nepal: Center for Entreport Trade

Nepal was a place for entreport trade till the opening of Gangtok route in 1904.[90] India's trade with China and Tibet was conducted through Tibet. Entreport trade between South Asia and Central Asia was carried through Kashmir, Kathmandu, Patna and Lhasa route which were connected by Kuti and Kerong passes. Nepalese traders acted as brokers between the traders from Tibet and India.[91] Katmandu became the place of trans–Himalayan trade because it was close to Kuti and Kerong passes. Nepal imported brocades, raw wool, yak tails, musk, herbs, bullion etc., from Tibet to re-export to India.[92]

After the opening of direct Gyantse and Chumbi Valley routes between Tibet and British India, Nepal's importance as a place for entreport trade declined. The trade traffics passing through Tatapani–Rasua and Kuti-Kerong were diverted to Kalimpong. [93]

1.2.4 Cultural Factor

On the cultural front, India and Nepal have intimate age-old ties. Nepal's cultural and social customs resemble those in India. Nepal is the only Hindu state in the world while in India, majority of the people follow Hinduism. Hinduism has been, and continues to be, perhaps the strongest common bond between India and Nepal.[94] Indian people visit Nepal since ancient time for a *darshan* of Pashupatinath, Muktinath, Janakpur Dham and Lumbini and Nepalese people too aspire for pilgrims to Varanasi, Badrinath and Gaya.[95] Hindus of Nepal are followers of Vishnu, Siva, Rama, Krishna etc., and also worship Parbati, Durga and Kali-Bhairavi.

The king of Nepal had privilege to mount the "Throne of Diamonds" at the Puri-Jagannath temple for worship, whereas the owner of that temple too is denied this privilege. The king is also entitled to worship in the centrum of the Rameshwar temple.

Since Shah dynasty, Nepal had been having a link with Rajasthan. Rajputs from Rajasthan had to move northwards and settle in Nepal. They unified Nepal and ruled over the whole of Nepal. The Shah dynasty has become the symbol of Nepal's national unity. [96] Socially also India and Nepal bear striking similarities. The cart structure in Nepal is almost similar to those of India.[97] A large number of families of both the countries are intermarrying. Matrimonial ties have been an important factor of continued relations between India and Nepal.

Notes and References

1. Bidhyut, R, Chalisey, Nepal's outlet to the sea, Article in Coronation Souvenir of Centre for Nepal Foreign Affairs Studies, Kathmandu, p. 99.
2. Perceval, Landon, *Nepal,* Vol. I, Constable & Co., London, 1928, pp.XII-XIII, Kathmandu.
3. Jawaharlal Nehru, India's Foreign Policy, selected Speeches, September 1940–April 1961, New Delhi, Publication Division, Govt. of India, 1961. p. 436.
4. S.K. Jha, British Indias Policy Towards Nepal, *Journal of Bihar Research Society,* Vol. IX Pts 1-4, p. 194.
5. Ludwig F. S. J. Stiller, A Note on Himalayan Trade, *Journal of Tribhuvan University, Kirtipur, Nepal*, Vol. VII, November 1972, No. 1, p. 7.
6. *Ibid.* p. 8.
7. Rishikesh Shaha, *An Introduction to Nepal*, Ratna Pustak Bhandar, Kathmandu, 1975, p. 91.
8. Asad Husain, *British India's Relations with the Kingdom of Nepal 1857-1947*, George Allen and Unwin Ltd., London, 1971, p. 32.
9. *Ibid.*
10. S.K. Jha, *op.cit.*
11. Ludwig F. S. J. Stiller, *The Rise of the House of Gorkha: A Study in the Unification of Nepal* 1768-1816, Manjusri Publication, New Delhi, 1973, p. 327.
12. *Ibid,* p. 367.

13. John Premble, The Invasion of Nepal, Oxford University press Oxford, 1971, p. 86.
14. S.K. Jha, *op. cit.*, p. 205.
15. *Ibid.*
16. *Ibid.*
17. Rishikesh Shaha, *Essays in the Practice of Government in Nepal*, Manohar Publisher, Delhi, 1982, pp. 79-81.
18. See Appendix II.
19. Asad Husain, *op. cit.*, p. 109.
20. Piers Blaike, *Nepal in Crisis; Growth and Stagnation at the Periphery,* John Cameron, *Oxford University* Press, Delhi, 1980, p. 37. David Seddon,
21. N. P. Banskota, *Indo-Nepal Trade and Economic Relations,* B.R. Publishing Corporation, Delhi, 1981, p. 24.
22. Asad Husain, *British India's Relations with the Kingdom of Nepal,* 1857-1947, George Allien and unwin Ltd, London, 1970, p. 64.
23. Kanchanmoy Majumdar, *Anglo-Nepalese Relations In the Nineteenth Century,* Firma K.L. mukhopadhyay, Calcutta, 1973, p. 11.
24. *Ibid,* p. 11.
25. *Jawaharlal Nehru, India and the World,* Allien and Unwin, London, 1936, pp. 251-53.
26. See Appendix VII.
27. Karan and W.M. Jenkins, *Nepal: A cultural and physical Geography* Lexington, University of Kentucky Press, 1960. U.N. Malla, *A Brief Geography of Nepal*, Kathmandu, Department of Publicity. H.M.G. 1667; Dr. Harka Gurung, Geographical Setting, (ed.) Nepal; A Profile, Kathmandu, Nepal Council of Applied Economic Research, 1970; Toni Hagen, *Nepal. The Kingdom in the Himalayas*, Berne. Kummerly Grey, 1961.
28. G.P. Bhattacharjee, India and the Politics of Modern Nepal, The Minerva Associates, Calcutta, 1970, p. 4.
29. So far as the boundaries between India and Nepal are concerned, they were fixed with a high degree of 'precision in a series of bilateral agreements between the Government of Nepal and the British Government of India in 1860 and 1875 and the surveys undertaken in accordance with their terms. However, independent India has no formal boundary treaty with Nepal, See: C. U. Aitchison, *A Collections, of Engagements, Treaties and; Sunnvds* New Delhi, Central Publishing Branch, 1929; S. C. Bajpai. *The Northern Frontier of India,* Bombay, Allied, 1970.
30. P. P. Karan and W.M. Jenkins, the *Himalayan Kingdom Bhutan, Sikkim and Nepal*, D.Van Nostrand Company, INC, Princeton, 1963, p. 19.
31. *Ibid.* p.108.
32. Ramakant, *Nepal–China and India*, Abhinav Publication, New Delhi, 1976, p. 33.

33. Dr. Vijaya Katti, *Indo-Nepal Trade: Post–WTO Dimension,* Kalinga Publication, Delhi, 2001, p. 14.
34. Jahar Sen, *Indo–Nepal trade in the Nineteenth Century*, Firma KLM Private Limited, Calcutta, 1977, p. 15.
35. Sylvain Levi, *Le Nepal,* Paris, 1905, Vol. III, pp. 181-85. In fact, Gautam Buddha never visited Nepal. One of the Buddha's disciples, Anand had travelled to Nepal and was warned by the Lord about risks involved in the journey. See, D.R. Regmi, *Ancient Nepal* Firma, K.L. Mukhopadhyay, Third Edition Calcutta, 1969, p. 59.
36. Kangle (11, p. 119) translated the passage of Kautilya's text as follows "The black bhingisi, made out of a collection of eight woven strands (and) the apsarak which keeps of rain that is woollen cloth from Nepal." Cited in Ibid, *Inscriptions of Ancient Nepal.* New Delhi, p. 19.
37. Balchandra Sharma, *Nepal Ka Aitihasik Rup Rekha,* Banaras, 1976, pp. 71-72.
38. Haripada Chakravarty, *Trade and Commerce in Ancient India.* (C.100B.C, C. 650 A.D.) Calcutta 1966, pp. 23, 26, 182, 184.
39. D.R. Regmi. *op. cit.* p. 262.
40. *Ibid,* p. 263.
41. *Ibid,* Inscription of Ancient Nepal, p. 19.
42. Haripada Chakravarty, *op. cit.* p. 254.
43. *Ibid, Ancient Nepal* p. 262.
44. *Ibid.*
45. Roughly extending one thousand years from the middle of the eighth century to that of the eighteenth century.
46. Yuktikalpataru of Bhoja mentions that sword making industry of Nepal was quite well known in India. *Rasaratnasamuchchaya* describes the superior quality of copper brought to India from Nepal. *Dhatumanjari*, a part of *Rudrayamalatantra*, mentions the location of copper found in Nepal. See, B. P. Majumdar. *The Socio-Economic History of Northern India:* Calcutta, 1960, pp. 199-201.
47. B.P. Majumdar, *The Socio-Economic History of Northern India*, Calcutta, 1960, p. 199.
48. *Ibid*, p. 201.
49. Clement R. Markham, *Narrative of the Mission of George Bogle to Tibet and of Journey of Thomas Manning*. Trumbes & Co *(IInd edition)* London, 1876, pp. i - iv.
50. Levon Khaceikian, "The Ledger of the Merchant Hovhannes Joughayetsi." *Journal of Asiatic Society.* Calcutta, 1966, Vol. VIII No. 3. pp. 153-86.
51. Clement R. Markham, *op. cit.* p. IX.
52. Filippo De Fillippi (ed.) *An Account of Tibet: The Travel of Ippolito Desideri of Pirtcrea S.J. 1712-1727.* London, 1973, pp. 317-18.
53. N.K. Sinha, *The Economic History of Bengal*, Firma K.L. M. Pvt. Ltd., Calcutta, 1956, Vol. I, p. 57.

54. *Ibid.*
55. N.K, Sinha, *The Economic History of Bengal*, Calcutta, 1970, Vol. III, p. 46.
56. K.K. Datta, *Survey of India's Social and Economic Condition in the Eighteenth Century* 1707-1813, Calcutta, 1961, P.47.
N.K. Sinha, "Administrative, Economic, Social History 1787-1793", *History of Bengal,* University of Calcutta, 1967, p.115.
57. D.R. Regmi, *Modern Nepal,* Firma K.L. Mukhopadhyay, Calcutta, 1960, p. 34.
58. *Ibid, Ancient and Medieval Nepal,* Kathmandu, 1952, p. 176.
59. Leo E. Rose, *Nepal Strategy for Survival,* Oxford University Press, Bombay, 1971, p. 25.
60. George Bogle mission of 1774 to 1779. Turner 1783, Purangir Gossain 1785 to Tibet and Hamilton mission to Blutak in 1775, were planned by Warren Hastings. See, Jahar Sen, *Indo-Nepal Trade in the Nineteenth Century.* Firma K.L.M. Pvt. Ltd. Calcutta, 1977, p. 20.
61. K.C. Chaudhuri, *Anglo-Nepalese Relations from the Earliest Times of the British Rule in India Till the Gorkha War,* Modern Book Agency Pvt. Ltd., Calcutta, 1960, pp. 59-60.
62. When Raja Chait Singh of the State of Bejaygarh revolted against the Company, Prithvi Narayan Shah came to the latter's aid. But before the Nepalese army arrived, Bejaygarh was captured. Asad Husain, *op. cit.* p. 33.
63. *Ibid.*
64. Ludwig F.S. J. Stiller, *Prithvi Narayan Shah in the light of Dibya Upadesh.* Kathmandu, 1968, p. 18.
65. See Appendix - I
66. M.C. Regmi, *A Study in Nepali Economic History,* Manjusri Publishing House, New Delhi, 1978, p. 148.
67. Jahar, Sen, *op. cit.,* p. 22.
68. M.C. Regmi, *op. cit.,* p. 149.
69. *Ibid.*
70. *Ibid.*
71. Asad Hussain, *op. cit.* p. 34.
72. K.C. Chaudhari , *op. cit.* pp. 90-91.
73. C.U. Aitchison, *op. cit.* p. 44.
74. *Ibid.*
75. B.D. Sanwal, *Nepal and the East India Company,* Asia Publishing House, Bombay, 1965, p. 112.
76. Asad Husain, *op. cit.* p. 40.
77. Kanchanmoy Mojumdar, *Anglo-Nepalese Relations In the Nineteenth Century,* Firma K.L. Mukhopadhyay, Calcutta, 1973, p. 6.
78. Chittaranjan Nepali, "General Bhimsen Thapa ka Tatkalin Nepal", Kathmandu, (2013 V. S.), 1956, p. 111.

79. Baburam Acharya, "Rajendra Vikram Shah Ka Shasan" *Purnima.* Vol. 27. Kathmandu, 1977, p. 174.
80. Foreign Consultant, 12 June 1834 No. 140. Cited in M. S. Jain, *The Emergence of New Aristocracy in Nepal,* Sri Ram Mehra, Agra, 1973, Fn. p. 9.
81. B. H. Hodgson, *Essay on the Languages, Literature and Religion of Nepal and Tibet,* London, 1874, Reprint. Manjusri Publishing House, New Delhi, 1972, p. 92.
82. A. Campbell, *Notes on the Agriculture and Rural Economy oj the Valley of Nepal,* Kathmandu, 1837.
83. W. W. Hunter , *Life of Brain Haughton Hodgson British Resident in the Court of Nepal,* John Murray, London, 1896. pp. 141-42.
84. N. K. Sinha, *The Economic History of Bengal.,* Firma K.L.M. Pvt. Ltd., Calcutta, 1970, Vol. Ill, p. 53.
85. Ramakant, *Indo-Nepalese Relations 1816-1877,* S. Chand & Co., Delhi, 1968, p. 125.
86. H. Ambrose Oldfield, *Sketches from Nepal,* W. H. Allen, London, 1880, Delhi (reprinted). p. 281, C. U.Aitchison, *A Collection of Treaties, Engagements, and Sunnuds, Relating to India and Neighbouring Countries.* Vol. II, Calcutta: Printed by G. A. Savielle and P.M. Cranenburgh, Bengal Printing Company Limited, 1863. p. 83.
87. C.U. Aitçhison, *op. cit.,* pp. 212-13.
88. Shankarman Rajvamsi, *Sahkalin Aitihasik Chittipatra Sangraha* (A Collection of Historical Documents of the Shah period), Department of Archaeology, Kathmandu, Vol. I 2023 V. S. (1966), p. 33.
89. D.R. Regmi, *op. cit.* p. 153.
90. N.P. Banskota, "Indo Nepalese Trade and Economic Relations" Ratna Pustak Bhandar, Kathmandu, 1974, pp. 186-187
91. K.C. Choudhary, *Anglo-Nepalese Relation from the earliest times of the British rule in India till the Gurkha war,* Modern Book Agency Private Limited, Calcutta, 1960.
92. *Reporting India,* 1976, (ed.), G. G. Mir Chandani, Abhinav Publication, New Delhi, 1977, p. 99.
93. B.P. Shreshtha, *An Introduction to Nepalese Economy,* Ratna Pustak Bhandar, Kathmandu, 1974, p. 174.
94. Shriman Narayan, *India and Nepal: An Exercise in Open Diplomacy,* Popular Prakashan, Bombay, 1970, p. 31.
95. Indu Shekhar, Cultural Collaboration between India and Nepal, United Asia, July–Aug., 1967, p. 21.
96. Y. N Khanal, *Reflections on Indo-Nepal Relations,* Rakesh Press, New Delhi, 1964.
97. E. B. Mihaly, *Foreign Aid and Politics in Nepal,* OUP, London, 1965, p. 7.

2

Transport and Communications

2.1 TRADE ROUTES

The movement of goods and men is dependent upon transport and communication. The provision of cheap and adequate facilities of transport is an essential prerequisite for the development of trade and commerce.

Transport means movement of materials (goods) and men from one place to another. It carries goods from the place of production to the place of consumption. The location of industry, the facilities available for the growth of cities, ports, domestic and foreign trade, all are influenced by transportation. With the improved means of transport, goods move faster and countries come very close to one another.

"The stupendous dispositions of nature overmatch the delicate provisions of science, and we must perforce accept such roads as nature points out and treat her indications with respect.,"[1] The ancient trade-routes across the Himalayas are "such roads as nature points out".

During ancient period rivers were the most important means of internal trade. Other trade routes such as roads, railways and canals are almost modern means of transportation.

The trade routes used by the traders of India and Nepal during 19th and early 20th centuries may be classified into four broad groups:

(i) Land routes (Road transport)
(ii) Railways
(iii) Water ways
(iv) Other Means of Communication

2.1.1 LAND ROUTES (ROAD WAYS)

Most of the border areas of Bengal and North-Western Provinces and Oudh were dotted with ancient trade-routes to and from Nepal.[2] A detailed description of the routes to, in and through Nepal, generally used in the 18th century, have been mentioned in Colonel Kirk Patrick's Book *An Account of the Kingdom of Nepaul.*[3] Hadson's Report has also mentioned various references of the routes of the Central Asian trade in the first-half of the 19th century.[4] The routes from Kesriah to Hitounda comprising 88 miles in nine stages meant for bullock's load and that from Hitounda to Kathmandu comprising 39 miles in six stages meant for hill porters have been mentioned, with amazing case by Hodgson.[5]

The oldest mode of interaction between the people of the two countries was land routes as people approached each other through personal interaction and traversed long distances through land route. The land routes emanating from India to the neighbouring countries can be broadly divided into three main channels:

(i) Trade between the British Indian provinces of Oudh and North Western and Western Nepal.

(ii) Trade between the British Indian district of Champaran, Muzaffarpur, Darbhanga, Bhagalpur and Purnea (All in Bihar) and adjoining Nepalese districts.

(iii) Trade between the British Indian district of Darjeeling and the Nepalese district of Ilam.

2.1.1.1 Trade between the British Indian Provinces of Oudh and North Western and Western Nepal

The important districts linking British India in the North western provinces and Oudh were Kumaun, Bareilly, Kheri, Bahraich, Gonda, Basti and Gorakhpur. The Nepalese districts in the vicinity of these places were Doti and Silgarhi in the western part of the hill. The places in the western terai region including Butwal, Banke, Bardia, Kailali and Kanchanpur called new country (Naya Muluk). The British captured these districts after the war of 1814-16 and restored to Nepal in 1860. The territories ceded were two hundred miles in area[6]. [The important routes are discussed in detail here.]

(A) Kumaun to Doti

These routes followed by people through their movement on the man-made foot points, river valleys and bunds through roads, carts and other means of transport. There were several points between Kumaun and Doti-Barmdeo, Jhulaghat,Gurjaghat, Barchula and Boondee. The route connected with Barmdeo was more important than all the other routes.[7]

The relevant routes of this district are given below.

In Kumaun:		In Dotee
1. Barmdeo	to	Silgarhi
2. Jhulaghat	to	Silgarhi
3. Gurjia Ghat	to	Silgarhi
4. Dar Ghula	to	Silgarhi
5. Boondee	to	Silgarhi

Means of Conveyance: All thẹ transportation was done by cooliès in Doti in Western Nepal because the roads in Doti were mere jungle paths, which were unfit for carts.[8]

(B) Bareilly to Western Terai

The routes between Bareilly and western Terai of Nepal were Doknabagh, Ghurrighat, Belauri, Nanda, Simara, Doti and Pooryna. Pilibhit, Madho Tanda and Purunpur were the main places in Bareilly district.[9]

The relevant routes in this district of Bareilly to Pilibhit are given below:

	In Barcilly		In Western Terai of Nepal
1.	Bareilly	to	Dakna Bagh
2.	Bareilly	to	Ghata
3.	Pilibhit	to	Belauri
4.	Pilibhit	to	Nanda
5.	Pilibhit	to	Simri
6.	Madho Tanda	to	Dotee
7.	Purunpur	to	Pooryna

Means of Conveyance: Ponies were used as means of transport for everything except timber between Bareilly and Western Terai of Nepal.[10]

(C) Kheri to Western Terai

Kheri district of UP in India and Western Terai of Nepal were connected through the route between Pullea to Pallian via Satyana and Chandighat through Khyraghur to Putda via Puchperwa, through Singahi and Simri to Golamandi via Bunberpur and Kakrowli Ghat and via Ramnagar Ghat. There were other roads via Mohna to Golamandi for example. Hallona and Kalaupur. The roads were usually unusable during monsoon but they were repaired by the traders themselves. Since the government in Nepal was not wakeful to the economic needs, it did not take any repair work.[11]

The relevent routes of this district are :

In Kheri		In Western Terai of Nepal
1. Pullea (via Satyana and Chandi Ghat)	to	Pullian
2. Khyraghur (via Puchperwa)	to	Putda
3. Singahi (via Bunbirpure)	to	Golamandi
4. Simri (via Ramnagar Ghat)	to	Golamandi

Means of Conveyance: Carts were the usual means of conveyance on the route from Kheri to Western Terai of Nepal. Salt, grain and tobacco were carried by pack animals such as buffaloes, ponies and bullocks.[12] The Deputy Commissioner of Kheri was of the opinion that there were two usual modes of conveying goods namely Garis and pack animals, mostly ponies. He suggested that the traders from British India must carry conveyances with them because it was difficult to find means of transport in Nepal.[13]

(D) Bahraich to Western Terai

The Important routes to Nepal of this district are as follows.[14]

In Bahraich		In western Terai of Nepal
1. Sujauli (via Kalania Ghat)	to	Golamandi
2. Sujauli	to	Dubra
3. Motipure (via Dharmapure) and Kalania Ghat	to	Golamandi
4. Motipure	to	Banki
5. Nanpara	to	Banki
6. Kutra Bazar (via Golaria) and Sibhanee Ghat	to	Banki
7. Bungaha	to	Banki
8. Bhinga (via Bhagoura) and Balapore	to	Banki

Means of Conveyance: Carts were the usual means of transport for the routes going from Sujauli to Dubra, Nanpara to Banke and Bhuga via Bhagoura and Balapur to Banke. But salt, grain and tobacco were transported on the back of buffaloes, bullocks and ponies.[15]

(E) Gonda to Western Terai

Between Gonda and Western Terai of Nepal there were altogether eleven passes which served as trade routes. These passes were Garia, Barchwa, Patali, Goron, Khabu, Bais Mata, Bhambhur, Jarva Byrat, Khangra, Sirya and Jarwa.These were the important passes in Nepal and they were earmarked by the tracks of trade.[16]

Means of Conveyance: The eight passes were being crossed by pedestrians with or without head load. These passes were Garia, Barchwa, Patali, Goranm Khahu, Baies Mata, Bhamphur and Jarwa Byrat. The last three passes were practicable for laden animals and none of these could be traversed by carts. The cart tracks led up to the passes in India. As the load arrived at the foot of the hills it was transferred to either pack animals or coolies. The communications in Nepal connected by these passes with routes in India were also mere tracks. [17]

Girdlestone, the British resident in Nepal, believed that the Dara pass which was not mentioned in the above list was one of the best routes across the hills.[18] During the memorable famine years 1873-74, the roads were made on the Indian side of the range. A metalled road was constructed from Nawabganj to Bahramghat. A high road emanated from a distance of one mile eastward of Nawabganj and it reached upto Bahramghat and this was a direct route from Lucknow to Bahraich and Gonda.[19]

Basti and Gorakhpur to Butwal: Although this route suffered during the rainy season but a considerable amount of business was transacted during the cold weather. This route connected North Western provinces and Western Nepalese Terai through Basti and Gorakhpur in India and Butwal in Nepal.

(F) Gorakhpur to Butwal

The important trade routes to Nepal in the district of Gorakhpur are as follows:[20]

	In Gorakhpur		In Butwal
1.	Bagohi	to	Puchmara
2.	Bataidiha	to	Makundghar
3.	Kurha	to	Piprahwa
4.	Kaulahi	to	Bagauli
5.	Bhundi	to	Tirlokpore
6.	Gorakhpur	to	Majharia
7.	Naikat	to	Bilarawaghat
8.	Neatanwa	to	Kadamahwa
9.	Pipra Bazar	to	Belahia
10.	Ranjita	to	Gopaloore
11.	Deoghati	to	Rajabari
12.	Mirchahwa	to	Sundri
13.	Nichloul (via Thunthibari)	to	Palhi
14.	Nichlaul (via Chetteach)	to	Bhujahwa
15.	Nichloul (via Sittapore)	to	Khairatwa
16.	Rengahia	to	Dharmanli
17.	Bahnar	to	Sanouli
18.	Baitambya Bazar (via Amra)	to	Khairatwa
19.	Baitambya Bazar	to	Tribenigbat

The route No. 13 was the best road in the Gorakhpur district. It was linked through Nichloul by a series of roads with Gorakhpur itself and other local marts of importance This route carried the highest amount of traffic. The route Nos. 8, 9, 11, 12 also carried considerable amount of trade. The route Nos.l, 3, 17 were fit only for pedestrians. Most of these routes even in India were only seasonal roads. Their continuations in Nepal were in 9 mess. The common means of transport were carts, pack-ponies and pack bullocks. [21]

Means of Conveyance: Carts, ponies and bullock were the usual means of carriage on the route from Gorakhpur to Butwal. The rate of cart was 1.5 pie per maund per mile and they did not hold more than 10 maunds. Grains exported from Nepal through the river Gandak were carried on carts to Narkulia or some other depots.[22]

(G) Basti

Other relevant roads of the Basti district were Basti to Nepal via Domriagang, Uska to Naugarh, Birpur and Nepal frontier, Lotan to Nepal frontier.[23]

An important route in the Nepal-Basti trade started from Sirsewa, Bahadurganj and Captainganj by way of the north west corner of the district of Kakrahighat on the Banganga above the river junction with Rapti. The prinicipal roads in the Bansi Parganah–(i) from Domariaganj to Nepal by way of Intwa, (ii) from Basti to Nepal by way of Bansi Dumdumwa and Birpur. These were unmetalled lines till 188. But in the beginning of the 20th century it was found that the route between Bansi and Basti were metalled lines. The same road was extended to the Nepal frontier by way of Uska. This road was crossed by a road traversing the north of Bansi to Kakrahwa Bazar in Nepal via Chillea.[24]

On the routes from Basti to the Butwal district of Nepal, the usual means of carriage were carts, pack animals such as ponies and bullocks. Large number of carriages were available on this route. The rates of pack animals were a little over one pie per mound per mile. Therefore the increased trade would not involve a greater relative expenditure for transport. Any grain imported in India from Nepal by the Gandak river would be carried on carts to Narkulia or some other depots.[25]

Means of Conveyance: For trade between Champaran to Chitwan, carts, bullock, ponies and porters were used as the means of transportation.[26]

2.1.1.2 Trade passing between the British Indian district of Champaran, Muzaffarpur, Darbhanga, Bhagalpur and Purnea (All in Bihar) and adjoining Nepalese districts

The trade between Bihar and Eastern Terai of Nepal was conducted via-Champaran, Muzaffarpur, Darbhanga, Bhagalpur and Purnea. They were connecting Nepalese districts of Chitwan, Bara, Rautahat, Sarlahi, Mahottari, Janakpur and Morang. The trade through these routes were sometimes referred into the British records as Bengal trade. This trade gained importance in course of time. From Kathmandu valley and eastern Nepal it passed over to Tibet. This route carried the products of Kathmandu valley with the principal items of export from the eastern Nepalese Terai, This was the corridor for imported items into Nepal from British India. There was no attempt to make account of the trade amount before 1875 by the British Government in India.[27]

(A) Champaran

The trade between Champaran district in India and Chitwan district of Nepal was carried through Bettiah via Tribeni, Thori, Raxaul. The trade between Chitwan district in Nepal to carried to Sugauli via Raxaul, Motihari via Katkenwa and Ghorasahan in Simroughur in Chitwan district.[28]

The Champaran district had no good roads before 1800 A.D. except one in Saran. The good roads were constructed for the passage of troops during Anglo-Nepalese war between 1814 16 as there was line of communication along the frontier in the 19th century.[29] The trade-routes of Champaran were only second in importance to those of Muzaffarpur. Routes from Champaran led directly to Kathmandu and.were also chosen for direct traffic with Calcutta and Patna.[30]

The important routes of this district are as follows :[31]

Champaran		Nepal
1. Bettiah (via Tribeni)	to	Chitawun
2. Bettiah (via Toree)	to	Chitawun
3. Bettiah (via Raxaul)	to	Semrabasa
4. Segowlee (via Raxaul)	to	Semrabasa
5. Motihari (via Kutkenwa)	to	Bereywah
6. Motihari (via Ghorasan)	to	Semrounghur

There was no significant traffic in Bettiah route via Tribeni. The trade routes of Bettiah and Sugauli via Raxaul and Motihari (via Katkenwa in Champaran in Sembrasa) and Banewati in Chitwan were in good condition, these routes converged at or before Semrabasa. It was 30 miles away from Sugauli by the direct route through Raxaul. From there all roads led to Kathmandu. In dry weather it could be traversed by tighly laden carts through the low pass in the Chiriaghat, a hill, and also through Hetauda to Bhimphedi. Bhimphedi was situated at a distance of about 60 miles from Sugauli, the distance between Bhimphedi and Thankote was nearly 15 miles and there were two steep passes in between these. There was low intensity traffic on the route going through Motihari via Ghorasahan to Semrounghur in Nepal. The road passed through Mukwanpur to Hetauda where it met the main road to Kathmandu. The routes which led from the Nepal border to railway and the bank of Gandak were the most important routes.[32]

Means of Conveyance: Officiating Magistrate and Collector of Champaran stated "During the cold season the roads leading from the Ghauts on the Gandak into the Champaran district and Nepal were busy with up and down movements of carts, ponies and donkeys. The route between Bettiah to Chitwan in Nepal via Tribeni was fit for movement up to Tribeni. The communication across Gandak by cart track led to Butwal in the west and to Chitwan in the east and bulk of traffic was carried on bullock cart.[33]

For movements of goods by the route of Raxaul in Champaran district to Kathmandu, carts, bullocks, ponies and porters were used. The carts were used for transportation from Raxaul to Churia, the foot of the hill and to Bhimphedi (via Hetauda) and Bhimphedi to Thankot, porters were used as means of transportation. The coolies were engaged at Bhimphedi due to unavailability of the carts in the valley to carry goods to Kathmandu.[34]

(B) Muzaffarpur

The trade routes from Muzaffarpur to Nepalese district of Bara, Rauthat, Mahottari were approached through Bairgania, Majorganj, Sonbursa, Bela Muchpakauni, Sursand and Madhwapur (in Muzaffarpur district) and Semrounghur, Sangrampur, Adamara, Muggurthana, Jaleshwar and Janakpur in Nepal. Roads were made along all these routes to the border. In between these border areas many village tracks intervened.[35]

The important trade routes from Muzaffarpur to Nepal are mentioned below:[36]

	In Muzaffarpur		In Nepal (Bara, Rotahut, Sirlahi, Mahotari)
1.	Bairagania	to	Semrounghur
2.	Majorganj	to	Sangrampur
3.	Sonbursa	to	Adamara
4.	Bela Muchpakauni	to	Muggurthana
5.	Sursand	to	Jaleshwar
6.	Madhwapur	to	Janakpur

(C) Darbhanga

The trade routes from Darbhanga to Saptari (Nepalese district) were through Basupati to Janakpur, two roads from Darbhanga via Jayanagar to Siraha, Madhubani via Jayanagar to Siraha, Darbhanga via Lawkoha to Hanumannagar. The roads although in good condition degenarated into tracks across the border.[37]

At the cost of Darbhanga Raj, a road was constructed from Darbhanga to Narah and Jaynagar on the Nepal frontier in 1872-73.[38] Roads from Darbhanga to Sitamarahi as well as roads to the frontier and to Simri passed through Kanstaul, about 15 miles northwest of Darbhanga.[39] Along with this route there were other roads proceeding from Darbhanga, Pandaul and Madhubani to the Nepal frontier.[40]

These routes can be summarised as follows :[41]

	In Darbhanga		In Nepal
1.	Basupati	to	Janakpur
2.	Two roads from Darbhanga (via Jainagar)	to	Siraha

3.	Madhubani (via Jainagar)	to	Siraha
4.	Darbhanga (via Lawkoha)	to	Hanumannagar

There was a considerable volume of trade between Darbhanga and Nepal. The trade was carried on by means of carts, pack-bullocks and to a certain extent by means of coolies. The roads were in good condition in India, but deteriorated into tracks across the border.

Means of Conveyance: The cart and pack animals were used between Muzaffarpur and Darbhanga districts to the Terai districts of Nepal. Where there were hills, coolies were more suitable than other means of conveyance. [42] The Sub-Divisional Officer of Madhubani once observed in 1889 that at least two hundred carts of wood laden with grain passed through Paduma Mahalia etc.[43]

(D) Bhagalpur

According to Girdlestone, new roads had been constructed in Khandauli and Birpur in the Bhagalpur district and the trade routes from Bhagalpur to Saptari passed through Khandauli to Hanumannagar and Birpur to Ameerpur. These two roads of Hanumannagar and Ameerpur in sub-terai area of Nepal were no more than tracks of footpath.[44]

In the Bhagalpur district there was a good road leaving the south emigration road at Balha near Sukhpur through Supaul, Chandipura and Dagmara. This road ended at Kundauli on Nepal frontier.[45]

In the east direction, a road ran towards Pratapganj to Nathpur (on the east bank of the Koshi) which entered Purnea. A road also ran to the north via Murliganj and Madhepura to Singheshwar. From this point one route turned to Supaul and other via Pipra and Pratapganj to Birpur on the Nepal frontier. A branch of south emigration road ran via Supaul to Kundauli on the Nepal frontier. Another road moved southward via Banganj to Khagaria in Monghyr. A branch from north emigration road ran into Nepal via Panchaparamia.[46]

Means of Conveyance: Though the roads from Bhagalpur to Hanumanagar and Ameerpur in Nepal were no more than tracks, yet carts were used freely. Bullocks were also used as conveyance for trade of valuable items such as spices and salt.[47]

(E) Purnea

The important routes to Nepal from Purnea are mentioned below:[48]

	In Araria Subdivision		In Morung (Nepal)
1.	Nawabganj	to	Dewanganj
2.	Amona (via Sahibaganj)	to	Dewanganj
3.	Mirganj	to	Sahibganj
4.	Kusambha	to	Pattardewa
5.	Rajola (Via Dhobi)	to	Gogra

6.	Megha (Via Harecha)	to	Jhontiaki
7.	Kursakata	to	Rangeli
8.	Sikti	to	Rangeli

The list of trade routes, provided by W.W. Hunter, mentions the Pathardeba, Mahaseri, Sauragadam and Kuari routes. But the routes (i) Amona via Sahibganj to Dewanganj, (ii) Megha via Harecha to Jhontiaki and (iii) Kursakata to Rangeli have not been mentioned in Hunter's list but have been mentioned in Girdlestones's list and O' Malley's list.[49]

	In Kishanganj Sub-Division		In Morung
1.	Dhubeli (Via Kochaha)	to	Chailghazi
2.	Phulwari (Via Teragach)	to	Chailghazi
3.	Khaniabad	to	Athmauza/Atbhgaon
4.	Bairia	to	Ultabari
5.	Karabari (Via Pulsa) and Beniant.	to	Mohabari
6.	Dighal bank (Via Tanganduba)	to	Jhilmilya
7.	Gandhaibdanga (Via Khudabhita)	to	Pautapara
8.	Tatpos Market	to	Lodhabari
9.	Simalbari (Via Ambari)	to	Kbatamani
10.	Bhawanjganj (Via Changhati)	to	Kbaniabhita
11.	Kalughat	to	Panthamari
12.	Bhatgaon (Via Dhobagachi Bholabari)	to	Dohnagiri

The route between Fathipur and Chaulghagi is mentioned in Hunters' list. However, Girdlestone's and O'Malley's lists have not mentioned this route.[50]

Hunter mentions three other routes connecting Purnea to Nepal. A road from Sahibganj to Bhopla - Tajpur emanating from the frontier of Nepal in the north-west corner of Purnea, which was 78 miles long and crossed the north emigration road near Matiyari and then ran through Basantpur, the headquarters of Arariya sub-division. It ran through Dalmalpur market, Amur-Kasaba police station across the Ganges, Darjeeling road, and the river Mahanada at Dengra ferry. It passed on through Raniganj police outpost and market, crossing the river Sadanu to the river Nagar on the Dinajpur frontier. This was the main line of communication from the north - western of the district to the eastern division. This route was used by people of Nepal during their journey to the Nekmard and other fairs of the Rajshahi Division.[51]

Two other roads- a 16 miles long road from Arariya to Sikti and a 15 miles long road from Araria to Kursakata, connected the headquarters of Arari sub-division with the police outpost on the Nepal frontier. [52]

Means of Conveyance: Carts were commonly used for transportation on the routes between Purnea and Morang district of Nepal. Since ponies were highly expensive, their use was not common.[53]

2.1.1.3 Trade passing between the British Indian district of Darjeeling (Bengal) and the Nepalese district of Ilam (bordering Darjeeling).

(A) Darjeeling to Ilam

Nepalese traders visited Darjeeling through three main routes:- (a) Ilam Garhi in Nepal to Nagree across river Mechi (b) via Mayoong in Nepal to Goong on the other side of the border (c) via Toonglong and Fulaloong in Nepal to Samaboong across the border.[54]

British Resident in Nepal, Charles Girdlestone stated (19 Sept. 1876) that there were various hill paths between Eastern Nepal and Darjeeling. Among them the best known was the route from Ilam across the Mechi near Thapalia. Though the trade was not very significant. He further remarked that as there were greater facilities of access from Purnea, it was not expected that any great result would be achieved from the direction of Darjeeling.[55]

The construction of road from Little Ranjit to the Nepal frontier was started in 1874 and it was completed in 1876 as far as Tongloo and extended northward along the frontier to Phalut. Here the frontier of Sikkim, Darjeeling and Nepal meet. In course of time, due to increasing need this road was also extended to a southward direction along the Nepal frontier to a point near Singhali Tea garden. Later it was proposed to take it across Balasan river to the projected terminus of the North Bengal railway.[56] The condition of the roads in north and south Nepal was good and an inspection bungalow was put up at Tangloo. This view was expressed by J.W. Edgar, the Deputy Commissioner of Darjeeling in a report submitted to the commissioner of Rajshashi and Coochbehar on 11 December 1878.[57]

As per the reports of the Deputy Commissioner of Darjeeling in 1886, the flourishing marts were situated at some convenient points along these roads. The trading community in this area wanted the completion of the roads from Siliguri to Naxalbari and Nepal frontier to be constructed on the proper scale.[58] After seven years, the Annual General Administration Report of Darjeeling for the year 1892–93 reported the completion of the road from Matigara to Naxalbari.[59]

Means of Conveyance: Coolies were the most common means of conveyance between Darjeeling and eastern Nepal as there were mostly hill paths in the area.[60] Transportation up to Bejanbari was by coolies from there to Darjeeling by rope way or via Palbazar by bridle path. The rail route was used in the Terai via Sanicharia in Nepal to Naxalbari via Bhadrapur in Nepal to Adhikari and via Garidhura. The trade up to Naxalbari was through both carts and rail. The trade between Siliguri and other stations were carried through the railway.[61] In response to the commercial needs of the district, the communication system of Darjeeling had grown rapidly. Moreover, in the closing years of the 19th century, the Terai area emerged as a promising economic unit, having a distinct character of its own with the completion of the chains of roads surrounding the southern part of the district and facilitating trade with Nepal.[62]

2.1.1.4 Important Routes

All the above mentioned routes were classified into some important routes by the respective Government of North-West provinces & Oudh and Bihar and Bengal. The Government of N. W. A. and Oudh classified following ten routes on the Indo-Nepal border.[63]

(i) The route between Nepal and Almora crossing the Kali river at Jhulaghat.

(ii) The route across the Sarda river from the Nepalese mart Barmdeo into Kumaun.

(iii) The route between Golamandi and the Bahraich district (a) via Sugauli (b) via Katgarh.

(iv) The route between the Nepalese mart of Golamandi and the Kheri district (a) via Ramnagar on the Kauriala river (b) via Singhai.

(v) The route between Pilibhit and Nepal across the Sarda by a number of ghats varied from year to year with the condition of the river. Most of this trade ran between Pilibhit and the Sarda in two lines via Neuriyaghat and via Madho Tanda.

(vi) The route between the valley of Deokhur and Dang and Gonda district via Derapass.

(vii) The routes between the Nepalese mart of Banke (Nepalganj) and Bahraich and Gonda districts (a) via the mart Nanpara (b) crossing the Rapti at Gulana (c) via Gobapur.

(viii) The route between Butawal and Gorakhpur districts marked by several tracks the main among them were Thundibaree and Bahuar.

(ix) The route between the Nepalese mart of Sirsewa, Bahadurganj and Captainganj (in the province of Sheuraj) and the Basti district, via Marni or Kakrahighat.

(x) The route between the Nepalese mart of Butwal and Basti district – (a) via Uska (b) via Lotan.

Other nine important routes between North Western Provinces and Oudh and adjoining Nepalese districts have been mentioned in another report.[64]

(a) The routes between Kumaun and western Nepal via Jhulaghat and Barmdeo.

(b) The road between the Golamondi and its vicinity and Kheri and Bahraich district via Palia (via Singhai, Kamnagar and Sujauli).

(c) The roads between the western part of Nepal Terai and town of Pilibhit via Nuria Husainpur and Sangadhi.

(d) The roads between the Nepalganj (Banke) and the Bahraich district via Katgarh and Babganj.

(e) The route between the marts of Bahadurganj, Captainganj, Sirsewa and Bas and Gonda districts via Marni, Materghat and Kakrahighat.

(f) The route between the Nepal Terai or Nepalese mart of Butwal and the Terai around it and the Gorakhpur via Jogiabari, Nautanwa, Jhesnthibari.

(h) The route between Nepal Terai and marts of Uska, Lotan and Sohas.

(i) The route passing through Gandak river water flow and through Banks.

Six important routes in Bengal and Bihar adjoining Nepalese districts were classified by the Government of Bihar and Bengal as follows: [65]

(a) The road entering the Nepalese land territory near Kutkenwa in Champaran district of Bihar.

(b) The road via Sitamarhi entering Nepal near Sonbarsa.

(c) The route via Madhubani in Darbhanga entering Nepal near Lowkahi.

(d) The road entering Nepal near Kuhnauli in Bhagalpur.

(e) The route entering Darjeeling of West Bengal near Naxalbari from Dhulabari in Nepal.

(f) The road from Ilam to Darjeeling entering Darjeeling near Ghumpahar.

For trade between India and Nepal, mostly country carts were used. Animals used in these country carts were pack animals such as ponies, donkeys, buffaloes, bullocks etc., and porters. The carrying capacity of porters and pack animals was two mounds and three and half mounds respectively (one mound is equal to 82 lb). The carrying capacity of carts was 10 mounds. Carts were used in the lowland of Nepal, whereas pack animals and porters were the main modes of transportation in the hill.[66]

2.1.1.5 Items of Trade

There were several commodities transacted through these routes and among them rice and timber were the principal articles imported to India through most of the routes on Indo-Nepal border. The two articles constituted more than two- thirds of total imports of India from Nepal through the route between Kumaun and western Nepal via Jhulaghat and Barmdeo and Pilibhit via Neuria,Husainpur and Sangadhi.[67]

The most important item of trade was timber, which formed one third of the total exports to India through the route between the Golamandi and its vicinity and Kheri and Bahraich districts via Palia and via Singhai, Kamnagar and Sujauli. Nepal imported cotton goods through these routes. Another item exported to India was oilseeds.[68]

Through the route of Nepalganj (Banke) and Baharaich district ghee, spices, timber, rice and oilseeds were exported via Katgarh and Babaganj. Nepal also imported cotton goods, salt, sugar and tobacco from India through this route in return. These routes were more significant for export of ghee, oilseeds and spices than that of other route.[69]

The route between Deokhari and Gonda district was used for the export of rice, the principal articles of export from Nepal. Two important lines of traffic merged in this route and both ran between Gonda and Basti and the Sheoraj district of Nepal. This route was famous for the export of timber and rice via Marvi. Most of the cotton and sugar were exported by this route.[70]

Nepal imported cotton goods and salt through the route between Nepal Terai and marts of Uska, Lotan and Sohas. The large portion of the cotton goods were of European origin and reached Uska and Lotan by road from Zamniah on the East Indian railway. The salt was principally Liverpool salt brought up by Gogra from Kolkata, Patna and other marts in Bengal. The cotton goods formed 76 per cent of the imports. This route carried the large import of non-intoxicating drugs and manufactured fibrous products. Nepal used to export rice and oilseeds through this route.[71] Major part of the export of rice took place through the route between the Nepal Terai or Nepalese mart of Butwal and the Terai around it and Gorakhpur district. It ran through Gorakhpur district via Jogiabari, Nautanwa, Deoghat, Baitaulia and Thunthibari. The Gandak river route was used for the export of timber.[72]

A study by E.C. Buck, the Director of Agriculture and Commerce of North Western Provinces and Oudh reported the total value of traffic passing in 1878-79 through the different routes as follows:-[73]

District	*Description of Routes.*	*Total Value of Traffic Passed in 1878-79 (in Rupees)*
Bahraich	.via Sujauli between Golamandi (Nepalese marts) and Motipur.	2,50,028
	.via Ratgarhi between Nepalese mart of Banke and Motipur.	3,43,725
	.via Babaganj between Nepalese mart of Banke and Nanpara.	11,33,413
Basti	.via Marni between Nepal marts of Bahadurganj and Sirswa and the Basti and Gonda district.	3,33,170
	via Uska between the British marts via Lotan and Nepal Terai	5,04,475
Gorakhpur	via Jogiabari between Nepal marts of Batiwal and Gorakhpur district	5,12,248
	via Bartaulia between Gorakhpur district and Nepal Terai and mar of Butwal.	2,90,178
	via Thunthibari between Gorakhpur district and Nepal Terai and mart of Butwal	3,22,442

Articles passing through the different routes in Bihar and Bengal were rice and paddy, cotton piece-goods, salts, sugar and kerosene. These articles entered the Nepalese territories near Kutkenwa in Champaran district of Bihar.[74]

According to a statistical report, Patna despatched 168 tons (i.e. 4587 maunds) of spices and ointments to Nepal during the six months ending in March 1876. This formed 26 per cent of the total exports. Other items were copper, brass and betel nuts. These goods constituted 16 per cent and 11 percent respectively. European cotton goods exported to Nepal amounted to Rs. 87,025 or 78 per cent and miscellaneous native goods to Rs. 10,935 or 10 per cent. All these exports were registered at Katkenwa in Champaran district. During the same six months of 1876 only 574 maunds or 21 tons of articles were received at Patna and tobacco formed 84 per cent of them.[75]

Several items entering Nepal near Sonbarsa by the route in Sitamarhi. Nepal exported rice, sakuwa wood, oilseeds and hides and imported cotton piece goods, salt, sugar and Kerosene oil.[76] In 1888-90 the sub Divisional Officer of Madhubani mentioned in his tour diaries that salt, cotton, castor sugar, tobacco, English cloth, silk etc., were the principal items of imports of Nepal. At the same time Nepal exported paddy, rice, linseed, saltpetre, timber, mustard seeds through the route via Madhubani in Darbhanga. Similar articles were exported and imported through the route entering Nepal near Kunauli in Bhagalpur.[77] By the route between the border of Ilam in Nepal and Darjeeling, Nepal exported blankets and cattle and imported various kinds of chintz.[78]

Items like rice, paddy, potato seeds and cardamom were imported through the different routes connecting Nepal with Darjeeling. Cardamom was imported through the Tista valley and Nepal frontiers Bazaars. Potatoes imported from Nepal were dispatched to West Bengal, South Bihar and Orissa.[79]

2.1.2 Railways

The Indo-Nepal trade relations entered into a new phase with the opening of the Indian railways in the districts bordering Nepal. The railways had great impact upon the markets and trade centres in the border districts of Nepal and India. The branch lines of the railways were entered to the convenient points at the frontier with a view to encourage and to facilitate trade with Nepal. Several new lines pushed up the growth of trade or affected its traditional passage.[80]

In 1885, it was proposed by the Bengal and North-Western Railway Company to extend the main line (32 miles) from Bahraich to the Nepal frontier near Nepalganj in substitution for the proposed branch line from Gonda to Bahramghat which formed part of the original project".[81] Gorakhpur was the headquarter of the Bengal and North-Western Railway. Though in May 1882, the main line was sanctioned, however, the traffic was opened on 15 January 1885. On 15 December 1886, a branch line from Gorakhpur to Uska Bazar was opened. Later it was extended from Uska to Tulsipur in Gonda.[82] Previously, the trade of rice from the Nepal Terai and Binayakpur was carried to Dhani Bazar on the Dhamela. Thereafter it was transported by boat along the Rapti and the Gogra to the markets of Bengal. Railways, to a large extent, superceded all these routes. The great revolution effected by the railway has been accompanied by practical abandonment of the rivers[83] to capture the large grain trade from Nepal and the north of Basti was the main aim of the Bengal and North-Western Railway. Subsequently, several railway lines were built to connect a number of towns on the Nepal-India border situated along important centres of trade in Nepal.

The Gonda-Tulsipur railway was opened in 1897 and later it was extended to Panshperwa and Uskabazar (Basti) with a branch from Gauauri to Harrwa in the bonest near the Nepal frontier.[84]

Previously, Bahramghat was one of the most important centres of trade between Nepal, Gonda and Bahraich on the North and districts south of Gogra. In 1890, Great Elgin Bridge at Chaukaghat was Constructed. This bridge carried over the Gogra, the main line of the Bengal and North-Western Railway, due to which the importance of Bahramghat as a trade centre declined.[85] Through this route of railway, gram, oilseeds and spices from Nepal to Bahraich and piece-goods, metals, salt, tobacco and sugar from Bahraich to Nepal were carried which terminated on the frontier close to Nepalganj. The main line of the Bengal and North-Western Railway passed through the extreme southern corner of this district. A branch line of this railway was terminated at Katarnian Ghat on the Girwa with a branch from Nanpara to Nepalganj Road on the frontier. Through this railway, a large trade with Nepal passed. Indeed, the opening of the railway gave a strong stimulus to the increase of trade in Bahraich.[86] Due to the development of railway, Pilibhit became a distributing centre for the products of the Terai and Nepal. But, on the other hand, the development of railway had disadvantages too. Before the advent of railway in this district a large timber business from Nepal was transacted. The extension of the railway system to the frontier from Mallanj in the Kheri District practically exhilarated this trade.[87]

Because of extension of the Indian railway system, Nepalganj (western Terai region of Nepal) was developed into a bustling town with a brisk construction activity, growing population and development of a rudimentary street-lighting system. With passage of time, there was a heavy influx of Indian traders, both seasonal and permanent into Nepalganj. In its journey of development the town accommodated nearly 45 permanent commercial establishments as well as more than 100 temporary stalls during November to May every year. These were operated by Marwaris and other traders from India.[88] The Assam–Bihar Railway opened its Purnea section from Kasba to Forbesganj, adjoining the market town of Rangoli in Morang district of Nepal (nuclear of the modern town of Biratnagar).[89] It changed the trade-route of the Western and Northen parts of the Araria and Sadar sub-divisions. Products were brought from Nepal to Forbesganj. After that it was taken to Manihari ghat and it was shipped and carried westward by rivers to Revilganj. The opening of the new railway stations at Anchraghat and Debiganj gave additional facilities for the trade of Purnea district. A good deal of traffic was attracted at Debiganj as it was an important trade centre near the Nepal frontier.[90]

The Tirhut State Railway was started in 1874 by the construction of a line from Muzaffarpur to the left bank of the Ganga opposite Mokamah ghat. This line was leased to Bengal and North-Western Railway Company in 1890. The system consisted of 1,468 miles occupying the whole country north of Ganga between Gogra and the Koshi rivers by the end of June 1905.[91]

Later the Tirhut State Railway was extended across the north of the Supaul-sub- division to Pertapganj and this altered the course of the trade in the Bhagalpur district to a considerable extent and diminished the importance of the river borne traffic. About the effect of the construction of Tirhut State Railway, the collector of Champaran stated in his report (1882- 83) "since the opening of the railway for traffic, piece goods have been imported exclusively and salt and hardware to a very great extent by rail." Before the opening of the railway, piece goods were brought from Muzaffarpur by cart, salt and other hardwares were brought from Patna. Since the line has been opened, it has been fully utilised for the export of sugar, indigo, saltpeter, chillies and makai (maize) the Goladars adopted the railway to avoid delay in the carriage by boat.[92]

On 24 February 1877, the Muzaffarpur branch of the Tirhut State Railway was opened. A survey in regard to the proposed railway line from Muzaffarpur through Motihari and Sugauli to Bettiah was completed in 1878. As it was thoroughfare for all the trade between Nepal and the districts lying south of it, the project was regarded as a financial success. F.M Halliday, the Commissioner of the Patna Division reported "very great traffic exists between Nepal and the adjoining districts of Muzaffarpur and Darbhanga. There is undoubtedly a very extensive trade in timber with Nepal and the grain traffic also not inconsiderable. All this will, of course, be enormously developed. When we have the railway extension from Muzaffarpur via Motihari to Beattiah- a line which is in course of construction."[93] The extension of the Tirhut State Railway from Muzaffarpur to Bettiah (79 miles) and from Darbhanga to Peepraghat (88 miles) was sanctioned in July 1880. These extensions covered the highly cultivated and populous districts and were expected to tap the products from the Nepal and north Bihar.[94]

The final survey conducted in 1885, reported to be in good progress of the line from Muzaffarpur to Sitamari. In September 1890, this branch line of the Tirhut State Railway to Sitamari was opened by the Lieutenant-Governor of Bengal.[95] Regarding the importance of the route, J.F.K. Hewitt, the officiating Commissioner of the Patna Division, reported in 1885, "the completion of this portion of the line will bring the railway communication into close connection with the Nepal frontier".[96]

In 1897, the construction of a feeder line from Raxaul on the Nepal frontier to the Tirhut State Railway at Sugauli was undertaken and which was completed during the year 1898-99.[97]

During the famine of 1897, the ground work of the Bengal and North-Western Railway line running from Sakri to Jaynagar on the Nepal frontier was completed for relief work. This line linked the larger area of hinterland, which was very far from the railway track. This route passed through Madhubani, an important trading centre in Darbhanga district, as it tapped large grain supply from Nepal. Nahra was also important trade centre and it acquired large grain traffic from Nepal and it was connected by road with the railway. Sakri, Jhanjharpur and Nirmali [98] Railways were connected with Darbhanga town and extended to the Nepal frontier. The spread of the Indian railway system to different market towns on the Indian side of the border gave fillip to the growth of towns on the Nepal side of the border as well-as the cities like Nepalgunj, Birgunj and Biratnagar all came into prominence through the spread of railways.

Champaran was connected from south to north by the Muzaffarpur-Bhikhna Thori branch of the Bengal and North- Western Railway. Starting from Muzaffarpur, it entered Champaran a few miles south of Mehsi, ran south of and parallel to the Sikrana river upto Bettiah and reached its terminus at Bhikhna Thori on the Nepal frontier. There was a 18-mile long branch line between Sugauli and Raxaul on the Nepal frontier. It was reported in the Champaran Gazetteer in 1907 that a third branch line from Bagaha (on the western boundary of Champaran) to Bairagnia (the terminus of the Darbhanga-Bairagnia branch) was under construction. "This line will convey the grain traffic of Nepal and the north of Champaran direct to Gorakhpur and the United Provinces without the present long detour through Muzaffarpur and Saran."[99]

Regarding the importance of extension of Tirhut State Railway in Champaran district, F.M Halliday highlighted in 1882 "In Champaran the railway has not yet been completed, and it is too early to say what its full effect will be. It may however, be safely said that it will enormously develop trade. A great deal of grain was brought from Nepal and kept here with the railway at Bettiah. Through improved communications between the line of rail and Nepal passes, there can be no doubt that an extensive trade in grains is likely to spring up and benefit the district generally". [100] The Magistrate of Champaran also accorded priority to the importance of railway as its effects are already beginning to be felt. It has helped reduce about 20 per cent in cart-hire in and around Bettiah and Motihari. It has attached to itself a fair share of export and import traffic of the district. It has made Bettiah the highway for travellers from Gorakhpur, Suguali and Motihari and for those from Nepal. It attracts light traffic from Gorakhpur, Saran and Nepal. It may absorb a portion of the traffic now borne on the Gandak.[101]

The North Gangetic State Railway connected the eastern and western limits of the Indian provinces adjoining Nepalese districts in Terai, and brought Muzaffarpur, Darbhanga and Champaran into closer connection with the rest of India. It also served as a distinct link in the chain of Indo-Nepalese trade. Champaran served as the principal trade route from Nepal to India. Raxual served as the trade point between Sugauli-Raxual branch. Railway served as the main arteries of commerce but the Gandak and the Burhi Gandak also carried much traffic.[102]

The local authorities in India near the Nepal border realized the importance of the construction and extension of the railway in specific directions to increase the volume of Nepal trade. They recognised utility of the railway for the effective trade across the frontier. Several officers suggested the importance of the railway.[103] In 1897, Fuller, the Assistant Director, Department of Agriculture and Commerce, argued that Nanpara should be made a terminus of light railway because it was the collection and distributing centre for a great portion of the Nepal trade. He also argued that "railway would act as a feeder to Gogra, if the river export traffic kept to its present figure. But the construction of Benares bridge would attract a very large portion of the present river traffic to the Oudh and Rohilkhand Railway.[104]

The Deputy Commissioner of Bahraich, Major de Montmorency suggested the route to Bahramghat, but the Deputy Commissioners of Gonda, Boys did not agree with this. On the other hand, F.N.Wright, the officiating Director, Department of Agriculture and Commerce, North-West Provinces and Oudh in his report dated 6 September 1880 to the Secretary to Government, North-West Provinces and Oudh stated, "Considered commercially, there is every reason to believe that the proposed line from Nanpara through Bahraich and Gonda to Faizabad would prove a success. If river traffic is maintained, the proposed line would act as a feeder to it, but it is more than probable, it is almost absolutely certain, that the whole trade of Nepal which crosses on the Bahraich and Gonda frontiers, as well as that of the Bahraich and Gonda districts themselves, will use the rail".[105]

The Faizabad conference on 26 January 1880, discussed the construction and extension of the railway system in the adjoining districts of Nepal. With regard to the improvement of the Indo Nepal trade through the Indian Railway system, the conference concluded "the direction in which first experiment could be most easily made appeared to be in the extension of a railway line from Bahramghat to; or towards, the mark or Banke or Nepalganj. The line as far as Bahraich forms part of the present government scheme and would lead to bring into closer connection with the two marts of Cawnpore (the most rising market of the Nepal side) and Nepalganj. The line is very short and not coming into competiion with river or with the Oudh and Rohilkhand railway to which it could act as a feeder. It was proved that railway carriage within nearer reach of the frontier marts was of the cost reducing nature, and thus constructing of the railways might be desirable even though the initial profits were not to reach the Government standard."[106]

Charles Girdlestone, the Resident of Nepal was of the opinion that the Durbar would require to make profit on material supplied. But the sleepers and fuel per railway would be in preferential rates as compared to those required in its ordinary dealings.[107] But the government of India waited for more definite proposals to be received from the Government of the North-Western Provinces.[108]

E. Buck, the Director of Agriculture and Commerce, North Western provinces had suggested. On 1 November 1877, that light Railway feeders might be extended from the main lines of rail through the North Western Province and Oudh either to the border of Nepal or if the Nepal border would permit it to the marts on the other side of the border. According to him, the most important of the two railway lines would be (1) From Bareilly to Pilibhit, to be extended possibly to Barmdeo, which would meet the requirements of Kumaun and Tibetan trade as well as the Western part of Nepal. However, if a railway would be constructed at Ramnagar or any other place at the foot of hills and western Kumaun, the extension of a railway to Barmdeo, would perhaps not pay because this line would absorb the greater parts of Kumaun and Tibetan traffic (2) The line through the Gorakhpur district parallel to the series of routes converging towards Butwal in Nepal. The railway through Gorakhpur would cater to the areas through which this route passes. The advantages of the railway was felt even by the Nepalese within their territory.[109]

The total traffic by the route connecting Nanpara, Bahraich and Gonda with Nawabganj was estimated at 20 lakhs of maunds. Fuller, the Assistant Director, Department of Agriculture and Commerce, North Western Provinces and Oudh opined, "For a portion of this traffic the railway would act as a feeder to the Gogra, if the river export traffic kept to its present figure. But the completion of the Benares bridge would in all probability attract a very large portion of the present river traffic to the Oudh and Rohilkhand Railway...,"[110] It was clear from the decline of the Ganges traffic and the opinions of native merchants, no river of these provinces could compete with a railway for the transportation of goods for long distance. The greater portion of the Gogra traffic consisted of grain and oilseeds destined to the port of Calcutta. Bahramghat and Faizabad were the two points at which Nepal trade brought into contact with the existing Railway system. Both were the terminals on the Oudh and Rohilkhand Railway. Bahramghat was connected with the main line by a branch line extended from Nawabganj. Faizabad was on the main line itself. The Bahramghat route ran through Nanpara and Bahraich. The Faizabad route ran through Nanpara, Bahraich and Gonda.[111]

On 20 October, 1892 Franklin Prestages presented a scheme for the second time for the extension of the Darjeeling-Himalayan Railway into Nepal.

Prestages opined that the line would help in cheaper and quicker transit and reduce the cost of transportation by two-third. It would give the most certain and cheap means by which food grains could be brought into the valley direct from the most productive districts of Bengal[112] at the time of scarcity and famine.This proposal of Railway extension was rejected by the Nepalese Government.

The supplies of primary products from the Terai region of Nepal particularly foodgrains and the timber, were the main reasons for the expansion and installation of branch lines connecting towns of the Nepal border with important trading centres in India. Indeed, scarcity of firewood in the Gangetic valley had been cited by British officials as early as 1850 as a justification for the construction of branch lines into the sub- Himalayan plains. It is well known fact that the commercial links between the Terai regions of Nepal and the adjoining areas of India, tradtionally close because of the absence of natural boundaries and the proximity of populous settlements on the Indian side of the border were further cemented by the extention of Indian railway system.[113]

During the closing years of the 19th century and the beginning of the 20th century, the Northern Indian Railway system played a vital role in the development of the Indo - Nepal trade. The river navigation still existed side by side as there is no evidence to suggest that railways completely displaced the river navigation for transportantion of goods. The major share of Nepalies trade in central sector passed through Raxaul the terminius of the Sugauli-Raxual branch railways,The Gandak and the Burhi Gandak also played an important role in the movement of commodities from the interior areas to railheads on the Nepal - India border. Timber, foodgrains and other commodities were brought to the nearest railhead and raliways helped them to send to diffenent parts of the country.[114]

Due to recurrent floods and changing course of the river, facilities were inadequate and Koshi river caused disorganised traffic in Saharsa and Darbhanga. In North Bihar, railway ran parallel to the courses of the rivers, mainly because of the difficulty in constructing bridge and danger of interference with the riverine drainage by railway embankments. As a consequence, transportaion between Muzaffarpur to Darbhanga and Motihari to Chapra was difficult.[115]

2.1.3 WATER WAYS

Between India and Tibet, the Himalayas consist of a massive chain of snow- clad mountains. These are carved into alternative ravines and ridges and gradually descends into the valleys of the Ganga and Brahmaputra. The distance between India and Tibet extends for over a hundred miles. The whole mountain system from the Indus in the west to the Brahmaputra in the east extends for nearly fifteen hundred miles[116]. Sir Sidney Burrand in his book "*A Sketch of the Geography and Geology of the Himalaya Mountains and Tibet*" divded the complex mountain system of Himalayas into four parts : The Punjab Himalaya, Kumaun Himalaya, Nepal Himalaya and Assam Himalaya. In addition to this division, Keneth Mason has mentioned two other parts of Himalayas– (I) Trans-Himalaya in the Kashmir mainly Karakoram and its associate ranges and (II) Sikkim Himalaya.[117]

The Nepal Himalya is sub-divided into three parts, embracing the basins of the Karnali, the Gandaki and the Kosi.[118] There were seven tributaries of all the three rivers.The tributaries were called the Sapta(seven) Karnali, the Sapta Gandaki and the Sapta Koshi. In the monsoons, roads were not of much use and these rivers and their tributaries carried the bulk of the country trade.[119]

2.1.3.1 Karnali

The Karnali system in the west consisted of the Kali (Sarda), the Seti, the Burhi Ganga, the Humla Karnali, the Bheri, the Sarju and the Rapti. The Seti, the Mugu Karnali and the Bheri pursue independent courses through the lower Himalayas. The Karnali, after piercing through the Mahabharat range, is reinforced by the Seti and is also joined by the Bheri in Dun. The combined water of the three rivers - the Seti, the Karnali and the Bheri penetrate the Siwalik range and enter into the Gogra of the Indian plains between Kheri and Bahraich districts of Uttar Pradesh.[120]

The seven tributaries of the Karnali river are the Seti, the Burhi Ganga, the Humla Karnali, the Mugu Karnali, the Tila, the Thuli Bheri and the Sani Bheri.[121] The most important place on the bank of the river is Faizabad, with Ajodhya, the sacred birth place of Rama adjoining it.[122]

The river Karnali is called Gogra (Ghagra,Gher -ghara Sarju, Dehwa) in India which rises in Tibet 30° 4' N and 80° 48' E and flows through Nepal by the name of Karnali. It meets the Girwa near the border just below the Saheli. The Saheli is one of the three branches of the Sarda. The Kuthi -Yankti and Kalapani, two rivulets rise in the Panch Chuli mountains in the north eastern parts of Kumaun. After a journey of few miles they combine and form the Kali or Kali Ganga. The Nepal and Kumaun are separated by this river. The Kali meets the Sarju or Sarda at Pancheswar at a distance of one hundred and six miles from the source. As it descends on the plains at Barmdeo, the name Kali is lost after it flows through Pancheswar. The river forms the boundary between Nepal and Pilibhit. After entering Kheri in Pilibhit it is joined on the right bank by the Chanka river. The Sarda has four district channels from south to north –the Ui is the Sarda or Chauko, the Dahawar, the Suheli. The Ui, one of the smallest streams which joins the Chauka again.[123]

Dahawar, the main branch of Sarda, joins the Karnali at Mallanpur, a few miles below Kataighat. At Bahramghat, another branch of the Sarda named Chauka meets it. The united stream is called Gogra or Sarju from this point.

After turning east it divides Gonda on its north bank from Barabanki and Faizabad on the south. It also separates Basti and Gorakhpur from Faizabad. It joins the Rapti and little Gandak from the north. This river also forms the boundary between Saran districts (Bihar) and Ballia districts (United Provinces) for about forty miles. This river joins Ganga in 26° 44' N and 84°42'E.[124]

Before the opening of the Bengal and North-Western Railway the traffic on the Gogra was considerable and of great importance. Large quantities of timber, grain and spices came down from Nepal through the Gogra [125]

2.1.3.2 Gandaki

The central Nepal is drained by the river system of the "Sapt Gandaki" or seven Gandak rivers. It rises in the central mountain basin of Nepal in 27°27' N and 83° 56'E. The Great Gandak, an important river of Northern India, has its source at the Sapt Gandaki zone.[126]

There are several names of Gandaki river it is known as Salgrami in Nepal and Narayani in the United Provinces. It enters into India at Tribeni and forms the boundary between Champaran (Bihar) and Gorakhpur (UP) for about twenty miles. It also separates Saran on the south west and Champaran and Muzaffarpur on the north-east. In Champaran it drains forty miles and joins the Ganga, opposite Patna at 25° 41'N and 85° 12'E after a course of one hundred and ninety two miles.[127]

The Gandaki river became a deltaic river soon after its entry in India. Below the Bagaha in Champaran district, it was navigable through out the year by country boat.

Logs and Rafts of timber grain and sugar were exported by the same route. During the dry season, the channel became narrow and winding, due to which navigation was difficult, however, during monsoon, it became a torrent and winded to two or three miles.[128]

The Little Gandak rises in the lower Nepal hills and flows from north to south through the whole length of Gorakhpur after then it joins the Gogra within the Saran District.[129] The Little Gandak becomes forbidden in dry weather.[130] A good deal of trade was carried on by the Little Gandak. If slightly improved, it would ply 500 maunds boats coming up all the year round.[131]

2.1.3.3 Kosi

The eastern part of Nepal is drained by the Kosi river which consists of seven main tributaries: the Milamchi, the Bhotia Kosi, the Tamba Kosi, the Likhu, the Dud Kosi, the Arun and the Tamur.[132]

In the south, the Tamur joins Arun a few miles downstream of the junction of the Arun and Sun-koshi. Then the combined waters of all three streams move through the Mahabharat range of the outer Himalayas and turn into the Kosi river of the Indian plains. It enters into India in the extreme

WATER WAYS

north- west of the Bhagalpur district. It has a course of a few miles along the boundary between it and the Purnea district. A few miles north of Anchraghat it enters Purnea. It runs about 84 miles in Bengal, then falls into the Ganga. A few miles before it joins the Ganga, it meets the Gogra from North Monghyr and Tilijuga and Bagmati from North Bhagalpur.[133]

The Kosi was navigable throughout the year for boats of 750 maunds or about 27 tons of load. It was navigable as far as the Nepal frontier for boats of 250 maunds or about 9 tons burden.[134] There are other streams in addition to the above mentioned streams, which orginate from the southern slopes of the Mahabharat lekh (lesser Himalayas). As compared to the great Himalyan strems, these streams are quite small but, during monsoon, they become very dangerous and devastating. Some of these minor streams draining from west to east in Nepal are the Mohana, the Bahai, the Rapti, the Ban Ganga, the Tinku, the Bagmati, the Kamla, the Trijuga, the Bakra and the Kankai.[135]

In the Churiya zone, scores of hills and rivulets arise to flow south, but except monsoon many of them have little or no water on the surface. The main reason was the porous nature of the region.[136] The Purnea, Bhagalpur, Darbhanga, Muzaffarpur, Champaran, Gorakhpur, Basti and Pilibhit districts on Indian side were catered by these rivers and rivulets. The Indian slopes of Himalayas were drained by three Nepalese basins of the Karnali, the Gandaki and Koshi, for a distance of 800 miles. [137]

Apart from these three rivers, many other smaller rivers played important role of commerce between India and Nepal. The role played by some of these rivers in different districts are discussed below

2.1.3.4 Purnea

The chief waterways, were the Kosi, the Bakra or Panar, the Kankai and the Mechi. These were mainly, used for floating down of timber. There were also smaller streams of the Rutwa and the Kowul. There was origin of Panar in the Matiyari police division in the junction of a number of hill streams coming down from Nepal. Through Sultanpur Parganas it moves south-east passing by Araria and also through Haveli Purnea approximately ten miles to the east of the headquarters town.

Then it turns southward through Kadba and Hatanda to the Ganges. It was navigable for boats of 250 maunds or about 9 tons in the neighbourhood of Purnea and above that stage for boats of 1OO maunds (about 3.5 tons) almost to the Nepal frontier. [138]

The lower Himalaya range of Nepal or the Madhubani taluk of the Morang was the origin of Bakra. It also joins the Panar river at Rampur which is five miles north of Araria. From Nepal huge amount of timber was brought down the Bakra river. [139]

2.1.3.5 Bhagalpur

According to Girdlestone, the Kosi was "the only practicable waterways" in this district.[140] But a special report drawn up during the famine of 1874 on the water-communication of Patna and Bhagalpur Divisions by Mr. T.H. Wickes contains some concerete information about other waterways of Bhagalpur-especially the Tiljuga and Dimra. The first stream rises in the hills in the sub-terai region of Nepal. It turns into Bhagalpur at the most northern point of Pargana Naridigar. Then it flows towards the western boundary between Bhagalpur, Nepal and Darbhanga. Near Tilkeswar, it receives great quantity of water from the Dimra. It also gets through the Katna the united waters of the Talabas, Parwan, Dhusan and Loran.[141]

2.1.3.6 Darbhanga

In Darbhanga district the Kamla and Tiljuga were the only streams that were navigable. The Kamla river was used to float down the timber[142] from former to Darbhanga during the rains.

2.1.3.7 Muzaffarpur

In the Muzaffarpur district, the Bagmati, the Bakaya, the Shorum, the Lakhandyi and the Hurdee rivers were only navigable in the rains.

2.1.3.8 Champaran

In the Champaran district the river Gandak was used for floating timber in rains. It carried boats of 1000 to 1500 maunds burden throughout the year upto a place, called Nillpur in Nepal. It was only navigable twenty miles above Tribeni. It had little carrying capacity and large boats rarely went beyond Bagha.[143]

2.1.3.9 Gorakhpur

The Great Gandak or Narayani was navigable in the Gorakhpur district and used for the floating of timber from Nepal. According to a contemporary account, it was navigable throughout the year for boats up to 350 maunds beyond the frontier of Nepal. But Girdlestone pointed out that there was water enough for such boats during the rains. But when the snow started melting the navigation became dangerous on account of its rapid currents. In the dry season a boat of 100 maunds faced difficulty over the shallow between Tribeni and Narkulia.[144]

2.1.3.10 Basti

In the Basti district the Rapti, the Banganga and the Kunra or the Dhamela otherwise known as Tenavi were the main waterways on the Nepalese side of the border. The Rapti was less used than the other two through which much timber was floated. By the Kunra the grain was also shipped to the local mart of Uska. The mart of Uska collected and distributed the rice of the surrounding country and the Nepalese Terai. Throughout its course in Basti, the Rapti was navigable for boats of 100 maunds. The Kunra and its continuation the Dhamela in months of flood bore country boats of any size.[145]

There were no river routes in Gonda, Bahraich, Kheri and Bareilly districts. But the Ferries maintained link between Bahraich and Nepal.

2.1.3.11 Pilibhit

The river Sarda enters Pilibhit in the extreme north of Pargana Puranpur, one mile above Mundiaghat. This Mundiaghal was the ferry point between Pilibhit and Nepal and formed the principal line of traffic between India and Nepal.[146]

2.1.3.12 Bridges and Ferries

On the Indo-Nepal border there were several wooden and rope bridges across different rivers.

Rope and wooden cantilever bridges were numerous in most of the streams. Later some of them were replaced by suspension and masonary bridges.

There were three main approches into Western Nepal from British India: two could be crossed through the bridge over Kali (Sarda) river at Jhulaghat and one[147] at Darchula in Nepal.[148]

The most important ferries were :

1. Ferries on the Gogra-Kamnagarghat, on a cart track from Nepal through Kates to Khairigarh, one small boat.
2. Ferries on the Rapti-Gangapur, on a cart track from the north of the Charda pargana to Nepal, one small boat.
3. Gulra, at the meeting of the boundaries of the Bhingor and Charda Parganas with the Nepal line, two small boats.[149]

The Teesta suspension bridge was very important in the development of trade through the route from Eastern Nepal to Darjeeling. According to the Deputy Commissioner of Darjeeling, there were two great works of the district, the suspension bridge and the road leading to Darjeeling and Siliguri and the road from the frontier at Naxalbari to Garidhura at the foot of the hills. He further stated that these works consisted of two systems. Firstly, that depended on the Teesta Suspension Bridge for opening up trade with Tibet and secondly, Naksabari - Garidura Road for opening the trade between the hills, plains and Nepal. This system has been completely successful and the roads are crowded with the carts and pack animals.[150] The roads of Nepal had been improved with the presence of bridges on the road. There was no need to reconstruct their surface.[151] Bridges on the larger rivers were rare. The passengers, carts, cattle and other commodities passed in ferry boats.These ferries were leased annually at auction for considerable sum.[152]

Tanakpur on the west bank of the Kali had no bridge to cross the border even though it was the larger frontier town of British India.The primitive boats were made of hollow tree trunk which could pass few articles.[153] The river Gogra in Oudh near the Nepal border was navigable by light drought streamers.[154] The Bahraich and Nepal WERE connected through ferries on the Ghaghra Rapti -Gangapur and Gulra.This route was connected with the cart tracks from the north of Chardo Pargana to Nepal. Gulra was connected at the meeting of the boundaries of the Bhingor and Chardo Pargana. All these rivers were crossed by small boats.[155]

During the monsoon when the water levels were high, a considerable quantity of traffic was carried in the country boats in the Gandak, little Gandak and Bagmati rivers. Thus, this route helped carrying the traffic between Muzaffapur and the adjoining districts of Nepal. Sal logs and large quantities of bamboo from Nepal were sent to the little Gandak and Bagmati.[156]

A few rivers in Nepal were not navigable due to swift current and were suitable only for floating of timbers. But these rivers were navigable in the

Indian plain. The little Gandak, the Bagmati and the Ganga in the rainy season were used to send goods directly to Kolkata. But in the dry weather the large crafts were navigated by the Great Gandak only. Hence, mainstream trade followed the course of Great Gandak to Patna and then to Calcutta.[157]

In Nepal, traffic through rivers was important and they were not much affected by the Indian Raliway system. Even during 1940's goods were transported between Hanuman Nagar in the Saptari distrct and the Indian Railway station at Nirmali by boat through Koshi river. In 1896, an engineer's services were requistioned (British Indian Government) to dredge the Karnali river in order to facilitate transportation of timber through the river.[158] A proposal from British India to construct boom on the Sarda river near Barmdeo for the purpose of catching the timber was accepted by the Prime Minister Chandra Shamsher, on the 15 October, 1912. But he wanted to discuss the project before its implementation.[159]

Water communcation was cheaper in comparison to the road[160] because the cost of maintainance and replacement of the orginal road bed would be higher than the former.[161] The Conservatt of Forest, Oudh, opined that if the river Mohan in Nepal were cleared, as they have cleared Suheli, a great deal of rice might be brought down to Bahramghat.[162] The traders of India and Nepal followed this route from the beginning because of this fact and it became the cornerstone of the commercial relations. It was the best means of communication for the poor and hilly country like Nepal which has plently of water resources.

2.1.4 Other Means of Communications

2.1.4.1 Postal Arrangement

Before 1881, there was only one line of postal communication between India and Nepal from Barewa to the capital of Nepal as there was no formal postal arrangement between the two countries.[163] Barewa connected the postal service with the Motihari in Champaran district. It passed through Hetauda via Chitlang to Kathmandu. It followed the same route as the Resident's post which started from Sujauli. Even the messages of the Darbar could not be forwarded due to lack of proper postal system, except by putting the cover in a cleft stick with the order that it was to be conveyed from village to village by whatever means available in routes which helped sending the message from one place to other. Thus the postal arrangement was slow and had uncertain procedure. Some Nepalese documents mention there were postal arrangements in Eastern and Western Nepal.[164]

In 1861 the Nepal government complained to the British Indian government about the serious loss of revenue owing to the constant receipt from and delivery to merchants at Kathmandu of some important articles which entered without no duty at the frontier. The Governor General in Council assured Nepal that Indian Post Office was not bound to deliver any letter or parcels in Nepal beyond the limits of the residency. An instruction was given to the Resident that he should refuse to receive any dispatch by the post or any haughty material from any persons living outside the Residency limits and this delivery should be accompanied by a custom house pass. Again, he was reminded that if this plan was adopted he would have no difficulty in making arrangements which would be satisfactory to the Nepalese government.[165]

The loss of revenue of the Nepalese government owing to the prevailing system of maneuver, which operated within the Residency, was reported by Charles Girdlestone in 1879. "If the system of money orders be extended to the post offices of this residency which is included in the Indian postal guides list, it is likely to be often recorded for the sake of evading the payment of duty in proportion to the receipts for money orders issued would be the loss of the Darbar by non- payment of its duty. Under these circumstances, Girdlestone submited the case for consideration whether the Nepal Post Office should be exempted from the new system just as the Residency Treasury has hitherto been from the system regarding money order.[166]

The government of Nepal organised internal postal line in the Nepalese districts, adjoining Indian territory. There were several lines opened for the postal sevices in Ilam near Darjeeling, Doti near Kumaun, Kerung and Kuti on Tibetan frontier. Besides, the branch line of these lines were connected with the outlying towns and the important military posts of regular staff appointed in the main lines to carry the despatches. As the postal operations started it took several days to reach the different places. British Resident was informed by the Nepalese Prime Minister that the dispatch reached Ilam in nine or ten days, it reached Silgarhi in the Doti district in ten or eleven days. As per the arrangement, the headmen of the village en route were always to have one or more men ready for the conveyance of a mail received. The facilities introduced were opened for general public and the stamps were available for purchase and stamps were manufactured locally.[167]

2.1.4.2 Rope Tram Way

As Bhimphedi and Thankot were separated by high mountain ranges and were not approachable through any means of conveyance, in 1902 Chandra Shamsher tried to establish a rope way from Bhimphedi to Thankot.[168] Before the rope way started, goods were carried on men's back and the transport was very slow and expensive. The Prime Minister, Chandra Shamsher had requested the British Government for material and technical assistance for the construction of rope tram way. The services of one or two European engineers were requisitioned to make preliminary survey and this rope way was erected on a similar model as existed in Cherrapunji.[169] In 1903 initial survey was carried out by the firm Martin and Company Kolkata but later a firm of Messers R.S. Underhill and Company of London took the charge of surveying.[170] The original rope way was supplied by Messers Keymer Son and Co. of London with Messers R. Pearson and A.J. Knight as consulting engineer, Mr. Underhill was in charge of the project and it was completed by mid summer 1925.[171]

Thus, railway, telegraph and postal services had helped to transform the independent states of India into British dominion. Though much pressure was put on Nepal for the extension of British telegraphic services it yet refused. It was clear that these provisions of civilization would affect their status of independent country.[172] The Nepalese government did not pursue a liberal policy regarding the extension of the railway or telegraphic system because that would have necessitated the employment of Europeans in their territories.[173]

2.2 TRADE ROUTE POLICY

The British Indian Government always insisted on better communication obviously for the expansion of trade to Nepal and through it to Central Asia. The road policy adopted by the Nepal Darbar was just opposite to the policy followed by the British Indian Government. The British Government always tried to compel the Nepalese Government to construct good roads but the Government of Nepal was hesitant to open all the roads for the British traders. The main reason for not giving concession was the fear of British aggression in Nepal. After the defeat of captain Kinlock in 1767, the British felt the need for constructing new roads for military movement. The Anglo- Nepal war of 1814-16 was the first landmark for development of roads and communication in Northern India. During the war, military roads had to be made. Communication lines were also established in the border areas. The revolt of 1857 in India witnessed another landmark in the history of development of roads and communications. To supress the revolt, the militray movement and particularly the march of the Nepalese army had been hampered.[174] The roads made to meet the military requirement, became the trade routes in the later period.

The Nepalese were fully aware of the fact that the hills being their fortifications and a good road over them would be a breach of their security.[175] The Nepalese Government did not want that the roads made by British India and extended beyond the frontier would reach Nepal. Nepalese were of the view that these neglected routes, with the passage of time, would either be forgotten or be made of forests which could prevent access. Thus, there would be a few roads which could be guarded easily by small force. Besides, the Government of Nepal also intended to open only a few roads for customs purpose. If there were several routes, the Nepalese would have to employ more officials and construct more customs houses. The Nepalese also did not want to allow them access to Tibet and aimed at frustrating every British move to obtain the transit route to Tibet. The Britishers always wanted to enter

Tibet through Nepal as the passes from Nepal were more suitable and lower than those of Kashmir, Lahaul and Karakoram and the main routes from Punjab to enter Turkistan. Government in India had realised that if Nepal provide access it would create a new trade avenue with all the territories north of the Himalayas.[176] The Nepal had privileged trade relation with Tibet which the Nepalese did not allow to misuse. The British claim for a rightful free passage to the Tibetan frontier for their merchants and goods in return for the full and free access enjoyed by Nepalese in British territories had no effect upon the Nepalese authorities.[177]

After several efforts when Nepalese refused to grant access, and there was no hope for the same, the British Indian Government approached London in 1875, to sanction the survey to be undertaken to ascertain the estimated cost of making a tolerable bridle path throughout that portion of the route from Darjeeling to Tibet which lay within the British territory. The road to Tibet from British India was completed ultimately in 1905 and to open this route was the only alternative.[178]

A great deal of conversation was held between the Nepalese Prime Minister, Ranodip Singh and the British Resident Charles Girdlestone for the improvement of roads in Nepalese territory. The conversation was based on the instruction given by the Government of India to the British Resident in Nepal in 1879. It was the duty of the Resident to bring carefully to the notice of the Nepal Darbar, the matters regarding the improvement of communication on the Nepalese frontier as one of the measures to increase trade between India and Nepal.[179] The Commissioners of the divisions bordering on the frontier between Bengal and Nepal were to enquire and report on the possibility of bridging at cheap cost the forest roads through which the traffic passed between these two countries.[180]

As instructed by the British Government in India, the then British Resident in Nepal requested the Government of Nepal to maintain better communications on the Nepal side of the border. The conversation between the British Resident Charles Girdlestone and Nepalese Government was put in writing on 18 July 1879. It was reported that there were several well maintained roads in India on which laden carts were able to move. But on the Nepalese side of the border, there was either no continuation or the continuation was very bad and as a result laden carts could not move along or the carts were moved with greater difficulty. If the road communications were good, the import of rice and hill products from Nepal would have been better and it would serve to increase the wealth of Nepal.[181]

The negotiation for the construction of road started on 7 August 1879, between the Prime Minister of Nepal and British Resident with several other Nepalese and British officials attending the meeting.[182] Mr. Ranodip Singh, the Prime Minister of Nepal, argued that Nepal being a poor country, there was no advantage in making roads and it was not possible to keep roads in good condition. He stated that the road made by the late Prime Minister Jang Bahadur, from Semrabasa to Bichakoh, and through Hetauda to Bhimphedi was destroyed every year. The Prime Minister also cited the example of the road from Kathmandu to a place within hills where there was a sulphur mine, but was destroyed by the rain. There was great difficulty in making roads from Hetauda to Bhimphedi and it was of no use if this road did not continue both sides. There was great difficulty in making the roads within the beds of rivers or on mountains. The urgency of establishing the metalled roads was emphasised in the negotiation. Both the sides accorded the importance of even earthen roads as they could be useful for carrying rice and forest products like medicinal herbs, dyes, iron, etc., as exports from Nepal and abroad like cloth and cash would be imported into Nepal. The Resident also suggested that to keep existing roads in good condition and to fill up the routes which would not cost annually more than 20 or 25 rupees per mile. The Prime Minister agreed that such repairs would be done.[183]

The existing road from the Nepal border to Banke was discussed between the Prime Minister, the Commander in Chief and Mir Suba Balwan Singh. They often enquired about the authority who had made it. The Resident told the Prime Minister that the road from border to Banke was in very bad condition and probably made by the British Government before the mutiny of 1857 as Banke was within the British territory. The Nepalese Prime Minister was told that the road was raised sufficiently and was well above the level of the surrounding ground and water could not overflow the road. The Resident took the permission to send list of 8 or 10 main lines of communication, which needed repairs. The Prime Minister had no objection whatever.[184]

According to Dr. H. Witwell, Officiating Residency Surgeon, "the subject of the inferiority of road communication in the Nepal border territory was evidently very unpalatable subject. The whole discussion regarding the construction of the road was more with a view to pacifying the resident and closing the discussion. It was far from the genuine conviction of their necessity and a real determination of having them carried out to the point continually being brought forward with increasing persisterce being the poverty of the country to support the strain of these burden. Further he added that the remainder of the subject under discussion seemed to have been carried on in much more earnest and honest manner".[185]

The Prime Minister of Nepal agreed on 12 August 1879 to repair the road leading to Banki Bazar. As a result the government of India directed the Governments of Bengal, Northwestern provinces and Oudh to send information to the British Resident with regard to the main lines of communication between these provinces and Nepal.

The government of Bengal prepared a list of six important routes running between lower Bengal and Nepalese territory. Similary, a list of following routes was sent by the Government of N.W. Provinces and Oudh.[186]

District	Description of Routes
Bahraich	via Sujauli between Golamandi (Nepalese mart) and Motipur.
	via Ratgarh between Nepalese mart of Banke and Motipur.
	via Babaganj between Nepalese mart of Banke and Nanpara.
Basti	via Morni between Nepal marts of Bahfletr-ganj and Sirsewa and the Basti and Gonda districts
	via Uska between the Indian marts and Lotan and Nepal Terai
Gorakhpur	via Logiabari between Nepal mart of Butwal and Gorakhpur districts

Via Bartauli between Gorakhpur district and Nepal Tarai and mart of Butwal
via Thunthibari between Gorakhpur district and Nepal Tarai and mart of Butwal

In 1880 a conference held at Faizabad, discussed the impact of different means of communication on the trade with Nepal. The view of charles Girdlestone that the improvement of road communication of Nepal side of the frontier was not possible without strong pressures from the British Government, was accepted by the conference. It was also concluded that the improvement of road would lead to better transportation of goods. These goods were meant for distribution among the hill tribes which were carried by coolies and ponies. All the roads leading to the important marts like Nepalganj needed adequate funds to maintain them, specially at the point where ferry approaches. It was also suggested that the Darbar should be asked to maintain the portion of roads on the Nepal side leading to marts to be traversed by carts.[187] The Government of India always tried to influence the Nepalese Government on the question of improving the communication. Consequently, the Secretary of State induced the Nepalese Government to maintain and repair the roads in good order. These roads always led to the interior of the country. The British Resident in Nepal, Girdlestone, informed the Secretary of State, on the basis of the report prepared by the Government of North Western Provinces, that the export from Nepal to North Western Provinces and Oudh was 215,199 mounds worth Rs. 258,731 when the road was bad between 1 April 1875 and 31 March 1880. But from 1 April to 31 March 1880 when the quality of road was upgraded, the export from Nepal to North Western Provinces and Oudh went upto 220,878 mounds and worth Rs. 927,688. Hence there was an increase in both volume and value when the road was good.[188] This was also mentioned by Resident in his memorandum to the Prime Minister of Nepal.[189]

The Resident had extensive correspondence with the Prime Minister of Nepal with regard to the improvement of roads in the Nepalese territory. It was calculated that more important roads leading from border to the prinicipal Terai marts of Nepal were at most 400 miles and Rs. 25 per mile was required to repair which gave a total annual outlay of Rs. 10,000. It would be a wise decision to devote a portion of the taxes for the maintenance of communications. The improvement would lead to enhancement of trade and thereby the advantage would accrue to the Darbar and to its subjects. Regarding extra burden on the poor for levying more taxes for construction of roads, the resident replied that he did not see any reason to impose extra tax upon the subjects because a little restriction on Darbar's expenses would generate sufficient resource for the repair of the roads.[190]

Nepalese officials holding the posts of Subha and Captain informed the Prime Minister that the estimate of Rs 25/miles would not be sufficient for the repair of roads in Nepal. As the rivers at the foothills had no depth, all the roads got damaged in the rainy season. The Prime Minister instructed the repair of roads leading to the Banka Bazar.The Nepalese Government was not inclined to meet the British request for the general improvement of roads on the plea of poverty and inablity to command the requisite labour.[191]

Charles Girldlestone rejected the Prime Minister's plea of poverty and argued that thousands of rupees had been spent by the Darbar for expenditure on a temple close to Kathmandu valley within the twelve months. Coolies in numbers up to hundred were employed to carry rice from the Terai to the valley. The rice was collected and stored as a provision against famine.[192] In his confidential dispatch dated September 1880, Charles Girdlestone mentioned "a yearly expenditure of Rs. 10,000 would probably meet all reasonable requirements of Nepal to maintain the roads which equals to interest at 5 per cent on half the sum i.e., for lakhs of rupees, which the Prime Minister is taking from the state treasury for expenditure on the tour in British India."[193] Girdlestone accepted the view expressed by Nepal Darbar that there were serious physical difficulties in the way of making and maintaining roads suitable for traffic throughout the years.[194]

The poor response from the Prime Minister, Ranodip Singh, made the British Resident irritated. He remarked about the Prime Minister that his excellency's character is such that he would agree to a proposal rather than continue a distasteful conversation. The Prime Minister often comes into influence of the bigoted officials by whom he is surrounded. So despite the appeal made by the British officials for the betterment of the communication and roads, the result was only to regret. The Prime Minister did not meet the terms of improvement of the roads and communication.[195] Mr Jang Bahadur Rana, the predecessor of Ranodip Singh wanted to construct and maintain good roads in the coming years but he did not initiate because he felt that in the near future there would be war between the British and Nepal.[196] Mr Jang Bahadur Rana was pressed to make the road but he replied that his countrymen were against the prop sal. The people were of the opinion that even if the roads remain in the same condition, no invading army could make its way to the valley. He added the cat and lion story "Though the cat can not fight on even terms with the lion, yet if the lion drives the cat into a corner the cat will scratch his eyes".[197]

Several efforts were made to persuade Jang Bahadur but without success. It was reported in 1862, that the British attempts to open Tibet for trade were viewed by Jang Bahadur as a threat to Nepal's own commercial interest in the Himalayan trade which Nepal had for long established in Tibetan trade.[198] The British Government in India had to give up the hope of Jang Bahadur's co operation. But the successive premiers of Nepal played the same card and policy of isolation. Thus, ultimately the British Government had to concentrate its attention on the routes from Darjeeling and Sikkim for trade with Tibet.

The Kerung and Kuti route via Nepal was replaced by the new route between Phari in Chumbi Valley and Kalimpong across the Jalep Pass. Kalimpong had replaced Kathmandu as the entrepot of trans Himalayan trade by the end of the Nineteenth century. The Phari route was very helpful. It provided direct contact of Tibet with the British India and helped in making obsolete the existing trade route that linked Tibet and South Asia via Nepal. This ultimately changed the behaviour of Nepalese merchants in Tibet, which were deprived of the margin of profit and stopped sending wool. Tibetan Government prohibited Nepalese to use the route as an artery of commerce. The traffic of 3,000 to 4,000 balls of wool by the Nepalese bound trades towards Darjeeling to Kathmandu was compelled to be diverted.[199]

It was widely accepted that due to difficult means of transport, the Indo- Nepal trade in general and Nepalese exports earning in particular suffered to a great deal. The trade was confined mainly to villages and most of the adjacent valleys. In conclusion it can be said that the Rana Prime Ministers of Nepal did not pay attention to investing money. The British Resident in Nepal Colonel H. Wylie in this regard wrote, "roads and bridges are being neglected while funds are squandered on a succession of palaces for himself and his sons". 'I am informed that these palaces were considered to be the Ministers' own private property and they can leave them to whom he pleases, although they are built from State funds.[200] No major roads existed in Nepal except some historical roads existing up to the boundary of the Nepal and British India. So naturally it was difficult to have more trade.[201] Charles Girdlestone did not subscribed to the view. He argued that the ordinary carts of Northern India did not require good roads. The construction of good roads was also affected by presence of nullah or water course. He suggested that the banks of nullah should be connected with rough wooden bridges.[202] Despite the weak road policy followed by Nepal, the Indo –Nepalese trade flourished over the time.

NOTES AND REFERENCES

1. The article on the physical aspects of India by T.H. Holdwich, *Imperial Gazetteer of India,* 1907, Vol. p. 5.
2. The article On the traditional routes of Central Asian trade by Jahar Sen "India's trade with Central Asia Via Nepal," Bulletin of Tibetology, Vol. VIII. No, 2. pp. 21-35.
3. Kirkpatric William, *An Account of the Kingdom of Nepal,* London, 1811, Reprint Manjusri, New Delhi, 1972, pp. 11-37, 107-143.
4. B.H. Hodgson, Essay on the language, literature and Religion of Nepal and Tibet together with further papers on the Geography, London, 1874, Reprint Manjusri Publication House, New Delhi, 1972, Part II, Section VIII, pp. 94-97.
5. *Ibid.*, p. 99.
6. Kanchanmoy Majumdar, *Anglo-Nepalese Relations in the Nineteenth Century,* Firma K.L. Mukhopadhyaya, Calcutta, 1973, pp. 78-79.
7. Revenue A. August, 1877, No 22. Girdlestone, Resident in Nepal to T. H. Thornton, Officiating Secretary to the Government of India. Foreign Department, No. 15 p. dated 19 September, 1876. (N.A.I.)
8. Shreeram Prasad Upadhyaya, *Indo–Nepal Trade Relation*, Nirala Publication, Jaipur, 1992, p. 53.
9. Revenue A. August, 1877, No 22. Girdlestone, Resident in Nepal to T. H. Thornton, Officiating Secretary to the Government of India. Foreign Department, No. 15 p. dated 19 September, 1876. (N.A.I.)
10. *Ibid.*
11. *Ibid.*
12. Revenue A. August 1877, No. 22.
13. The Deputy Commissioner of Kheri to the Commissioner, Sitapur Division No. 681A, dated 6 April 1876 (N.A.I.).
14. Revenue A. August 1877, No. 22.
15. *Ibid.*
16. *Ibid.*
17. *Ibid.*
18. *Ibid.*
19. Jahar Sen, *Indo-Nepal Trade in the Nineteenth Century,* Firma K.L.M. Pvt. Ltd., Calcutta, 1977, p. 52.
20. Revenue A. August 1877, No. 22.
21. Jahar Sen, *op. cit.,* p. 50.
22. Jahar Sen, *op. cit.,* p. 43. Cited Champaran District Records, Serial No. 76 of Register 75. Vol. I: page 23-24, Govt. Circulars, Orders and Letters commencing.
23. H.C. Conybeare, Gazetteer of N.W. Provinces, Vol. II, Allahabad, 1881, p. 699.
24. *Ibid.*
25. *Ibid.* No. 22.

26. It was common practice among the traders to enter into an agreement with the cart owners to carry the commodities. There were leaders among the cartmen who took leases for supply of carts. They were called Chaudhuries. see P. C. Raychnudhury, *Bihar District Gazetteers*, Champaran, Patna, 1960, p. 337.
27. Krishnakanta Adhikari, "Brief Survey of Nepal's Trade with British India during the latter half of the nineteenth century", *Contribution to Nepalese Studies*, Vol. 2, No.1, February 1975, Kathmandu, p. 191.
28. Revenue A. August 1877, Vol. 22.
29. L.S.S. O'Malley, Bengal District Gazetteer, Champaran, Calcutta, 1907, p.120.
30. W. W. Hunter, *Statistical Accounts of Bengal, Tirhut and Champaran,* Vol. VIII, London, 1877, p. 249.
31. Jahar Sen, *op.cit.*, p. 48.
32. Revenue A. August, 1877, No. 22.
33. Jahar Sen, *op. cit.*, p. 43.
34. P. C. Roy Choudhary, *Bihar District Gazetteers*, Champaran, Patna, 1960, p. 337.
35. Revenue A. August 1877, No. 22.
36. Jahar Sen , *op. cit.*, p. 47.
37. Revenue A. August 1877, No. 22.
38. Administration Report of the Patna Division for the year 1872-73, p. 153 (N.A.I.).
39. W. W. Hunter, *Statistical Account of Bengal, Tirhut and Champaran* Vol. XIII, London, 1877, p. 6.
40. *Ibid.*
41. Revenue A. August, 1877, No. 22.
42. *Ibid.*
43. P.C. Roy Chaudhury, *Bihar District Gazetteer* Darbhanga. Patna, 1964, p. 304.
44. Revenue A. August, 1877, No. 22.
45. W. W. Hunter, *op. cit.*, p. 177.
46. The General Administration Report of the Bhagalpur Division for the year 1881-82. (N.A.I.).
47. Revenue A. August 1877. No. 22.
48. Morung—An old name for the Nepal Terai lying north of the Purnea District. "The name is an old one being mentioned more than once in the Alamgirnamah and in the annals of the Koch Kings. It is shown in Van den Broucke's map as comprising the whole Himalayan tract from Bihar to Assam and in Rennell's map of 1779, the Nepal Terai between Muzaffarpur and Jalpaiguri is entered under this name." L.S.S. O'Malley, *Bengal District Gazetteers*, Purnea, 1911, p. 198.
49. Revenue A. August, 1877, No. 22.
50. Jahar Sen, *op.cit.*, p. 45.

51. W. W. Hunter, *Statistical Account of Bengal,* Purnea, Vol. XV, London, 1877, p. 351.
52. *Ibid.* p. 253.
53. Revenue A. August 1877, No. 22.
54. Krishnakanta Adhikari, *op. cit.*, p. 192.
55. Revenue A. August 1877, No. 22.
56. Jahar Sen, *op. cit.* p. 43, Cited from Proceedings of Bengal Govt. Gen. Mis. August, 1876, File No. 120, S. No. 1-2. p. 24 (N.A.I.).
57. Ibid, cited from Darjeeling District Records, General Department English Correspondence 1841-1879.
58. *Ibid,* collection XXXXII. File No. 48 of 1885-86, No. 241 G, dated 25 May 1886.
59. *Ibid,* cited from Collection XXX, File No. 55 of 1893-94 dated 9 June 1893.
60. Revenue A. August, 1877, No. 22.
61. Arthur Jules Dash, *Bengal District, Gazetteers*, Darjeeling. Alipur, 1947, p. 169.
62. Jahar Sen, op. cit. p. 43.
63. Report on the Foreign Trade of North Western Province and Oudh, during the year 1877-78. N.W.P. and Oudh Government. Pvt. Allahabad, 1878, p. 4 (N. A. I.)
64. The Report on the Trade of the N.W. Provinces and Oudh from 1879-1885. (N.A.I.).
65. Foreign Department Political, A. March I880. No. 303, Rajendra Nath Mitra, Assistant-Secretary to the Government of Bengal to Girdlestone. No. 816 dated, 15 November 1879 Calcutta, (N.A.I.).
66. Revenue A. August 1877, No. 17.
67. The Report on the Trade of the N.W. Provinces and Oudh from 1879-1885. (N.A.I.). p. 55.
68. *Ibid.*
69. *Ibid.*
70. *Ibid.*
71. *Ibid.*
72. *Ibid.*
73. Political A. March 1880 No. 305. E. C Buck, Director of Agriculture and Commerce of N. W. P. Oudh to C. Robertson, Secretary to Govt. of N. W. Province of Oudh, dated 2 December 1979. (N.A.I.).
74. L. S. S. O'Malley, *Bihar Orissa District Gazetteers*, Champaran, Patna, 1938, p. 92.
75. W. W. Hunter, "A Statistical Account of Bengal", Patna and Saran, Vol. XI, London, 1877, p. 197.
76. L.S.S. O'Malley, *Bengal District Gazetteers.* Muzaffarpur, Calcutta, 1907, p. 157.
77. P. C Roy Chaudhury, *Bihar District Gazetteers,* Darbhanga, Patna, 1964, p. 304.

78. *Imperial Gazetteer of India,* 1908, Vol. VIII p. 268, also see Sunil Kumar, Geography of transport in Eastern India, under the British Raj, Calcutta, 1980, p. 50.
79. Revenue A. August 1877, No. 22.
80. Jahar Sen, *op. cit.,* p. 77.
81. Bengal Administration Report for 1883-84. p. 220.
82. H. R. Nevill, (ed.), District Gazetteer of the United Provinces. No.XXXI. Allahabad 1909. p. 82
83. Ibid., pp.76-77.
84. H. R. Nevill, (ed.), *The District Gazetteer of the United Provinces*, Basti. Vol. XXXII, Calcutta, 1907. p. 259
85. H. R. Nevill, (ed.), The Gazetteer of the United Provinces-Vol XLVIII Allahabad 1904. p. 189.
86. *Imperial Gazetteer of India* 1908. Vol. VI. 213.
87. H. R. Nevill, *District Gazetteer of the United Provinces.* Allahabad, 1909. p. 213.
88. M.C. Regmi, "The Impact of India's Railway System on Nepal's Economy During the Closing Years of the 19th Century." *Regmi Research Series*, Year 15, No. 5, Kathmandu, 1883, p. 72.
89. *Ibid.,* p. 72.
90. Jahar Sen, op. cit. p. 71.
91. Sunil Kumar Munsi, op. cit. pp. 91-92
92. *Ibid.* p. 92. Cited from Annual Report on the Administration of Bengal Presidency,1880-81, p. 46.
93. Annual General Administration Report of the Patna Division for 1890-91, p. 39.
94. Jahar Sen, op. cit. p. 72. cited from Bengal Administration Report for 1880-81. p. 270.
95. Annual General Administration Report of the Patna Division for 1890-91, p. 39.
96. *Ibid.,* for 1884-85. p. 47, para. 167.
97. Annual General Administration Report of the Patna Division for 1898-99.
98. *Imperial Gazetteer of India*, Provincial Series Bengal, Vol. II. 1909, New Delhi, Reprint 1979. p. 132.
99. L.S.S.O' Malley, *Bihar and Orissa Gazetteers,* Dist. Champaran 1907, p. 122.
100. Annual General Report of the Patna Division for 1881-82. pp. 38-39. para 31. (N.A.I.).
101. *Ibid.*, for 1884-85, para 31.
102. Annual General Report of the Patna Division for 1884-85. p. 23. (N.A.I.).
103. Revenue A. August 1877. No. 22.
104. Appendix C. Annual Report of the Foreign Trade of the North-West Province and Oudh for the year ending 31 March 1880 (N.A.I.).

105. Annual Report of the Foreign Trade of the North-West Province and Oudh for the year ending 31st Match, 1880. (N.A.I.).
106. Political. A. July 1880, No. 196. Proceedings of a Conference assembled at Faizabad on 26 January 1880. (N.A.I.).
107. *Ibid.*
108. *Ibid,* Nos. 196-98. K.W. No. 1. (N.A.I.).
109. Revenue A. December, 1877, No. 2, E. Buck, Director of Agriculture and Commerce. N.W. Provinces and Oudh to C. Robertson, Esq., Secretary to Government of North Western Provinces and Oudh. No. 187C Allahabad, dated 1 November 1877. (N.A.I.).
110. Annual Report of the Foreign Trade of the North-West Provinces and Oudh for the year ending 31st March 1880.
111. Jahar Sen. *op. cit.,* p. 76.
112. External B. February, 1893. No. 30. Franklin Prestage, the Chairman of the Darjeeling Himalayan Railway to the Foreign Department Government of India, Simla, No. 103. dated 20 October 1892. (N.A.I.).
113. M.C. Regmi, *op. cit.* p. 72.
114. *Ibid.* p. 73.
115. R.R. Diwakar, *Bihar Through the Ages*, Orient Longman, New Delhi Patna, 1959, p. 50.
116. Kenneth Mason, *Abode of Snow* (London 1955), p. 3, B.C Law (ed.), *Mountains and Rivers of India* (Cal. 1968), pp. 59-61.
117. Kenneth Mason, *op. cit,* p.10.
118. Jahar Sen, *Indo-Nepal Trade in the Nineteenth Century*, Firma K.L.M. Pvt. Ltd., Calcutta, 1977, p. 63.
119. *Imperial Gazetteer of India, Provincial Series.* Bengal Vol. I. 1909. Reprint, New Delhi, 1979, p. 98.
120. *Imperial Gazetteer of India, op. cit.* p. 210.
121. J.B.S. Burathokey and U.M. Malla, The Physical Aspects of the Kingdom of Nepal, Seminar paper on the Ecology of the Tropical highlands, Nepal National Commission for UNESCO, 1968, p.12.
122. *Imperial Gazetteer of India, op.cit.* p. 211.
123. *Ibid.*, p. 210.
124. *Ibid.*
125. *Imperial Gazetteer of India* 1908 Vol. XII. pp. 302-303.
126. J. B. S. Burathokey and U.M. Malla. *op. cit.*
127. *Imperial Gazetteer of India, op. cit.* p. 212.
128. *Ibid.*
129. *Ibid.*
130. *Ibid.*
131. W.W. Hunter, *Statistical Account of Bengal*, Tirhut and Champaran, Vol. XIII, Calcutta, 1877, p. 51.
132. J.B.S. Burathokey and U.M. Malla. *op. cit.*

133. Imperial Gazetteer of India, *op. cit.* p. 225.
134. *Ibid.*
135. *Ibid.*
136. J. B. S. Burathokey, *op. cit.*
137. *Ibid.*
138. W.W. Hunter, *Statistical Account of Bengal*, Bhagalpur, Vol. XV, Calcutta, p. 226.
139. *Ibid.* pp. 229-231.
140. *Ibid.*
141. Jahar Sen, *Indo -Nepal Trade in the Nineteenth Century,* Firma K.L.M. pvt. Ltd., Calcutta,1977, p. 67.
142. Revenue A. August 1877. No. 22.
143. W. W. Hunter, *Statistical Account of Bengal*, Tirhut, Champaran, p. 222.
144. Revenue A. August 1877. No. 22.
145. Jahar Sen, *op. cit.* p. 69.
146. Ibid., pp. 69-70.
147. Northey W. Brook, *The Land of the Gurkhas,* John Lane, London, 1933, p. 139.
148. *Ibid.,* Darchula is some three days march above Jhulaghat, The route across the bridge over Kali at Darchula runs to Bajrang and Bajura, the two northerly provinces of Western Nepal.
149. *Gazetteer of the Province of Oudh.* Vol. I, A to G, Lucknow, 1877, P. 103.
150. Jahar Sen, op. cit. p. 43. Cited from Darjeeling District Records. General Department English Correspondence. Collection XXXII. File No. 8 of 1885-86, No. 241 G. dated May 1886.
151. Perceval London, Nepal, Vol. II. Constable & Co., London, 1928, p. 200.
152. *Imperial Gazetteer of India*, provincial series Bengal Vol. I 1909, Reprint 1976, New Delhi, p. 100.
153. Revenue A. August 1877. No. 22.
154. Orfeur Cavenagh, *op. cit.* p. 95.
155. Jahar Sen, *op. cit.* p. 69.
156. Imperial Gazetteer of India, *op. cit.* p. 114.
157. L. S. S. O'Malley, Bengal District Gazetteers, Muzaffarpur. Calcutta, 1907, p. 94.
158. M C Regmi, *op.cit.*
159. Register No. 147, Foreign Ministry of Nepal, dated 15 October 1912.
160. "It is estimated that on a good wagon road a single horse power will drag about 3000 lbs at the rate of 3 feet per second, on a railway about 30,000 at the same rate, in water as much as 200,000 lbs." K.T. Shah, *Trade Tariffs and Transport in India,* National Books Bombay, 1923, p. 370.
161. *Ibid.*
162. Revenue A. August 1877. No. 14. Conservator of Forest, Oudh to the Junior Secretary to the Commissioner of Oudh. No. 113 dated 28 March 1876. (N.A.I).

163. The line from Barewa to Kathmandu was introduced in 1875. See Divya Deo Bhatta, "Mass Communication in Nepal". Nepal, The Himalayan Kingdom. His Majesty's Government, Ministry of Communication, Kathmandu, 1982, p. 16.

164. However, some Nepalese documents mention that there were postal arrangements in Eastern and Western Nepal. In 1850 there were over-whelming majority of the 4,979 Hulaki households who used to provide mail services from Kathmandu to Dhankuta in the east and Doti in the west. Arrangements were made in western hill region to provide each Hulaki households with a rice-land allotment of between 40 and 100 muris, depending on the size of the family. On the eve of the Anglo-Nepal War, these arrangements were extended to Hulaki porters in the eastern hill region also. This does not mean that each Hulaki household in these regions possessed a rice land allotment. Later on the system was discontinued. Hulaki porters were compensated through exemption from taxes and were given security of tenure without any provision for rice land allotments. On the whole, the postal arrangements of Nepal were not well organised as in British India, Register of Kagate—*Hulaki Households in Nepal*, 1909 (1852), in Regini Research Colleciion, Cited in M.C. Regmi, *Thatched Huts and Stucco Palace*, p. 96; "Hulak Regulations for Areas between Dharmathali and the Jamana River" Ashadh Sudi 4, 1866 (June 1809). Cited in *Ibid.*, p. 97; *Hulak Regulations for areas Between the Bagmati River and Vijayapur.* Baisaku Sudi, 4, 1866 (May 1814); Arrangements regarding Hulaki Households in Dailakh's Bhadra Badi 6, 1886. (August 1839). Cited in Chittaranjan Nepali, *op. cit.*, pp. 328-39. "Register of Kagati-Hulaki Households in Junla" Falgun Sudi 1O, 1949 (March 1883), *Regmi Research Collection* Vol. 22, pp. 349-80. Cited in M.C. Regmi, *op. cit.* p. 98.
General B. October, 1881. No. 109. Charles Girdlestone, the Resident in Nepal to the Officiating Secretary to the Government of India in the Foreign Department, Simla. No. 71 p. dated 27 September 188l. (N.A.I.).

165. Foreign Department. Political, A. November 1861. Vol. 49. Colonel H.M. Durand C.B., Offg, Secretary to the Government of India, Fort William to the Resident in Nepal. No. 114, dated 19 November 1861. (N.A.I).

166. General B. November, 1879. No. 356. Girdlestone, Resident in Nepal to the Secretary of Government of India, Foreign Department, Simla dated 20 Oct. 1879. (N.A.I.).

167. General B. October, 1881, No. 109.

168. Bhimphedi is at the foot of the first range of hill and Thankot is at the head of the Kathmandu Valley. It is also the main entrance of the capital.

169. External. P. 1 June 1902, No. 6. Lieutinant Colonel T.C. Pears, Resident in Nepal to the Secretary to the Government of India, Foreign Department. No. 4 p. dated 8 January 1902. (N.A.I.).

170. Secret E. September, 1903, No. 95, Lieutenant Colonel C.W. Revenshaw. Resident in Nepal to the Secretary to the Government of Indian Foreign Department, dated 11 April 1903. (N.A.I.).

171. Perceval London, Nepal, Vol. 2, *op. cit.* p. 203.
172. Abrol Mridula. British Relations with Frontier States. (1863-1875). S. Chand & Co., New Delhi, 1974, p. 41. Cited from the f n, of K.M, Panikkar, Indian States with the Government of India, London, 1932, p. 82-83.
173. Shreeram Prasad Upadhyaya, *Indo–Nepal Trade Relations*, Nirala Publication, Jaipur, 1992 p. 57.
174. P.C. Roy Chaudhury, *Bihar District Gazetteer*, Champaran, *op. cit.* p. 336.
175. Political A. December 1880, No. 38. Charles Girdlestone British Resident in Nepal to A.C. Lyall, Esq., C. B. Secretary to the Government of India, foreign Department. No. 32 p. dated 25 September 1880. (N.A.I.).
176. Political A. February 1875 No. 30. G. E. R. Girdlestune to H. Le Poer Wynne, Officiating Secretary to Government of India, Foreign Department, dated 9 June 1874. N. 18 p. (N.A.I.).
177. Niranjan Sharma. Nepal Foreign trade, (unpublished Ph.D. Thesis), Delhi School of Economics. University of Delhi, April 1968, p. 29.
178. *Ibid.*
179. Revenue A. February 1879, No. 2. A.C. Lyall. Esq. C.B., Secretary to the Government of India, Foreign Department to the Resident in Nepal. No. 1R, dated 14 January 1879. (N.A.I.).
180. Political A. October 1879. No. 132. H.L. Harrison, Officiating Secretary to the Government of Bengal to the Secretary to the Government of India, Foreign Department No. 351, dated 7 June 1879.
181. *Ibid.* No. 136, Charles Girdlestone, Resident in Nepal to A.C. Lyall, Esq. Secretary to the Government of India, Foreign Department. No. 37. p., dated 18 July 1879.
182. The Nepalese Officers present in the talk were General Dhira Shumsher Jang Bahadur Rana, Commander-in-Chief, Sirdar Laxmi Bhaga i.e. confidential adviser of the Prime Minister, Colonel Ran Singh, Commissioner of Police, Kathmandu, Major Captain Mahabeer Singh, Orderly officer, Mir Subha Balwan Singh, Private Secretary to the Prime Minister. Dr Whitwell, Residency Surgeon and Shew Shankar Singh, Mir Munsi of Nepal Residency were two important British officers. *Ibid.* No. 137. Report by Shew Shanker Singh, Mir Munshi of the Nepal Residency, of a conversation between the Prime Minister of Nepal and the Resident on the 7 of August 1879.
183. *Ibid.*
184. *Ibid.*
185. *Ibid.* Notes of a conversation held between the Maharaja Prime Minister of Nepal and the Resident on the afternoon of August and prepared by H. Whitewell, Residency Surgeon, on 8 August 1879. (N.A.I.).
186. *Ibid.* March 1880, No. 305, B.C. Buck, Director of Agriculture and Commerce of N.W.P. and Oudh to C. Robertson, Secretary to the Government of N.W.P. and Oudh No. 1413 C–C.T.V. dated 2 December 1879, Kanpur, (N.A.I.).
187. *Ibid.* July 1880. No. 196, Proceedings of a Conference assembled at Faizabad in North Western Provinces and Oudh on 26 January 1880.

188. General A. January 1882. No. 15. Charles Girdlestone. British Resident in Nepal to Grant, Secretary to the Government of India, Foreign Department No. 69 p. dated 23 September 1881.
189. *Ibid.*
190. Political A. December 1880. No. 44. A Memorandum from the British Resident in Nepal to the Prime Minister and Commander-in-chief of Nepal, dated 2 February 1880.
191. *Ibid.* No. 45. Abstract translation of a memorandum from the Prime Minister and Commander-in-Chief of Nepal, to the Resident in Nepal dated 30 Magh, Samwat 1930 (25 February 1880). (N.A.I.).
192. *Ibid.* No. 38. Charles Girdlestone, Resident in Nepal to A.C. Lyall, Esq. Secretary to the Government of India. Foreign Department No. 32 p. dated 25 September 1880 (N.A.I.).
193. *Ibid.*
194. *Ibid.*
195. *Ibid.*
196. Orfeur Cavenagh, Reminiscences of an Indian Official. London, 1884, pp.175 -176.
197. William Digby, 1857: A Friend in need 1887, Friendship forgotten, Indian Foreign office Administration, London, Indian Political Agency, 1890, pp. 25-26.
198. Ravuri Dhanalaxmi, *British attitude to Nepal's relations with Tibet and China 1814-1914,* Bahri Publications, New Delhi, 1981, p. 86.
199. Prem R. Uprety, *Nepal Tibet Relations 1850-1930, Years of Hopes Challenges and Frustrations*, Commonwealth Publishers, Kathmandu, 1980, pp. 166-167.
200. Secret E. July 1897. No. 76. Colonel H. Wylie, Resident in Nepal to the Secretary to the Government of India Foreign Department, No. p. 13 -3027, dated 16 June 1897. (N.A.I.).
201. Asad Husain, British India's relations with Kingdom of Nepal from 1857 to 1947 (unpublished Ph.D. Thesis), University of Minnesota, U. S. A. 1965 p. 174.
202. Revenue A. August 1877, No. 22.

3

Commercial Policy and Taxes

3.1 Introduction

Commercial policy plays an important part in the development of a country. It may be defined as the one that helps in accelerating the pace of economic development : (i) by enabling a country to have a larger share of the gains from trade, (ii) by augmenting the rate of capital formation, (iii) by promoting industrialisation, and (iv) by maintaining equilibrium in the balance of payments.

Regulation of foreign trade is the fundamental principle of commercial policy. The most widely used form of commercial policy instrument is the tariff or customs duty.

The trade relation between India and Nepal knocked the bottom after the establishment of the Gurkha hegemony in Nepal in 1769. Prithvi Narayan Shah, who is considered as the father of modern Nepal, was a "nationallist to the core of his heart."[1] Since the trade between India and Nepal ceased to thrive, East India Company attempted several times in the second half of the eighteenth century and the first-half of the nineteenth century to establish trade relations with Nepal. However, no significant result came. In the second-half of the nineteenth century, the diplomatic and political relations between India and Nepal improved slightly. Trade relation between the two countries registered a steady and phenomenal growth. The Indian Government followed free trade policy with Nepal.[2]

The commercial policy during the period under review was more or less the same as was during the whole period of Ranas. They were convinced that if the British were allowed to stroll freely in the country or their merchants were allowed to carry on trade in the country. This would ultimately lead to the subjugation. Particularly the Rana Prime Ministers understood that throwing open their country to foreign capital would in no time end their feudal system and would eventually lead to their decline.[3] Though the British Indian government had assured the same government that they had no desire to conquer their country, but Nepalese Government did not believe that.

The British Indian Government regarded Nepal as a growing captive market for manufacturing goods[4]. The secretary of the society for the encouragement of Arts, manufacture and commerce informed in writing to the Secretary of State for India that it was essential for Indian Government to use every efforts to obtain from Nepal free passage for the British merchants and goods to the frontier of Tibet in return for the full and free access enjoyed by Nepal in Indian territory[5]. Colonel G. Ramsay, the British Resident in Nepal, cited an example of Subha Dharma Narayan, a Nepalese merchant, owner of several shops in the Indian province.[6] The British Resident tried much to bring Jang Bahadur back to the term of engagement of 1839, but did not succeed. Only alternative for the Resident was to negotiate a fresh and new treaty with Nepal. But he had no hope of achieving this because India had nothing to offer Nepal as inducement to enter into a new treaty, he believed.[7]

With regard to diverse commerce relations, G Ramsay, the British Resident in Nepal had a frank discussion with Jang Bahadur, the Nepalese Prime Minister. Ramsay convinced the Nepalese Prime Minister that the Durbar exercised ceaseless vexatious interference over all the branches of trade within its own dominion. Durbar made Indian traders to conform to a particular line of policy detrimental to their own interest. This restrictive trade policy was due to personal attitude and disposition of Jang Bahadur himself, greed of Sardars, want of opposition in Nepal and the prevalence of the monopoly system.[8]

A section of the British officials had always viewed the fact that Indo-Nepal trade is an unrewarding business. Dr. Danial Wright, the British Residency Surgeon, remarked "as regards trade, I am aware on this point that this is generally believed that there is great field for European enterprises in Nepal along with Tibet. I suspect however, that this is an erroneous idea. Despite vast poverty, the peoples wants are not supplied by their own country. There was only small export trade from Nepal, and it was difficult to imagine that it could be increased because of the poor, rugged, mountainous land, producing hardly enough to meet the needs of its populations.[9] But Charles Girdlestone, the British Resident in Nepal, contested the views and stated that there was a good trade prospect for European goods in Nepal and Tibet. Though the government of Nepal was confirmed in writing by the Secretary of State (for India) yet, considering the natural resources of the country, the trade with Nepal was very small.[10] British Government in India could do little to press Nepal on its commercial policy because the British Indian Government had disclaimed all the rights to interfere and even to advice for giving up the protecting systems generally observed in western part of the country and the policy of isolation throughout the country. In respect of this one top ranking British Official observed, "Nepal in this matter is in her right it may be short sighted but we have no equitable standpoint for protesting."[11] Charles Girdlestone also stated that, "there was no native state in alliance which laid greater stress on declaration of British Government than Nepal. The Nepal Durbar showed intense fondness in all its communications, for precedent and an inclination to interpret the clauses of the treaty in the strictest sense. This feeling was so deeply rooted on the part of the Darbar, I could not conceal my fear that if occasion required "the words of 1859 would be brought up in judgment against us."[12]

The Nepal Durbar was told in 1859 that the British Indian Government had no right to interface with or to advise on the commercial policy of Nepal. Girdle Stone, the British Resident in Nepal, reminded the Indian Government about the existence of such a declaration in 1874 and 1877.[13] In the presence of such a declaration, any representation to the Durbar to alter a system which it believed to be for its own advantage and within its own right was very unlikely to have any effect.[14] It was not possible to grumble the incidence of taxation as levied in Nepal and also the effect of protective system in certain marts of western Terai.[15]

It was also pointed out that the whole tone of the letter which contained the 'declaration' was a remonstrance against the policy of the steps to take which the Nepal Durbar had threatened in the particular instance.[16] To exclude Indian traders entirely from Nepal, the Government was adopting indirect means. The British Government in India in its letter containing this declaration accepted that they had no wish or right to dictate Nepal. Nevertheless, they remonstrated pretty strongly.[17] The Foreign Department of Government of India opined in 1880 that the declaration of 1859 was not an express agreement. Evidently, the remark was simply a diplomatic phrase to ease out possible difficulties.[18] By treaties it gained the advantage of "free reciprocal intercourse" and full liberty of commerce with Sikkim.[19]

Charles Girdlestone organised a conference at Faizabad. High ranking officials like E. Buck, Director, Department of Agriculture and Commerce, North Western Provinces and Oudh; R. Speeding, Collector, Gorakhpur; R. Demoutmrency, Deputy Commissioner, Bahraich; J. Woodburn, Deputy Commissioner, Faizabad; J. Hooper, Assistant Commissioner Gonda; E. Wood, Conservator, Oudh Forests and D. Pitcher, Assistant Commissioner, Lucknow attended this meeting.The Development of Indo-Nepal trade was the main objective of the conference. It was widely discussed in the conference about the potentiality of trade and transportation system between India, Nepal and Tibet.[20]

The Faizabad Conference debated the question of the effect of the protective system observed in the marts of the Western Terai of Nepal. The removal of the protective measures by which Nepalese traders were prohibited from crossing the border and Indian traders were forced to use shops in the Nepalese marts was one of the agenda for discussion. It was suggested by the Faizabad conference that representation should be made to the Durbar on the subject by the Resident. The conference further recorded though, indirectly, nothing more would tend to break down the system than the existence of large depot that would necessarily spring up at the terminus of a railway.[21] It was suggested by the officials in the foreign Department of the Government of India, that the Resident should be asked to do his best to persuade the Durbar to remove the trade restrictions.They opined that Girdlestone's exertions would not be effective. "...but it seems desirable that such letter should issue in order to complete the file of enclosures we are sending to the Secretary of State and to show him that we have done something. Otherwise, our proceedings will have rather the appearance of ending in the air".[22] The indifferent attitude became more evident in the statement : "I do not see that we can usefully do anything more in the matter at present." This was noted in the relevant file.[23] The Resident was informed by the Government of India that he should convince Nepal Durbar, through his influence, for removal of restrictions of traders. The Durbar should be ready to recognize the advantage to both countries, resulting from expansion of trade.[24] The Secretary of State was also informed that it was desirable to remove troublesome restrictions imposed by Nepal on traders. The British Government requested to the Resident to exert effectively his influence to convince the Durbar to cooperate in arrangements for reciprocal advantages of both countries.[25]

The resident informed the Durbar on July 12,1880 about the evil effects of the restrictions and pointed out the advantage of free trade.[26] The Prime Minister of Nepal in reply said, that the Nepalese traders were not prohibited from going to India. They had been ordered to go first to the Nepalese marts and pay the duties on their goods and thereafter they might go with their commodities where they wish." Indian as well as Nepalese shopkeepers in the Nepalese marts were more advantageous than those who had no shops there in that only shopkeepers could purchase the commodities brought in the market. The Durbar asserted that there was no rule by which the Indian traders were disadvantageous in comparison to the Nepalese traders in the matter of shops.[27]

On August 16, 1880, the British Resident in Nepal conveyed the message of the Indian Government through following arguments[28] : (i) the Nepalese law should not compel the Indian traders to occupy shops at the Nepalese mart (ii) Indian traders should be free to make their own arrangements for purchasing and exporting commodities after paying duties (iii) having shops at Nepalese markets deterred many traders from engaging in trade. But, the Durbar declined the offer on the following two grounds : (i) liberty to the traders would deter the number of inhabitants in the marts from increasing and consequently there would be depopulations in the marts (ii) the occupants of the shops had some advantages over others for a long time.[29] The Resident informed the Government of India that the Durbar was not intended to sacrifice present source of revenue because it had no faith in the prospective advantage. The Resident referred to the decision taken at the conference of Faizabad that nothing would tend to break it down except the existence of such a depot on the Indian side of the frontier as would be brought into existence by a railway terminus.[30]

Before 1848, Nepal was hesitant to the British in India. However, in the latter period, Ranas had followed the policy of cooperation with British India. During the period of Jang Bahadur, Nepal's relations with British India became friendly and Gorkha troops were offered services in the British Army.

3.2 Commercial Policy of Ranas

The Rana rulers maintained their grip for about a century by crushing the national upsurge in Nepal. The restricted commercial relations between India and Nepal thus gradually became intense as the Ranas earned a lot due to the monopoly trade with British India.

3.2.1 Commercial Policy of Jang Bahadur

In 1850-51 Nepalese Prime Minister, Rana Jang Bahadur visited England and helped suppressing the Sepoy Mutiny of 1858. It ensured British Government that he would introduce certain liberal measures to promote Indo- Nepal trade.[31] Free trade between India and Nepal got a top priority in British India's foreign policy during the period of Jang Bahadur Rana.[32] However, like his predecessors, Jang Bahadur Rana was also not ready to adopt liberal and free trade policy which he had observed in England, because he was aware of the fact that free trade and unrestricted commercial intercourses might result in economic and political subjugation of Nepal.[33]

In South Asia and Indian sub-continent, Nepal was the only country where Europeans were not permitted to enter in trade.[34] Mr. Cameron, an English merchant, was not allowed to enter into trade in Nepal in 1856-57. Colonel Ramsay, the British Resident in Nepal, pressed Jang Bahadur to allow Mr. Cameron to enter in Nepal. Jang Bahadur answered politely that Nepal is independent, as British Government used to say that they had no desire to interfere with the internal affairs of Nepal and not even advise them in this regard. He added that we attribute that independence solely to our own peculiar policy. He did not want to alter it to please the British, though he knew that British have the stronger power like a lion and can forcibly change the policy of Nepal if they want. However, we have preserved our independence as a nation, so, Mr. Cameron will not be allowed to come into the country, except as a private gentleman and your guest and upon your assurance that he will not attempt to engage in trade or make any enquires into the resources of the county.[35] On February 13, 1856 at the time of the annexation of Oudh, Jang

Jung Bahadur Rana (1857-1877)

Bahudur met the British Resident and said that, if the kings of Oudh have only acted as we have done and had refused to mix themselves with you in any way, you would not have had any excuse for taking their country. He also said, "I know very well that in early few years Nepal would acquire much advantages if the British officers and British merchants were allowed to come and open the trade and even if we double our country's income for 10 or 20 years, what good would that do us ? At the end of that period you would probably take the country." In this respect he had often pointed the case of Sikkim. In this regard British Resident had reminded him that the Rajah of that country wantingly seized and barbarously ill treated Dr. Cambell and Hooker. Then Jang Bahadur said, "well but if they had not gone there to gather Rhododendrons, that could not have had happened and the Rajah would not have lost his country. He also said that some of our officials through ignorance and enmity to myself may irritate some British subjects, and then you would take half, if not the whole of country. All the other native states have either fallen entirely under your rule, or you interfere with their management that would so on happens here."[36] A timber merchant of North Western Provinces named Mr. Welliu Norris met Jang Bahadur in 1858-59 in Allahabad and asked for permission to carry timber trade with Nepal. Viceroy of India, Lord Canning, personally wrote to the king of Nepal in this favour. Such a high price[37] was quoted by Jang Bahadur that he decided not to do trade with Nepal. Colonel Walker and his team were also refused to enter into Nepal for exploration work in 1869 and 1874 though Jang Bahadur was pressed by the Governor - General.[38]

The British Resident was not allowed to travel in the country in accordance with his will. On the question of the entry of British and Europeans into Nepalese territory, Jang Bahadur tactfully succeeded in keeping them out, and saved his country from their impact.[39] The Governor General of India Lord Canning informed Jang Bahadur that Calcutta would restore the section of the Terai taken from Nepal because of the cooperation provided by Jang Bahadur in the mutiny of 1858. Lord Canning thought that the Nepal Government would be satisfied with the old Nepal-Oudh boundry, but he was wrong in this regard. Jang Bahadur took number of steps to express his dissatisfaction. He requested to recall Ramsay as Resident, but Calcutta refused to do so. Later he moved to restrict the activities of the British subjects engaged in commerce in Nepal.[40]

Jang Bahadur decided to expel Iraqi traders of India from Nepal in 1856. In protest, the British Resident in Nepal drew the attention of the Durbar to the Engagement of 1839. This stand of the Resident was supported by the British Government in India. The order was rescinded by Jang Bahadur.[41] But in 1858 he again ordered the expulsion of the Iraqi traders on the ground that they were source of intelligence prejudicial to the interest of the British Government. But, as the Iraqi merchants had large claims and as long as the claims remained unsettled, the original expulsion order was kept suspended.[42] The Nepalese Government asked the Iraqi traders to restrict themselves only to cash transaction. It was notified by the Nepal Durbar that the civil courts of Nepal would entertain their claims of debt incurred prior to August 21, 1858. This step of Nepalese Government was biased and discriminatory because no one would purchase from Iraqi traders on cash what could be purchased on credit from other traders. This measure of Nepalese Government ultimately compelled Iraqi merchants to leave Nepal.[43] This order was also applicable to other Indian traders.[44] Furthermore, these traders were called upon to sign a bond agreeing to sell their articles on cash only. The complaint made by these traders would not be entertained if they sell their products on credit.

G. Ramsay, the British Resident in Nepal, enquired this matter and asked about the reason of their signature, the principal Iraqi and other merchants in Nepal answered that it was the order of the Minister and his wish could not be disobeyed. They would inform us from Kathmandu if they had not signed the paper. They had outstanding debts in the city to a considerable amount. These merchants were willing to leave country provided they recovered their outstanding debt.[45]

The British Government in India believed that the main purpose of the measures was to monopolise the whole trade of the country and to make abnormal profit by Jang Bahadur, his family and other Sardars. Indian traders were obstacles on their way and thus they tried to drive them out of Nepal. The Secretary of State was informed by the Government of India that if the Durbar desired to shut its subjects out from all its intercourse with the British subjects, "it would be far better to effect this by adopting the policy which China and Japan have now abandoned than to bring about indirectly the same system of discouragement and ultimate exclusion of foreign traders by requiring from them such engagements as that which had formed the subject of correspondence."[46] The step taken by the government of India was approved by the Secretary of State, who urged it to renew friendly protest.[47] According to London, such restriction would have been considered as "an act of undisguised ill-will" among the European states. The goodwill showed by the Durbar to the British Government was too recent and too strong. But the wide difference exisited between the spirit of the bond lately taken from the Indian traders and that of the orders issued by the Durbar in 1839 to its court of law. The British Government in India opined that the recent step should be considered as "a commercial one only and not as a political one."[48] The Government of India stated that there was no good reason to suppose that it had renounced the rights which it had acquired under the Engagement of 1839. The British Resident in Nepal was informed by the British Government to remind the Durbar about the Engagement of 1839 and to the inexpediency of any departure from the commercial policy then initiated.[49]

In December, 1862, the British Government asked the Nepalese Government to restart negotiations for a less restricted trade. G. Ramsay got an opportunity to press the Nepalese Government and asked them to follow the provisions of the engagement of 1839. But, nothing could be done due to the absence of original documents. Jang Bahadur, the Prime Minister of Nepal, demanded the copies of the engagement from the Government of India. It was found that the engagement was perfect. It only mentioned export from and import to Kathmandu. Export and import regarding leather and hides were not mentioned in the list, which were the principal commodities of export and import.[50]

In 1860, the territory of Naya Muluk was restored to Nepal by the British. It thrived under the rule of Jang Bahadur. Nepalese Government induced and encouraged the British Indian subjects to settle in the new territory by providing them many facilities and concessions like free grant of land, lifting taxation on goods sold for one year.[51]

Jang Bhadur imposed a comparatively lower custom duty on imports from British India to Nepal and heavy duty on exports. On all valuable articles, livestock and other goods, a cess of one anna per rupee was imposed. A tax called Chungi was also imposed. In addition, Mahsuli Nikasi, transit duty, was imposed on exports to India.[52] The merchants and other people of Jagarkot, Salyan, Dang, Phalabang, Piuthan and Udaypur were asked, in a order, to sell their goods in the market of Naya Muluk.[53] In this way British Indian subjects were compelled to reconstitute the new Nepalese market to sell their articles. The policy also created hardship for the Nepalese traders who used to sell the hill products in the Indian markets freely before opening of these markets in Banke district.[54] On the other hand, Indian merchants were forced to live and to visit in the Nepalese market to get the hill products which were in great demand by Indians.This policy badly affected the bazar of British territory which carried flourishing trade with Nepal before the mutiny of 1858. Jang Bahadur informed the British Resident in Nepal that the king of Baharampur forbade the merchants who were residing in his jurisdiction to cross the border to trade with Nepal. After the restritictive policy, which was imposed by Nepalese Government, the King of Baharampur had to suffer a loss of fifteen to twenty thousand rupees per year, because he used to collect duties. The British Resident in Nepal protested against the restriction and duties imposed by the Nepalese Government, but Jang Bahudur had said that the Nepalese Government had every right to do so,[55] beacuse the engagement of 1839 nowhere mentioned that the rate of duties could not be revised. Nepal only engaged to forward a statement of authorised duties and assured that unauthorised duties not mentioned in the list would not be levied upon the Indian traders. In 1859 the Political Secretary had written on behalf of Lord Canning that the Governor-General "assumes no right to interfere with or even advise upon commercial policy of Nepal.[56]

The free trade policy was introduced by Sir Robert Peel in England which was witnesed by Nepalese Prime Minister Jang Bahadur. But he found it was useless for him and his country.[57] On matter of unauthorised duties, G. Ramsay told Jang Bahadur, that the trade in Britsh provinces was quite free and that no duties were levied by the Britsh Government upon the borders of Nepal, but Nepalese Government had imposed such heavy duties in its own markets at Nepalganj which greatly exceeded the amount fixed in the engagement of 1839. In response of this remark, the king stated that his government was free to make any rules for its own markets. He had liberty to levy from its own subjects any taxes that he thought proper to impose. The Prime Minister further stated that the duties imposed upon the goods at Naya Muluk were not concerned with the British Government because it was not intended to bear upon the subjects of that country.[58] Upon this the British Resident countered that British subjects were also invited to do trade and were the victims of "vexations" charges which were injuring the trade between the two countries.[59]

Jang Bahadur promised him to send the names of merchants who were not allowed to come into Nepal from British territory by the British Indian Government.[60] On request of the British Resident in Nepal to open the door for free trade, Jang Bahadur said. "The two countries cannot be compared because their Governments are quite different and refused the idea of free trade. The British Government had a series of sources for collecting wealth but he does not. He said to the British Resident that he is wiser and can understand this. By making apparent present sacrifices, British will gain later. The people of Nepal are not so wise and if I were to make any change in our commercial policy as British India hinted at various points of time, I would lose my Prime Ministerships."[61]

Since the power of Jang Bahaur was rested primarily on the support of the army and the feudal chiefs, therefore it was quite natural for him to close his country against foreign trade and capital. In fact, in a nation where the people were so sensitive, it was too much to expect the Prime Minister to throw open the country.[62]

On July 6,1864, G. Ramsay personally remarked about the Prime Minister, Jang Bahadur, that he was so suspicious that we are merely biding our times, waiting for an opportunity to introduce the point of the wedge. The British Government may gradually obtain a firm footing in the country that I think, the Prime Minister would rather counsel the cession to us of a considerable slice of it than consent to a system of free trade and permit British merchants to have transaction in Nepal.[63] The Resident also remarked that the Prime Minister had no fear of his people and Sardars, but he was himself main obstacle to implement free trade between Nepal and India. All the restrictions emanated from himself, not from Sardars becauase he was the chief spring and director of Gorkha's policy. Prime Minister did all according to his will, his word was law and his Government was the most perfect autocracy. He quickly could throw open the permission for English merchants to trade if he desired it, not a dissenting voice could be heard but he did not want to do so. The Resident further added that he could not go one yard further from the residency in any direction and it was solely owing to the Prime Minister's suspicious distrust that these restrictions were then kept up.[64] In 1862, the Indian merchants, who trade goods, were levied a special duty named *Chumanee*. It was levied in addition to the transit duties. The rate of this additional duty was one anna in each rupee upon the price of flocks of goats which were valued by the Nepalese authorities. According to Jang Bahadur, this special duty was levied due to the fact that the tax had been levied for many generations and that it was paid without demur by the Bhotes and all other traders from Tibet. He further added that if this special duty was abolished, heavy loss would accrue to his Government.[65]

According to Dr. Satish Kumar, the economy of Nepal seemed to have remained stagnant for about 104 years right from the beginning of nineteenth to the middle of the twentieth century. It was hardly different from those prevailing in the pre-Rana period.[66]

The British Resident in Nepal was directed by the Governor General in Council to forward a copy of agreement of 1839 to the Durbar. Under this agreement, Nepal Government made an authentic statement of all the duties leviable in Nepal shall be delivered to the Resident, unauthorised imports not entered in this list shall not be levied on the Brtish subjects. Governor-General also asked the Resident to be aware of the existence of such agreement "because if it be not abrogated by any subsequent convention, it will be incumbent on you to remonstrate against its insuration".[67] The Resident replied on this point that he was well aware that such a document had been obtained from the Maharaja of Nepal by the then Resident but it had been lost. He also said that document would have been without exception, the most important that had ever passed between the court and the Residency if their terms had, at the time been strictly acted upon. The British subjects trading with Nepal would undoubtedly, in such case have been upon better footing than they now are. It doesn't appear that the Durbar has ever been firmly held to them and to the best of his belief they were not once referred to in the dispatches of any one of his four predecessors in office.[68] The supreme Government ignored the agreement as a definite commercial one and that it was not deemed expedient to make any stand upon it. The Nepalese Prime Minister remitted a portion of the tax on the remonstrance of the Resident and this act satisfied the goat merchants of British Indian Provinces.[69] The British failed to negotiate a commercial treaty with Nepal though they made several efforts. G. Ramsay reported that the Gorkhas had nothing to gain by such agreement, but as they become accustomed to lose, they knew that the British had abolished the transit duties that were in force when the former negotiations failed, and that, since then our trade had been entirely thrown open. Through this agreement Nepalese traders could trade in British provinces freely as their own merchants do.[70] Nepalese Government was of the view that no advantage would be gained in concluding any commercial treaty with the British Indian Government. The British Indian Government also was not ready to implement a retaliatory policy. But in the opinion of G. Ramsay, a relatory policy would, of course, soon drive the Nepalese Government to a reciprocal treaty. The Chief Commissioner of Oudh stated, in this regard, that the Nepalese authorities would never have adopted the course complained of, had they not been well aware that the British Government would not resort to the same illiberal policy.[71] The England pressed the British Indian Government on commercial interest that they should abandon their policy of non - interference in Nepal because Nepal offered a good prospect for tea gardens, orchards, plantation, woolen mills, saw mills and such other productive industries, and could be profitably developed with European enterprises. The Resident was informed by the Governor General in Council that he might do something to facilitate and encourage trade between the two countries without entering into any such negotiations. The Durbar might be induced to improve the communications on the Nepalese side of the border and to remove as far as practicable any inconveniences arising from the Nepalese systems of farming revenue. The Resident was also suggested that in doing so he should carefully avoid things which might lead the Durbar to suspect that the Government of India desired to interfere in the internal administration of the country. The Resident was also told that while using his influence with the Nepalese authorities he would make it clearly apparent that his suggestions were limited to the adoption of measures obviously as favourable to the Nepalese interest as to those of the British Government.[72] The policy of liberal trade between India and Nepal, as tried by British Government in India, showed clearly the imperialist designs of the British. Free trade between India and Nepal was beneficial for the British. However, Nepal had her own fear and national interest. Nepal, a poor country, was fearful to throw open herself to an imperialistic power as the British had conquered the whole of India within a century made it a matter of national concer.[73] These types of statements were thrown by the Prime Minister at several occasions. Behind the demands for immediate justice for their traders showed the clear activities of British imperialism and how all the Indian states caught in that net. His restriction on free trade was not so much for the protection of Nepalese industries but to save the independence of his country.[74] On the commercial policy of Jang Bahadur, the Resident stated that he did not see any hope of stablishing Free Trade Treaty with Nepal during the period of Jang Bahadur's Prime Ministership, the Resident predicted that the Rajah would not consent to enter into any forward engagement with us and he will in future be more cautious in interfering with trade upon the border and other mischievious innovations will be averted.[75] All the Residents of British in Nepal like Hodgson, Lawrence and G. Ramsay felt irritated on the restrictions imposed by Nepal but they could not realise about the feelings of ignorant country which was poor and so weak, which had a strong sense of independence and where political power rested in the hands of the feudal elements.[76]

Only Charles Girdlestone tried to know the feelings of Nepalese Governments and their difficulties in developing Indo- Nepal trade. He refused to press the Nepalese Government for less restrictive trade as he was not in favour of any political pressure on the Nepalese Prime Minister to overcome self insulating and distrustful policy of Nepal.[77] Charles Girdlestone did not find any complain against Darbar and the courts of Nepal. He was in consent that Nepal Government and the Darbar were fair and clear in their judgments as was supposed by his predecessor. Darbar had ordered special courts composed of some of the highest officers in the country to do justice with regard to the cases which were rather intricate and expensive.[78] Charles Girdlestone stated on 19th September 1876 that the complaints of traders were peacefully settled if reasonably referred to.[79] In the eye of Girdlestone, there was no decline in trade and he took optimistic view about it. He also defended the trade policy of the Nepal Darbar during the period of Jang Bahadur's Prime Ministership by writing : "We do not appreciate the protective tendencies of American and Australian colonies neither we need to interfere with them nor we had right to interfere with Nepal which like ourselves imposes and maintains duties not in order to protect a branch of industry but for revenue purposes only".[80]

Regarding the trading system prevalent in Golmandi and Nepalganj, Girdlestone, the then British Resident in Nepal, stated that restriction was imposed only in the western part of Nepal. There was no such general prohibition in the eastern part of Nepal because in that region prosperity was secured. Girdlestone further stated that the protective policy was necessary to promote trade in the western part, which was also know as Naya Muluk, as this part was an underdeveloped and sparsely inhabited tract. There was no evidence of declining trade, on account of the protective policy. He further opinioned that it was improbable that the Indian traders would settle or resort year after year to the Nepalese marts, unless they realized substantial profits. Girdlestone pointed out "the difference between France and the caucasus is not more marked than that between British India and Nepal." The strange and unsuitable circumstances of these two countries, India and Nepal, prevented the adoption of a liberal policy by Nepal. Girdlestone did not agree fully with the policy of remonstrance but upheld the policy of persuasion and argument. He did not recommend any formal treaty. According to him, "Treaty is an unrealistic instrument and nowhere more so than in Nepal."[81]

The Nepalese Prime Minister, Rana Jang Bahadur, never accepted to introduce British proposal for unrestricted or less restricted trade and to negotiate a commercial treaty. According to the British Resident G. Ramsay, "Jang Bahadur is not open to reason upon points connected with the internal policy of his Government, nor will he receive as disinterested any advice that we may offer him."[82] At the time of abrogation of the Muchulka he tried to do justice with British traders and avoid any friction with the British Government on the issue of trade. He wanted to maintain better and smooth relations with British Government in the hope that they would not force him to admit European traders in Nepal and he could succeed in his policy towards the British.[83]

The British Indian Government also did not want to make commerce an issue with the Raja Rana Jang Bahadur.[84] They maintained value of their strong and friendly regime which had kept the turbulent tribes of Nepal in lease.[85] The British kept his hands off in the internal administration and affairs of Nepal. During the period of Jang Bahadur's rule a stable foundation of relations between the two Governments of India and Nepal were laid.Lord Lytton, the Governor General, after his death viewed," rather an opportunity than an occasion for anxiety."[86]

3.2.2 Commercial Policy of Ranodip Singh

In 1877 Rana Ranodip Singh became the Prime Minister of Nepal after the death of Jang Bahdur[87] in accordance with the law of succession,[88] which had been made in 1856.[89] He made, in the same manner, the friendly gestures to prove his honesty to the British, but he also refused to accept anything which might increase British influence in Nepal.[90]

In the report on its foreign trade during 1877-78, the Government of the North Western Provinces outlined the following restrictions on the free trade with Nepal : (i) Instead of allowing export trade to take its natural course to the North –Western Provinces direct from the place of production, the Nepalese Government forced the export trade to pass through the Nepalese frontier bazaars; (ii) Different methods to calculate customs duties, and (iii) Compelling Indian traders to take shops in the frontier bazaars in Nepal.[91] Ranodip Singh informed the British Government in 1885 of Nepal's willingness to offer military assistance just in the same style of diplomacy as was of Jang Bahadur's "should the rumour prove true that Russians intended to continue their advance through Afghanistan."[92] But the British Government politely declined the offer.

Nepalese Government's policy was to encourage their traders to manufacture and produce sufficient clothes,food and drinks, etc. The Government also wanted to keep its subjects ignorant of the outer world. Poverty and poor living standard of the people made them unable to purchase foreign goods, so they did not depend on foreign goods. They were well nourished, well housed and clothed in home spun clothes. For favourable policy of Government about trade, it was stated that people can exchange home products among themselves which they could not produce. Though Charles Girdlestone wanted to turn the balance of trade in favour of British Indian accord, he was in favour of material improvements in the export trade from India to Nepal through a radical change in the country's national policy and its character.[93] Charles Girdlestone reported that it was necessary task for the British Indian Government on account of balance of trade by getting Nepal to ready to take more articles of British product. He suggested further that it was the best chance to adopt British by increasing the import trade and by placing such goods near the border at lower cost than prevalent.[94]

The Secretary of State was of the view that the trade was "no doubt greatly hampered by the levy of heavy and variable duties."[95] This matter was brought to the notice of the British Resident in Nepal on 1 May 1879.[96] It was reported by Bengal that the executive officers of the frontier districts were ordered to report periodically, the amount of and mode in which the Nepal Durbar levied taxes and imposts. They were also directed to report directly to the Resident about the cases of oppression and exactions by the Nepalese authority.[97]

It was reported by Girdlestone that a few Indian traders were ignorant of the rates charged on different items of trade. All the traders whom he met specified the places and the amount of duty and there was no complaint of overcharge or extortion. In exchange for the produce of the Terai and also of the fertile valleys of Dang, Deokur and Pokhra, the Darbar received precious silver from the Indian traders. Girdlestone further asserted that the trade and the traders enjoyed a strong safeguard.[98] An offical of Kumaun reported that the Durbar, levied taxes according to the recognized schedules of rate.The District Officers of Kheri, Bahrich,Basti and Gorakhpur maintained that reduction, remission, modification and system attestation of duties were likely to improve the frontier trade.[99] The Departments of Agriculture and commerce, North-Western Provinces and Oudh were highly doubtful on this point.[100]

Nepal's policy of protection was unlike Canada, meant for increasing revenue and not to stimulate home industries.[101] Charles Girdlestone in his memorandum with Prime Minister suggested many ways and means to improve the trade of Nepal. He firstly advised to improve the roads to connect Indian and Nepalese business centers. Secondly, the freedom of merchants to meet freely and also to abolish the market system so that Indian subjects could visit the interior of Nepal. Thirdly, the methods of farming and the collection of revenues from the farmer should be improved and the British Resident in Nepal should be made known about the duties and customs levied by the Nepalese Government. At last he requested the Prime Minister for detailed information about the 'timber trade'.[102] In response, the Prime Minister promised to fulfil some of the demands of British Resident in Nepal and agreed to send information regarding the rate of custom duties and timber trade.[103] But the Prime Minister did not do much for the improvement of trade facilities between the two countries in spite of continued pressure from the Resident.He gradually provided small concessions for the improvement of trade. During this period the trade volume between the two countries increased, due to the reforms made by the Prime Minister on the suggestion of the British Resident. Charles Girdlestone was not satisfied with this reform and suggested coercive measures to secure the concessions.[104] This proposal of Charles Girdlestone was not accepted by Indian Government. It wanted to make a mutual policy for concession, as it was urgent need to recruit Gorkha for Indian Government. On the suggestions of Girdlestone, Governor General decided to give arms and ammunition to Nepal as a free gift so that the Durbar would agree to improve the facilities of trade and also provide freedom of movement for the British Residents in Nepal. It would also get a chance for British to recruit Gorkha army.[105]

The Faizabad Conference, held on 26 January 1880, compared the taxation system in Nepal with the taxation in India. The conference also discussed the effect of Nepalese transit duties on the trade to Tibet.[106] The conference concluded that the duties on imports into Nepal on cotton piece goods were somewhat arbitrary. For European and Indian cotton fabrics, the rates of duty were fourteen annas and nine annas per score *thans* respectively. The incidence of rate varied as the prices of *thans* varied. The incidence of rate generally fell between 1 and 1.5 per cent. The Conference was of the view that these rates were not more excessive than the octroi rates in India and thus, they were not prohibitory. But the rates of duty on the articles like sugar and salt were rather heavy.

The Conference observed that the rate of duty on the export of forest product from Nepal varied between 10 to 15 per cent and were not prohibitory. The rate of duty on grain export varied between six to seven per cent. This too was not considered prohibitory. Tax on rice and oilseeds was a form of land revenue levied by the Nepal Durbar. The rate of duty on ghee varied between nine to ten percent. This rate, in fact, did not hinder the production or export of ghee.[107] In brief, we can say that the Faizabad Conference was not of the view that the rates of duty were serious obstacles to trade.[108] The duties levied by the Durbar were, by and large, not excessive and in no way prohibitory.[109] But, the Finance and Commerce Department objected to this conclusion and stated that this was an expression of opinion which perhaps the Government of India, as a Government favouring a liberal fiscal policy, could hardly utter with consistency. It further argued that the Government should not accept this view of the Conference that the taxes did not unduly hamper trade. If the taxes prove to be quite wrong perhaps, it would be advisable to say that for an Eastern Government the taxes were not exceptionally heavy and restrictive.[110] The Secretary of State was informed : "from the proceedings of the conference held at Faizabad, it appears that for an eastern Government, the duties levied by the Nepal Durbar are not exceptionally burdensome and that the trade is not hampered to the extent previously presumed. On the contrary, the enquiry maintained to show that the Nepalese duties are seldom heavy, and in no case prohibitory, and that so far as taxation is concerned, the Nepal state accords to commerce a large measure of freedom as can be expected for the present."[111]

All the drama came to an end when the regime of Ranodip Singh overthrown by coup d'etat in 1885 and the new Prime Minister Bir Shamsher took over the regime.

3.2.3 Commercial Policy of Bir Shamsher

The second generation[112] of Rana dynasty, the Shamsher family, had the reputation of being hostile to the British. Bir Shamsher's father Dhir Shamsher had anti-British opinion. He had strongly opposed the support given by Jang Bahadur to the British during Indian mutiny. Bir Shamsher was politically forced to be friendly with British. Jang Bahadur's son and relatives, who had fled to India after the coup d' etat of 1885, were enemies of the Prime Minister in the Indian soil because they were claiming for the post of the Prime

Minister. They tried their best to change the policy of Indian Government in their favour, but could not succeed. Jit Jung, the son of Jang Bahadur, was informed by the British Government that the new Prime Minister had been recognised by them and the refugees would not assist to overthrow the regime of Bir Shamsher. Though Bir Shamsher tried to strengthen the relation between the two states but he was not in a position to accept the policy of free trade because he did not want to lose the traditional policy of isolation and opposition of free trade. After the end of Charles Girdlestone's tenure in 1888 as Resident, Major Durand was appointed as his successor, but the trade relation between the two countries suffered a lot. Towards the end of his tenure, Girdlestone reported to the Secretary to the Government of India that Bir Shamsher used to examine British merchants' letters before dispatch.[113] Since the relation of Girdlestone with Nepal was not good, he was recalled. Major Durand had also great distrust of Nepal. He stated that all measures," short of war should be taken to settle the vexed issue. The only result of the war was that Nepal could get complete defeat.[114]

Girdlestone as well as Major Durand were annoyed to see that Nepal presumed to limit trade, ban Europeans, restrict movemements of British Resident, complain about Resident's, behaviour and conduct directly to the Governor General. This kind of mutual distrust between Residents and Nepalese Government was not to the advantage of either country.

Colonel Wylie, who believed in the policy of conciliation and compromise, succeeded Major Durand as Resident in 1891. The previous policy was one of suspicion and hostility. Between 1891 and 1899, Colonel Wylie regularly submitted brief reports on the progress of Nepal, which showed a clear picture of Nepal's internal as well as external affairs.[115] He further reported that there appeared to be an increasing trade between the two countries.[116] Like H. Wylie A.C Lyall, the Secretary to the Government of India, also believed in friendly relations with Nepal. Opposing Major Durand's policy he once stated that the policy of aggression was imprudent, unwarranted, once dangerous and also morally indefensible. Further he said that they had no commercial interest in that country and the British subjects entered in the country at their own risk. It did not seem humiliating to him that they should be let in as harmless while they were excluded as formidable visitors.[117] According to Lyall, Nepal was an independent country and it had the right to adopt any policy to safeguard her interest. If it allowed for the free movement of British merchants in Nepal, it might create embrassing problems for both the countries. Lord Ripon, the Viceroy and the successor of Lord Ripon, also did not want any forward policy which was opposed to Lyall's views.

Regarding relations with Nepal, the British had four main objectives:

1. to increase the facilities for obtaining Gorkha recruits;
2. trade liberalization;
3. removal of restriction on the free movements of Resident; and

4. abolition of the system of isolation under which the country was closed for Europeans.

They wanted to achieve these objectives in their future negotiations with Nepal. The Government of India explained in writing to the Secretary of State for India that the second and third objectives are more important than the last one. It was also mentioned that the British merchants were harassed by uncertain heavy duties and the trade with Nepal, and through Nepal with countries beyond would become larger than it is.[118] But the Government of India laid more emphasis on obtaining Gorkha recruits than others.[119] The aim of British to recruit Gorkhas was fulfilled during the period of Bir Shamsher because before him none of the Prime Ministers allowed to recruit Gorkhas freely.[120] The Nepalese Prime Minister allowed to buy arms and ammuntions in the open market in lieu of Gorkha recruit concessions. Bir Shamsher requested Colonel Wylie to supply a price list for arms and machinery. For this purpose, the Nepalese Prime Minister was ready to spend eighteen lakhs of rupees in a year.[121] He further submitted a list of large quantities of arms and ammunitions to be purchased alongwith another list of the machinery needed for manufacturing military equipments in Nepal. In response, Wylie mentioned that if the war materials mentioned in the list are purchased, Nepal will be better armed in some important respects than we are in India.[122]

Bir Shamsher started to deposit money into foreign banks as contrary of late Prime Minister Jang Bahadur and Ranodip Singh. In this way he started to exploit the situation in his favour, glancing the wretched situation of finance of exiled son and relatives of Jang Bahadur. He thought that if there was a similar coup d' etat in the country his sons and relatives might use the money kept in the foreign banks for their support.[123]

It was clearly a climax of exploitation of the Nepalese people during his Prime Ministership. Bir Shamsher directly engaged in silver and gold trade. He also visited the British Resident in Kathmandu in May 1893 and stated that he had possessed gold worth Rs.7,50,000 which was purchased at the rate of Rs. 21or 22 per tola. He expressed his desire to the Resident that he would like to send Colonel Mahabir to sell the gold in Calcutta. Bir Shamsher requested Colonel Wylie to issue licenses enabling Colonel Mahabir and his party to carry arms and ammunition. The Resident promised to issue license immediately. The Resident stated that the Maharaja too was now carrying on trade.[124] It was an ironical remark on the conduct of the Prime Minister.[125] The Prime Minister expressed that he wanted to sell the gold which was lying idle. He also said that he would buy it, if its rate goes down. He sent silver worth Rs twenty lakh to Calcutta via Sugauli to buy gold in November 1896.[126] The Resident informed about this to the Foreign Secretary of the Governments of India on 11 August 1897 that the Maharaja was willing to buy silver with the huge money deposited by him in the Bank of Bengal.

The Secretary of the Foreign Department, the Government of India received a report from the Resident that Bir Shamsher, the Nepalese Prime

Minister referred him in a news that published on the 14th or 16th June in the Pioneer that the British Indian Government had purchased a large amount of silver for export to Afghanistan and Kashmir on free duty. If it was true he wanted to know whether the same privilege would be given to Nepal.[128] In reply, the Assistant Secretary stated that duty free silver was exported to Kashmir in accordance with the treaty of 1870, to develop trade with Eastern Turkistan while Afghanistan did not have the same privilege Nepal Government also did not allow to import of silver from India duty free.[129]

During the tenure of Bir Shamsher, luxurious goods were used in large scale and the import of cheap goods of foreign origin discouraged the native products. In the words of Lieutenant Colonel G.H.D Girnlettee, the Residential Surgeon and acting Resident "the cheaper and more flimsy Indian and European cloths are rapidly taking the place of native made articles in Nepal, though cotton cloths are also made for use in country which are very stout and durable."[130] The trade policy of the then Prime Minister was not favourable for Nepal but it was favourable for the merchants who were exporting large quantities of European and Indian goods. Muslim and Kashmiri merchants were mostly involved in this lucrative trade.[131] The Prime Minister was informed by the Nepalese official from the border districts that there were large number of wine shops close to the border and it caused the primary confrontation between the people of both sides. The British Government of India was requested by the Prime Minister to shift all these shops to a distance of two miles from the border to ease the tension.[132] To remove the wine shops at the border, the Bengal, North Western Provinces and Oudh Government were asked by the Deputy Secretary of Indian Government to give their opinion. The Chief Secretary, the Government of Bengal replied that the wine shops in Darjeeling district on the border were located on the main road within two miles from the Nepalese border and if these shops were removed, a heavy loss of revenue would occur. He also said that there is no such dispute between the people of India and Nepal.[133] According to the Commissioner of Excise, North Western Provinces and Oudh, "reports of disturbances between the people of the two countries were baseless. After detailed enquiry it was found that there was no need to alter the existing arrangements."[134]

It was stated by the Secretary to the Government of the North Western Provinces and Oudh that there would be no objection on the part of this Government if all the wine shops were shifted to a distance of one or two miles from the border area, provided that strict measures were taken to secure observance of the terms of the agreement by the Nepalese contractors.[135] It means that the chief feature and objective of this policy was to maintain peace and order in the border areas and discourage the production of liquor in the country. Due to lack of grains in the country, the Prime Minister issued an order to prohibit wine production because the people of hill and valley used to produce wine with rice and other grains. A reformist and economist of Nepal, Bhuwan Singh,[136] sent an application to the commander in Chief, Dev

Shamsher, mentioning that some people of poor clans and low castes would not give up the habit of taking wine and liquor and so they should be encouraged to prepare wine and liquor with fruits which were found in large quantities in the nearest forests. In this way the rising prices and scarcity of grains could be checked.[137] This constructive suggestion was not accepted by the Nepalese Government.[138] The Government only imposed restrictions on the export of food grains to control the rising price.[139]

The Prime Minister Bir Shamsher had been successful in maintaining good and cordial relations with the British. During the regime of Ranodip Singh, there was some suspicion and hostility between the two countries, but they were replaced by mutual understanding and co-operation during the period of Bir Shamsher.[140] The friendly relations between India and Nepal were also strengthened by Colonel H. Wylie. It was at his initiative that in 1892, Bir Shamsher invited the Commander-in Chief of India, Lord Roberts to visit Nepal. This was the first time that a British Officer of such a high rank visited Nepal.[141] During the regime of Bir Shamsher, the volume of trade and commerce also increased between India and Nepal. That is why the Prime Ministership Bir Shamsher is regarded as a landmark in the history of Indo-Nepal relations.

3.2.4 Commercial Policy of Chandra Shamsher

Dev Shamsher became the head after the sudden death of Bir Shamsher on 5 March 1901, but he was replaced by Chandra Shamsher within three months of the same year in a bloodless coup. He ruled over the country for the next 28 years. Chandra Shamsher further strengthened the policy of mutual understanding, co-operation and concession between Nepal and British India which had started during the reign of Bir Shamsher.[142] During his rule, Indo - Nepal trade relations took a new turn. The main reason was the British mission of 1903 -04 led by Colonel Francis Young Husband who reached the capital of Tibet on August 1904.Chandra Shamsher helped the British to succeed in their mission.[143] He helped the British on both the physical and diplomatic front. Physically, the Prime Minister gave 500 yaks immediately.[144] By the end of October 1903 Nepal handed over 3500 yaks to the British to fulfill the mission.[145] The collection of yaks and furnishing them with saddles and gothalas (drivers) were not an easy task.[146] Nepalese Government also assisted the mission in the supply of armed troops. As far as the diplomatic steps are concerned, Nepal strictly told Tibet that in case of British invasion, Nepal was in no position to come to aid because the political crisis was Tibet's own creation. Nepalese Prime Minister, in his letter to the Tibetan Government, assured Tibet that the British did not have any evil designs towards their country. The British were not only tolerant with their religious beliefs but also democratic in their diplomatic policies. He warned Tibet not to run into an unnecessary confrontation with the British government.[147] On this, Tibet told Nepalese Government to be neutral in Indo - Tibetan dispute and not to supply and assist the British with troops and transport carriers. During the year 1903-1905 Nepalese Prime Minister and a Nepalese advocate Jit Bahadur K.C. started to solve the dispute of Indo - Tibetans when the British troops entered Lhasa. Both the Nepalese officials and Prime Minister played an important role in this regard. In September 1904 a convention was finally concluded between Tibet and Great Britain to remove the difficulties in the Anglo-Chinese convention in 1870 and the Indo - Tibetan trade relations of 1893. Tibetan Government had promised not to station foreign representatives in Lhasa and not to cede sell or mortgage its land or give any concession for building of roads, railways and telegraphs in respect of rights to a foreign power. So they had to pay a war indemnity of Rs. 75,00,000 and also to allow the British to build trade marts in Gyantse, Gartok and Yalung.[148] The articles of conventions No-II did not satisfy the Tibetan Government which permitted British to establish trade marts and station British officers in Nepal.They asked Nepalese Government for the modification in the terms of the convention with the British Government, but the Nepalese Government were not be able to appreciate Tibetan approach. In Jan 1905, the British-Indian Government reduced the war indemnity of Rs. 75 lakhs to Rs. 25 lakhs on the vigorous efforts of the Prime Minister of Nepal and also agreed to occupy the Chumbi Valley for three years only.[149]

Though the British Government was happy by obtaining help of the Nepal Government during the disputes and negotiations,[150] the general people of Nepal were unhappy with the Nepalese Prime Minister for the help given to the British and forcing Tibet to accept the British commercial overtures. The report in this connection confidentially despatched to the British Indian Government read "the people were not in favour of present policy of the Government for the opening and improvement in trade routes between Tibet and India because this tends to seriously impair the trade.[151] Lhasa was of great importance to Nepal. In Lhasa thousands of Nepalese whose activities were extended throughout Tibet engaged in trade and business. They got special privileges and patronage from theTibetan Government. Accomodating British-Indian traders in Lhasa might affect adversely the interests of the Nepalese subjects and therefore, they were critical of the conduct of the Nepalese Government.[152]

On the proposal of helping the British during the Young-Husband Mission in the council of nobility, a large number of nobles pointed out that such a step would not only jeopardize Nepal's traditional, political and commercial rights in Tibet but would also pave the way for another war with Tibet. In his letter to the British Resident in Nepal the Prime Minister made discouraging remarks, saying that the nobles were opposing his plan and called them 'Little Nepalanders' as compared to the 'little Englanders' of Britain whose ideas were narrow and limited to the personal affairs of their country.[153]

Nepalese people and nobles blamed Chandra Shamsher for the destruction of trade which his predecessors had zealously guarded for 150 years. But he had his own fear and prejudice.[154]

Russia was expanding her territory in the beginning of twentieth century over Manchuria and Western Turkistan..She annexed Pamirs and absorbed Chinese Turkistan and Mongolia.[155] Czar believed that a friendly and controlled Tibet was necessary to protect the Russian supremacy over Singkiang and the Pamirs. It seemed that a secret treaty was made between Tibet and Russia in which the Czar promised to check British in Tibet. On August 2, 1902, this rumour was corroborated by the British Minister in Peking. It was a challenge for British imperialists that there were Russian activities in Tibet. It was believed by the British that the prestige of British would be undermined in South Asia by the presence of Russian army in Tibet. This rivalry of Anglo-Russian had its impact on Nepal and her commercial privilege and political influence in Tibet were also affected. Nepal had to adjust its policy and remain a strong element in Tibetan affairs, though it was not in the position to meet the situation. In case of invasion in Tibet, Nepal was bound by the treaty to assist Tibet. National security was the major factor which compelled the Nepalese Prime Minister to assist the British Mission. Chandra Shamsher felt that the privileges and patronage obtained from Tibet would be affected by the presence of Russia in Lhasa.[156] However, the policy of Chandra Shamsher was not favourable to the commercial interest in the country, and he had to sacrifice a profitable position for commerce to achieve the political leaverage in Tibet. He also knew that the British Government had nothing to give him in reward in proportion to what he had done in order to prevent the growth of Russian influence in Lhasa. It was perfectly a foolhardy act from the commercial point of view of Nepalese Government.The major loss of Nepal was in the profit on the entrepot trade through Kathmandu and the Nepal Government's revenue from it.[157] Thus, the foreign trade of Nepal was largely oriented towards India in the beginning of the 20th Century. A French paper "*monittur official de commerce*" mentioned that the Prime Minister of Nepal Chandra Shamsher in his Royal Palace (Thapathali Durbar) created an important bureau of external commerce. The head of this bureau was his brother. It had a good deal of correspondence with foreign countries, because the Prime Minister had regular business relations with Hong Kong and Shanghai Banking Corporation. Professor Sylvan Levi of the College de France had entered into intimate relations with the Nepalese Government.The Prime Minister had often asked for the catalogues and samples of French goods. It was clear from the paper, that the trade relationS between France and Nepal would secure profit through the desire of Nepal Durbar, because it was also mentioned in the paper that Nepal would be an interesting market for French merchants and articles.[158] The British did not bear the good commercial relations of Nepal with any other country because they were jealous commercial people. They had put many restrictions on free commercial intercourse with other European countries.They were already responsible partially for the traditionally exclusive policy of Nepalese Government. The policy of exclusion and non-intercourse of Nepal with foreign countries was, for the British, an insurance against foreign intrigue in this strategically important country, and that is why Nepal was not allowed to maintain any contact relating to commerce and trade with any western country. The British Indian Government warned Jang Bahadur in 1862, when he wished to meet the rulers of France, Austria and Russia as an ambassador of an independent State, that political relations with these countries would be prejudicial to Nepal's interests. British Government discouraged Europeans from visiting Nepal.[159] Hence, after knowing the possibilities of Western powers specially French engaging in trade with Nepal, an enquiry was made by the British through British Resident in Nepal. Colonel C.W. Ravenshaw wrote to the Officiating Secretary, the Government of Indiaon this, that there was no such commercial bureau in Nepal as written in the paper of France. There was certainly a Foreign Goods Department attached with Government Public Works Department which dealt in certain goods only in the domestic requirement of Prime Minster's family by the name of Jinsi Adda. Few French articles like glasswares, furnitures etc., were obtained by the department for trade from Paris. Jinsi Adda Department was dealing with only one French concern "*Au Bon marche,fillot Bicois Lucet and Cie Paris*" and *Monsieur Levi's* good offices had been used to see that it was worth the price. It did not appear that any such action was to promote commercial relations between France and Nepal. The British Resident also reported that the foreign trade in Nepal regarding import of goods from European Manufacture was almost exclusively monopolized by M/S D.J. Keymer & Company of No.1, Whitefairs Street, London.[160]

Chandra Shamsher took steps to remove liquor shops near the border areas of both the countries like his brother Bir Shamsher. Since Indian wine was costlier than Nepalese spirit, so there was a tendency of smuggling of Nepalese liquor. The Government of India also wanted to shift these shops from the border,[161] so that the border area becomes a 'zone free of country spirit', a distantce of two miles during this period. The Nepalese Government informed that the leases of the spirit shops would expire after a year. The Nepalese Government was prepared to remove the shops before the lease terminated. Though it caused a certain amount of hardship to the leasee. It was informed by the Nepalese Government that the Prime Minister, Chandra Shamsher would like to have timely notice of the dates for shifting of wine shops. In this way the work of shifting might take place simultaneously on both sides of the border and accordingly issued the necessary instructions to the officials.[162] But this proposal was not implemented in toto. Chandra Samasher had not noticed about the development of trade and commerce in the country. His objective was neither large scale economic development nor was it feasible.

It was much expensive to construct the means of transport in the hilly region which had numerous rivers and streams.The average annual revenue of Nepal was only fifteen million rupees. Under the Ranas' economic system, entire amount of revenue went to the private treasury which was a great impediment to economic development. The treasury became empty after the death of the Prime Minister and the succeeding administration started without money, so the progress of the country totally depended on the ruling premier and was determined by the amount of money he had been able to keep.[163] Indo- Nepal trade continued to flourish during the period of Chandra Shamsher despite all these impediments. The export of grains and jute had decreased[164] but the import of piece goods, twist and yarn and salt increased.[165] There was a favourable balance of trade for Nepal.[166] The upward trend in export from Nepal which was set in 1905 continued till 1914, upto the outbreak of the First World War, except the year 1906-07.[167]

During the period of Chandra Shamsher, the composition of export was changed. The forest products and herbal plants which were predominant in the overall exports of the country in the earlier decades had been replaced by food grains. Rice emerged as the major export commodity.[168] Apart from the Younghusband mission of 1904, Indo-Nepal trade was also affected by the First World War. Indo-Nepal trade became stagnant during the first three years of the World War. Nepal's exports and imports were recorded at around the stationary level of Rs. 3.95 crores and Rs. 2.00 crores respectively.[169] After 1912-13, Bihar-Nepal trade was on a decline. This period was marked by restrictions on trade, strain on the foreign exchange front, and restricted trade with neutral countries, etc. Indo-Nepal trade had been interlinked with Indo-European trade since Nepal was highly dependent on India for its trade. For example, during 1912, the export of linseed from Nepal to India decreased by 28 per cent because of small demand in Europe. Likewise, during 1913-14 the export of hides and skin from Nepal to India decreased by 63 per cent mainly due to less entrepot trade from Calcutta. Thus, so far as the international market movements were concerned, India and Nepal suffered in matters of foreign trade.[170]

3.2.5 Commercial Policy after the First World War

The Indo-Nepal trade was conducted largely on informal basis. The treaty of 1923 was the landmark in the Indo-Nepal commercial relations. Prior to this, there was no uniformity in conducting trade because there were variety of taxes in different markets at different rates discriminating resident and non-resident traders. For Nepal's scanty overseas trade, India provided transit facilities. But in 1950 soon after independence, a Treaty of Trade and Commerce was signed by the two countries. This treaty exempted Nepal from the custom duties of Indian ports. Nepalese goods imported into India were levied duty equivalent to Indian excise duty, which was refunded to Nepal with the view of helping her financially and to nullify the competitive disadvantages of Indian manufacturers. But this Treaty of 1950 did not satisfy Nepal.[171]

3.3 Government Monopoly

Monopoly is a market condition in which there is only one seller of a commodity having no substitutes in the market. Monopoly seller has absolute control over the market and price at which he sells.[172] In Nepal, monopoly was a long established institution. According to B.H. Hodgson, government authorities were the holders of the monopoly.[173] It was reported by Girdlestone in 1856 that raw cotton, tobacco, salt, opium, grain and ghee were government monopolies.[174] Timber, ivory and copper piece were also in general, government monopolies. The Nepalese Government also monopolized the export of cardamom from Kathmandu valley and imports of tobacco and Tibet salt.[175]

Traditional system of monopoly was followed by the Rana Government too. Fresh restrictions were imposed on internal trade and monopolies were created day by day. A monopoly of rice was given to Dharmanarain by an order issued by Jang Bahadur in 1863. The coolly system between Kathmandu and India was also monopolized and the authority was given to the same person, i.e., Dharmanarain. A retail shop in Kathmandu was opened by Jang Bahadur himself, though; ostensibly it belonged to a Newar merchant. The profits of the retail shop were credited to Jang Bahadur. The general public could purchase articles from this shop. This was a kind of disguised monopoly.[176] There were two types of monopoly: (a) direct monopoly (b) indirect monopoly. The first system of monopoly was popularly known as *Amanat* for which Government officials were appointed to carry out the business and the second system involved the contract system called *Theeka* which was generally used as *ijara* which was controlled by Theekedar.

The forest products such as *bunkus,* wax, honey and lac and the medicinal herbs like *pipal,* bay leaves, chiretas,musk and *dhup* wood as items of government monopoly were mentioned in the reports from Bareilly,Darbhanga and Purnea.[177] The Indian merchants who dealt in these articles imported from India, were affected by this system.[178] G. Ramsay, the British Residentin Nepal disliked this system because the system of monopoly was contradictory to the spirit of the engagement of 1839. Instruction from the Government of India as to what steps his excellency the Viceroy and Governor General in Council sought from the Resident which he might desire to take in cases in which monopolies already had been and hereafter might be, established in Kathmandu in articles of imports from British provinces.[179] The Resident was informed by the Governor General that he did not wish to move him in the matter of monopolies which he had complained.[180] Because monopoly in some articles such as salt[181] and opium[182] in India was imposed too by the British Indian Government.

It was reported by the Resident to the Indian Government that new monopolies were created and fresh restrictions were imposed by Nepalese

Government in absence of opposition. According to the Resident, merchant named Subha -Dharma Narayan had a great influence on the Durbar and acquired monopolies. The Prime Minister Jang Bahadur established monopoly upon oil, tobacco, sugar, grains of all kinds, cotton, salt, ghee and other necessary items of life. Most of the Sardars had monopoly in the trade of timber on behalf of Durbar and were engaged in trade one way or the other. Some had advanced money to the Newaer merchants who dealt in all kinds of sundry goods from British Provinces and shared the proportion of profit which was acquired by the merchants.[183] It was reported by the British Resident that the Sardars were playing an important role to monopolize the trade. He further stated that the monopoly was less profitable to them but it was ruinous for the poor classes, so the system of monopoly seriously affecting the well being of the citizen and the progress of the country. He also cited an example that it was like "the killing of the goose for the sake of its golden eggs".[184]

In an attempt to control the price of soap in the country, the Prime Minister, Jang Bahadur induces Iraquis to sign *muchalkas*, in 1863 to sell their soap at the rate of two tolas weight for a piece. The initial rate was 1.5 tolas. Muchalaka was initalilly for one year only and that is why Iraquis singned Muchalkas. But after the termination in 1864, Jang Bahadur again called Iraquis to sign similar Muchalkas. This time Iraquis refused to sign the new Muchalkas. In reaction, the Prime Minister issued an order that the soap trade would be controlled by Subha Darma Narayan. It was also stated that any one who sold soaps without license or sold at higher price than the fixed price, would be punished.

The Prime Minister Jang Bahadur cancelled the order later and said that the Iraquis were free to carry out their business as they wished. He wanted to reduce the price by encouraging the merchants to sell soaps at low price. On this proper act of the Prime Minister, the British Resident was happy and stated that it would promote the trade rather than impede trade.[185] The trade of tobacco was also controlled by Sudha Dharma Narayan through acquiring monopoly power without licence, none was allowed to sell tobacco. According to the Resident, tobacco of inferior quality was imported by Sudha Dharma Narayan and was mixed with other leaves. The Resident also reported that the price was disproportionately high.[186]

The timber trade was under the monopoly of Nepal Government.There were different contractors formed in 1858 in all the districts of Nepal. The agents of both the seller and purchaser arranged the trade of Timber.[187] The Nepalese Government employed their own officials according to Amanat System of monopoly in 1868 to cut down the timber and afterwards it was sold by auction at different depots.[188] No longer the timber was sold to the contractors in the forests after 1877. An agency of Durbar did the business of timber and they carried the timber to depot where the timbers were sold by auction.[189] The Government used to sell these timber at twenty-two forest depots in Nepal. Indian merchants were not allowed to cut trees and remove them out from the forest for themselves. Nepalese Government reported the British Resident on 11 November 1850 that the form of transaction in timber trade in all the depots could not remain always the same.[190]

A sub-overseer in the Public Works Department (PWD), Nabgopal Mukherjee in 1861, was in need of 6,000 sal wood for Government use. Regarding this the British Resident was requested by Major Parse, commissioners at Sugauli, to interfere in this matter. The Resident refused to interfere and said that the Durbar would not enter into any direct dealings with, or order the delivery of a single log of wood to any parties be they private traders or contractors on the part of our Government. He also suggested that the sub- overseer should make his own arrangements to obtain these timbers from different agents at the border who were engaged in this trade.[191] Because Government of Nepal had already appointed many agents from east to west of the border and Nepal frontier for this trade arrangement.

Fire wood was also the subject of Government monopoly. Due to the monopolized trade the prices of fire became double and therefore poor wood cutters suffered heavily. They had to spend four or five days in a week away from their family to sell fire wood. Hike in price of fire wood made much hue and cry and therefore after about a month, system was changed and then the price of fire wood came to nearly its ordinary price.[192]

The commissioner of Bhagalpur reported that timber, cardamom, bee wax, *Manjit* and *chireta* were government monopolies. It was also mentioned that "with the exception of timber, the trade in none of the articles is considerable".[193] The system of monopoly affected the individual interest of the traders. It was against the spirit of the engagement of 1839.[194]

Jang Bahadur's cousin General Bhat Jang had established monopoly over the forest from Kalia Peak (the north of the British Residency) to Bagdowar on the Sheopuri mountain. He got it for the payment of Rs. 18000/- annually and was permitted to do necessary arrangement with the help of wood cutters. But wood cutters were not allowed to get and cut a single piece of wood in absence of license which was issued by General Bhat. The license getting procedure was much difficult due to its high cost which was imposed by him. Former wood cutters were exploited because they used to sell these types of wood in the market and they became unable to support their family needs.[195] The system of monopoly exploited the people living in and around the Kathmandu valley. The supply of charcoal to the Government was obligatory for the inhabitants of Bulu area of Lalitpur district in the Kathmandu valley. In the course of the revenue settlements of the year 1854 and 1868, the arrangements of charcoal supply was reconfirmed. Instead of the obligation to supply charcoal, levies totalling Rs. 4 or 4.5 were imposed on each household in 1871. It continued for sixteen years till 1887. The standard of living and economic condition of the inhabitants in this areas was going worse. Not a single piece of rice land was left to them and they could not produce much to meet their families' needs for the whole year through *pukao* land that was barren land. They had much risk of bears, monkeys, birds and rats to come on these lands. If they ignored it for a moment the crops were destroyed by wild animals and birds. They could not satisfy their family needs for six months in a year even if they could successfully harvest the crops. They had to depend on wild fruits and roots collected by hard labour to feed their members. All these problems were faced by them for they had been discharging the obligation to supply charcoal to the Government.The villagers were kept under obligation to pay levies of Rs. 4 to 4.5 as well as to supply fire wood as usual. In this way they had to perform double obligation. A petition in this connection was submitted by the villagers to the Government against that extra obligation. The government then abolished former obligation on cutting and supplying of fire wood and a proportion of tax amount was remitted.[196] The Government had monopolized over the wax and paper production[197] and issued a notice in May 1862 to the village headman and the producers in which they had to supply wax of pure quality (Galawal) everyday in required quantity and more at the rate of Rs. 2.5 per Dharani under the obligation of monopoly. Similarly, the monopolists were under the obligation to supply writing paper to the palace at the rate of one anna per dhup (20 sheet) in the required quantity. It was also mentioned in this notification that *Jagirdar* and *Birta* owners did not let the monopolists to produce wax and paper produced in the areas under their jurisdiction. Government warned these *jagirdars* not to do so.[198]

Sahu Ram Das, the monopolist of paper and wax, reported in June 1879 that these articles were being sold elsewhere against the monopoly regulations.The Government official also procured papers from various sources. On this he asked how he could manage this monopoly and pay the stipulated amount of tax to the Government if the practice to sell continued to exist. He requested the Government to issue an order of prescribed fine to the double of profit that had accrued to the monopolist and confiscation of the commodities. He was assured by the Petition Officer *(Hukum Nikasai Jhagada Patti Ek lambur Adda*) that it would be issued according to Section 25 of the law on revenue contracts (*Rairakamka*) which was mentioned in civil code (*mulukiain*) and the terms and conditions stipulated with the monopolist.The council *(Bharadari)* admitted that recommendation and directed the court of customs to issue a notification accordingly.[199]

Monopoly on copper product was also exercised by the Government. Though in June 1900, the *Amanat System* for the management of copper, iron and lead mines in the eastern hilly region of Nepal was abolished, in the other parts it remained unchanged. Dittha Bhaktadhwaj Chhetri was deputed as the monopolist under *jara* basis for a period of three years. He had to pay Rs. 10301/- to the Government every year. He was ordered to supply copper and lead in the required quantities to the *Sadar Jinsi Khana* in Kathmandu at the rate of Rs. 3-12 *dhaiaui* for copper and Rs. 1-12 for lead. The monopolist was allowed to use inferior quality of copper for the manufacture of utensils.

However, he was denied the authority to mint coins.[200] In the eastern hilly region of Nepal, monopolizing the copper led to a scarcity of the raw materials for the manufacture of utensils. Even its inferior quality (scrap) for this purpose required a permission from the monopolist. So the coppersmith had to go on a journey for eight or nine days to acquire copper. The local coppersmith requested the Government that they be allowed to import copper from India on a payment of import duty, but refused by the Government reconfirming the ban on the import of copper.[201]

Jamaluddin Ranke, the Iraqi merchant was given the monopoly for exporting goat and sheep by the Nepal government in the valley of Kathmandu. He obtained monopoly for procurement and export of hides and skin *(charra rakam)* in Eastern Nepal north of the Churia Hills. The South Churia Hills were monopolized by others. The Iraqi merchant was not allowed to extend his operation in the South Churia Hills jurisdiction.[202]

There were many offers received from Iraqi merchants and Muslims for monopoly system and export of goat skins by *Rokam Bandobasta Addu* (Revenue Contracts Office). It was for Mahottari, Sarlahi and Rauthat districts of Nepalese Terai. At last, in November 1904 the monopoly was given to Mahmud Raki, residing at Indra Chowk in Kathmandu. He was obliged to pay Rs. 5,751 for the period of 2 years 7 months and 8 days. The highest amount for the contract was offered by Mahmud Raki on behalf of Makhu Miya, a real dweller of Gorakhpur in India. He was permitted to procure skins of goats and sheeps slaughter for meat or for natural death at the prices prescribed above. The monopolist was allowed to procure,[203] but he had no right to demand skins consumed by the owner of goats or used by him for agriculture and domestic purposes. Only that skin which was actually offered for sale could be procured. The monopolist got power to seize skins which were being smuggled to India and to hand over the culprit at Birgunj Revenue Office for further justice or action. He was also said to pay the prescribed export duty on skins which was exported to India.[204]

Two persons of Kathmandu *Kharidar*, Krishna Prasad and Bhairaw Prasad had been granted monopoly of cigarette business. They were required to pay the total stipulated amount of Rs. 100 for a year for obtaining monopoly power only for two districts, Lanjung and Kaski. Chandra Shamsher, the Prime Minister of Nepal, issued an order on November 19,1904 stating that the monopoly be granted to the Principal Babu Batukkrishna Maitra without inviting bids. He was required to pay Rs. 258.30 yearly for taking the monopoly power. It was Rs. 774.88 for the three years. The regulations which were promulgated by the name of the monopolist and provided articles that any other person who was found doing trade in cigarette business in his jurisdiction area, should be taken at the office of the *Rakam Bandobast Adda* (Revenue Administration) for legal action. On his first offence he would be punished with confiscation of his holding goods and if it was repeated by him, his holding goods were to be confiscated and also be charged with a fine equivalent to imposed duty. No duly would be collected on cigarettes brought for the use of the Prime Minister and his majesty. If cigarettes were smuggled in by Nepalese or British Indian post or otherwise, punishment would be imposed as mentioned above. Custom Offices were ordered not to collect any duty on cigarettes imported by the monopolist, but consignments were to be opened for custom inspection. The stipulated amount was payable in four installments during the three year period. No rebate was allowed to them in any circumstances. Monopolized trade of cigarettes in the other parts of the country had been given to Upadhyaya brothers: Subha Kalidas Upadhyay, Bhairav Prasad Upadhyay and Krishna Prasad Upadhyay. The first got monopoly in the Valley of Kathmandu on yearly payment of Rs. 7000 in Nepalese currency and remaining two brothers got the same in the hill except Kaski and Lanjung and in Terai districts respectively on payment of Rs. 720 for hill region and 2,530 (Indian currency) yearly for Terai districts. New bids were to be invited after the expiry of the terms of three years. Prinicipal Babu Batukrishna Maitra offered a highest bids of Rs. 22551. 83 Nepalese Currency for the Kathmandu Valley, Rs. 1135.28 for hilly sectors and Rupees 3584.10 for the Terai area. According to highest offer, the Prime Minister Chandra Shamsher ordered to grant that monopoly to the principal. The order of monopoly was issued for a period of 3 years. The amount of monopoly was payable in four installments every year.[205] It was an interesting matter that a principal of a Nepalese college in the capital was involved in the monopolized business.[206] The Rana autocratic regime wanted to control intellectuals by providing monopoly to the higher authorities like college principal.

The law of revenue collection *(Rairakam Ko),* contained in the *Muluki Ain* (legal code) promulgated in 1854, governed the Government monopoly of cardamom In this regulation it was provided that "in case it is proved that cardamom and other commodities which must be sold only in *golas* and other government establishments are sold elsewhere" shall be confiscated and the seller and the purchaser shall each be punished with a fine amounting to half the value thereof.[207] Chandrabir Bista Chhetri was appointed as captain in November 1861 with seven *golas* and Udaypur Gadhi under his jurisdiction to carry on business in cardamom. The trading of cardamom and other commodities also included in his duties. A depot for cardamom *(Alainchi - Kothi)* was established by the Prime Minister at Patna in Bihar to export cardamom. The regulations were issued in the name of Chandrabir Bista Chhetri. It was mentioned in the Section B of the regulations that the purchase on behalf of golas of such commodities which were arrived there from the hilly region can be traded at profit at current prices according to the season. The purchase of the commodities such as cardamom, wax, fish, soap nut (ritha), *pindaolu, laung*, pepper and other medicinal herbs and drugs like *piplamul, bikh*, Bikhma. *jatamasi, silajit, lac*, musk, yak - tails, *ganja, charas* and *borex* etc., were to be dispatched to Patna after making arrangements of payment of wages to porters and boatmen.[208] Due to the system of monopoly, the Nepalese Government sometimes, suffered loss of revenue, especially in the case of cardamom trade. The stock of cardamom at Nepalgunj Bazar Adda amounted to 824.25 maunds in January 1901. The cost price estimated was Rs. 29 per mound. The entire stock of cardamom was offered to purchase by the firm of Ramphal within eight months at the rate of Rs. 23 per maund. The *Nepalganj Bazar Adda* was ordered by Sardar Dhundi Raj Shahi of the *Naya Muluk Goswara Adda* to invite bids. However, other than Mahabir Ramphal, no tender was received. Mahabir Ramphal offered only Rs. 19, 421 at the rate of Rs. 23.9 per maund. Thus, a loss of Rs. 4,481 was suffered by the Nepalganj Bazar Adda.[209]

In far Western Nepal, the State Trading Authority, at the Brahmandeo Mandi, had monopoly to export cardamom. Central Government, sometimes, also sent officials to collect cardamom in Eastern and Western Nepal.[210]

A resident of Chilli in Dang district named Bidual was given monopoly in March 1886, for three year period on the payment of Rs. 500 every year in addition to export duty. The monopoly was bound to purchase hides sold by the inhabitants of Dang district willingly.[211]

All the Rana Prime Ministers thus monopolized the lucrative Indo-Nepal trade. The commercial policy was guided by them according to their desire. All the senior civil officials and military officers of the country were involved in the monopolistic trade. The right of monopoly was sold to their favourite merchants, who used to remit a share of their super profits to the Prime Minister. When scarcity of goods was made artificially by the monopolist, the Nepalese Government used to request to the British Government to help by supplying those articles from India at reasonable prices. But the British Government usually gave refuge to help in such matters.[212] There were two reasons behind it, the first was to give such help meant playing through the hands of monopolists and the second was against the commercial interest of the British Indian merchants in Nepal. The system of monopoly was regarded by the British Resident as one of the crying abuses of the administration in Nepal.[213] One of the officiating British Resident in Nepal Mr. F. Fenvey reported that Dhurba Narain and Company, a banking concern in Nepal was closely related and connected in pecuniary matters with the late Sir Jang Bahadur, the former Prime Minister of Nepal, enjoyed a contract for the exclusive sale of tobacco to prepare it for the chewing and smoking and for dried fish. Consequently, the cost of these common articles and food articles increased manifold. Sir Ranodip Singh abolished monopoly but he started to take off the toll tax at one pice on every person entering the valley for one year. Thus, the state was involved in a loss of Rs. 13000/- per annum upon these concessions.[214] The system of monopoly was followed by all the Rana Governments in this way. According to the law of revenue collection *(Rakam Tahasil Ko)*, "no person could sell any commodity which had been monopoly of the Government elsewhere. They must sell the articles at the prescribed place." The value of the commodity would be realized by the monopolist only if he acted as prescribed above, otherwise he shall be punished with a fine of an equal amount, or with an amount ranging between Rs. 20 and Rs. 500 or an imprisonment of four months to nine year, according to the degree of offence, at the discretion of Prime Minister.[215]

The monopoly system in Nepal was created by the Ranas to divert the attention of the Sardars, Government officials and intellectuals from politics to commerce and industry. These people raised their voice against the Government when their commercial interests suffered.[216]

3.4 Commercial Taxes

Commercial tax implies the duty levied on goods when they enter and leave the national frontier or boundary. Commercial taxes can be expressed in absolute or in relative terms, they may be either discriminatory or non-discriminatory, and can be imposed on imports or exports, of goods. They also may be prompted by considerations of revenue or protection to domestic industries.

3.4.1 Arrangements of Customs

The most important feature of Indo-Nepal trade was that despite the old commercial traffic, there was no customs arrangements as such on the long open border and there was a network of trade routes all over the border. Nepal maintained certain convenient *bazars* on the border areas to facilitate trade with India. Except few goods, the imports of goods into British territory from Nepal, other than through the Nepalese *bazars,* was strictly prohibited.[217] In each important city, there were customs officers called '*Bhansaries'*.

3.4.2 Different Taxation System

On the border of India and Nepal, various types of taxes were levied by the Nepalese Government which included customs and transit duties, license fees, house rent, market taxes etc. These taxes were termed as *Sair.*[218] During the British period, the multiplicity of taxes and varied ways of calculating them were the common features. There was no uniform system on which taxes were levied, besides, the rates of taxes for residents and non-residents were different. On bankas grass the duty was levied both in kind and cash. Customs Posts did not exist along the edge of the Gonda district. A custom duty on grain was imposed as there was no transit tax on grains.[219]

The Nepal frontier was divided into a certain number of sectors known as *'Sair Mahar'*. These *Sair Mahars* were farmed-out for a term of certain years to *thekadar*. The Nepalese Government imposed high export duties on Nepalese traders and very light import duties on Indian traders. This discrimination was done to attract the Indian traders to promote trade in the new region. Besides an export and transit duty called *Mahasuli*[220] *Nikasi* was levied on export from Nepal to India.

In addition to the customs and transit duties, there were two other taxes. Firstly, a tax was taken from the non-resident traders on their entry into the town. It was also known as *'Khunt'*. Secondly, there was a tax called *'Chungi'* or *octroi*. The *khunt* was meant to induce traders to take up their residence in the *bazars*.[221]

3.4.3 Taxes in Different Bazars

The rate of customs and transit duties varied from bazar to bazar in the border areas.

A. Kumaun

The rate of duty in Nepal adjoining Kumaun was 10 per cent *ad valorem* for both export and import. The duty on animals was clearly defined but on other items it was only guess work.[222]

B. Bareilly

The duty was levied not on *ad valorem* but on lump-sum basis on the commodities exported from and imported to Bareilly. The rate of duty was 10-12 per cent. On payment of the duty a pass was issued which protected goods from further charges. The estimate of duties on the imports into Nepal was not possible as the trade was in the hands of the Nepalese.[223]

C. Gonda

The rate of duty on trade between Western Nepal and Gonda districts was *ad valorem* and on the load for the most part. The duty on import was not as high as to discourage trade and the export trade was not significant in amount.[224] The rates of duties levied on the goods passing Dandwa range by the Dara pass opposite Gonda district were as follows:[225]

Table-3.1
Rate of Duty on the Goods Exported from Nepal to India through Gonda District

Name of Article	*Rate of Duty*			*How Levied*	*Percentage on Average Value*		
	Rs.	*a*	*p*		*Rs.*	*a*	*p*
Oil seeds, Lahi	0	3	0	per horse or bullock load	4	2	8
Linseed	0	3	0	"	4	2	8
Rice (husked)	0	2	6	"	3	14	6
Other grains	0	2	0	"	5	9	0
Ghee	2	0	0	"	6	4	0

Table-3.2
Rate of Duty on the Goods Imported into Nepal from India Through Gonda District

Name of Article	*Rate of Duty*			*How Levied*	*Percentage on Average Value*		
	Rs	*a*	*p*		*Rs*	*a*	*p*
Salt	0	6	0	per horse or bullock load	2	5	6
Coarse sugar (Gur)	0	6	0	,,	4	2	8
Molasses (Shira)	0	4	0	,,	6	4	0
Tobacco	0	2	0	,,	0	8	9
Potatoes	3 or 4	annas				Not known	
Onions	0	2	0	,,		Not Known	
Cloth country	0	0	3	,,	1	14	0
Cloth European							
Markin	0	2	0	,,	1	14	9
Nainsukh	0	1	0	,,	1	12	7

D. Gorakhpur

For the whole of the border to the north of Gorakhpur district, the duties were levied through one contractor. The levy was imposed according to cart loads for articles brought by cart and as per the weight for the rest of the articles. The import duty was levied on several bases instead of one. *Firstly*, it was levied for crossing the frontier and others were for the jurisdictions of different tax gatherers through which the goods might pass to their destination. This complicated system did not exist in other parts of the country. For exports 1.5 per cent and for imports 2.5 per cent *ad valorem* duties were initially imposed at the border. According to the Deputy Collector, "the aggregate charges on imports were 5 per cent or even more."[226]

E. Basti

The duty on trade between Nepal and Basti was levied by weight, load and *ad valorem*. Grain was taxed in the villages or markets where it was despatched. At Butwal duty was collected by peasants from the purchaser and accounted for it to the Government with his rent. Contractor was responsible for collecting the tax and remitting amount to the local treasury.[227]

F. Bahraich

The Deputy Commissioner of Bahraich estimated on December 13, 1875 that the Nepalese Government earned an average income of Rs. 55,000 in Banke district through various duties which were as follows:[228]

Duties earned by Nepalese government in 1875

		Rs.
1.	Import duty paid chiefly by British traders	8,000
2.	Cesses Paid by hillmen	4,000
3.	Mahsuli Nikasi (export duty) paid mainly by Indian traders	41,000
4.	Rent for shops paid by Indian traders located there	1,500
5.	Baithaki Mahsul (licenses to sell)	500
		Total: 55,000

G Kheri

On Nepal side of the border, there were a few custom houses but duties were generally imposed at the marts. The duty was levied by *ad valorem* and by the load, but the duty on cloth was levied by the piece.[229] Municipal institutions levied *'chungi'* almost in every town. The people were aware about the rate of tariff which was based on exact calculation in respect of anticipated profits. High ranking officials and persons had the privilege of purchasing goods duty-free.[230]

The rate of duties on trade between western part of Nepal and British districts of Kumaun, Gonda, Basti and Gorakhpur were not similar.

Following two tables indicates diversities in the taxation system.[231]

H. Champaran

Three types of duty were levied on trade between Nepal and Champaran district of British India. They were *ad valorem*, by load and by weight. Except *Chaukidari* duties nothing was paid *en route* till the goods reached the capital. In Champaran district no taxes were levied on the merchandised export by Nepalese subjects from Nepal. British-Indian subjects engaged in the trade of grain had to pay 6.25 per cent on the value of paddy and 15 per cent on the value of oilseeds brought down by river. When these products were brought down by land route, the rates were 10 annas per cart-load for paddy and Rs. 1.80 per cart-load for oilseeds. On timber exports, no special tax was imposed but 25 per cent *ad valorem* royalty was paid for every timber when cut down. In favour of a class of merchants known as the *bathis kathi* merchants, there was a provision for reduction of taxes on imports of different classes of goods from India to Nepal.[232]

I. Muzaffarpur

The SDO of Sitamurhee in the Muzaffapur district asserted that no duty was levied directly by the Nepalese Government officials. But high charges were levied by the *thekedars* of different *hats* and bazars in that territory. Ten annas per hundred rupee worth of things was levied for cloth sold and grain purchased in Nepal. In addition, road tax was also imposed at the rate of two

Table-3.3

Taxes Levied on the Commodities Exported from British Provinces to Nepal

Commodity	*Rate of Taxation per Maund on the Frontier of*											
	Kumaun			*Gonda*			*Basti*			*Gorakhpur*		
	Rs.	*a*	*p.*	*Rs*	*a*	*p.*	*Rs.*	*a*	*p.*	*Rs.*	*a*	*p.*
Salt	0	2	0	0	6	0	0	4	0	0	6	0
Sugar	0	2	0	0	6	0	0	4	0	0	6	0
Potatoes	0	1	6	0	4	3	0	10	0	0	6	0
Tobacco	0	2	0	0	2	0	0	4	0	0	6	0

Table-3.4
Taxes levied on this commodities imported into British Provinces from Nepal

Commodity	Rate of taxation per maund on the frontier of														
	Kumaun			Gonda						Basti			Gorakhpur		
				For Resident			For non-Residene								
	Rs.	a	p.	Rs.	a	p.	Rs.	a	p.	Rs.	a	p.	Rs.	a	p.
Iron-Ploughshares	Not Known			1	5	0	1	12	0	Not Known			0	6	0
Ginger	1	9	6	1	3	0	1	7	9	"			0	3	0
Honey	1	9	6	1	3	0	1	12	0	"			0	6	0
Cardamon	2	4	0	1	4	0	3	0	0	5	0	0	0	3	0
Turmeric	1	7	0	Not Known			Not known			1	12	0	0	3	0

lohiya paisa per pack bullock and four lohiya paisa per cart load. This tax was known as *Dhoor Urai.*[233]

The custom duties on export and import was levied on the basis of entry point. According to the Collector of Muzaffarpur, there were following rates of duties at the different points of entrance.[234]

Collector of Muzaffarpur asserted that the transit duties levied by the Nepalese Government were so moderate that they did not affect the trade to very serious extent.[235] The Nepalese Government in 1886-87 introduced the following fixed scale.[236]

The duties on imports and exports were abolished by the Nepal Durbar from 1889 and *dhururai,* the impost on grain, was also abolished. Only a duty on hides was imposed. *Sair,* an impost, was levied at varying rates on export and import of certain articles. Another impost known as *bhinsar* was levied on the goods which were carried up to the hills. Certain tolls were levied by contractors at the *ghats* near Sonbarsa and Bela on the articles like *Sabey, Kharh,* bamboos, leaves of *Molhan* and foodgrains exported from Nepal.

J. Darbhanga

From Darbhanga it was reported that with the exception of Sabai grass and *tejpat* (bay leaves) no other articles were being taxed by the Nepalese Government.[237] It seemed that transit duties were levied with a view to revenue and not to protection. The imposition of duty was according to cart load or bullock load and not by the weight or value of the goods. Foodgrains and tobacco were exempted from any import duty. The traders were free to pay customs duty at the *kachahari* in the village where they carried on their trade.[238]

Customs duty which was known as *bowri* was regulated by no fixed scale or principle. According to the SDO of Madhubani, the persons engaged in the trade between Nepal and Darbhanga districts of British India could be classified into the following three categories : (*i*) those traders who imported the Nepalese product as wholesale traders and exported some items from British India to Nepal; (*ii*) traders who were involved in export trade of grains from Nepal; and (*iii*) traders who had shops in the tarai and exported such articles as species from India. Both Indians and Nepalese people constituted the first group. The last two categories consisted of only Indian traders. Traders in the last category paid duties for their sales at *hats* and taxes for their shops as were levied upon all such traders.[239]

K. Bhagalpur

Without paying duty, no goods could pass from Bhagalpur to Nepal. The duty was levied partly by load, partly by animal per head and partly *ad valorem*. A shopkeeper had to pay one *pie* in one rupee on his sale. The rate of duty was arbitrarily fixed. One farmer alongwith his subordinates collected the dues. The export dues were collected according to the rates in schedule, but the imports were levied whatever the parties could pay. In Nepal, the duty was levied on all imports and exports. The SDO of Supaul reported that other than *batti* or *chungi*, no other impost were levied in the interior of the sub-tarai district of Nepal.[240]

L. Purnea

All exports and imports to and from Nepal on the other side of Purnea were subject to customs duties. The contractor with the help of subordinates collected the dues. Dues were collected only in cash and not in kind. According to the SDO, the export duty was on an average 7 per cent. The pedler had to pay for a license at the cost of the goods. The pedler had to pay toll in kind besides his license fees in cash. After paying fees, the pedler was free to sell his goods without any inteference.[241]

The duty was not levied directly on imported goods. Traders had to pay duties according to the size of his shop or extent of his transactions. In January 1882, the Government of Bengal published the duties levied in Morung district of Nepal which have been shown under the following heads.[242]

(*a*) Duties charged at *chaukies*;
(*b*) Duties levied at *hats* from shopkeepers;
(*c*) Duties levied by contractors on exports from person purchasing goods on market days;
(*d*) An export duty called *Tangiana* collected by farmer within his *sayer mahal*;
(*e*) An import duty called *Chadhti* was taken at fairs at Barahchhetra;
(*f*) Taxes on grazing
(*g*) *Bajra bila, i.e.,* Indians coming into Morung to settle down and lease for one year.

M. Darjeeling

Before 1882, the Nepal Durbar did not levy any duty on articles imported from Darjeeling to Nepal. Even after 1882 there was no duties on exports. But, in 1882, the Nepalese Government levied duties on traders entering into Nepal from British India. In 1882, the Deputy Commissioner of Darjeeling listed following duties[243]:

There were four stations in Nepal tarai on the Darjeeling frontier and five stations on hills. The imports levied varied considerably at these stations. The rate of duty on the import of raw cotton per load was four annas in the hills against only 3 pies in Nepal Terai. Metals, except brass and copper, paints, colours, spices and sugar were levied at the rate of eight annas per load in hills, whereas, it was three pies per load in Terai.[244]

The Deputy Commissioner of Darjeeling reported in 1885 that in the Terai duty was realized per loaded pony or cart and per head of cattle irrespective of the quantity and quality of the imported or exported items. The rates in the hills were uniform everywhere for both imports and exports and on all traders, British, Nepalese or foreign.[245]

To sum up, it can be said that the Nepalese Government imposed differential and preferential policies regarding taxes on Nepalese subjects, and there was no scientific system of registration or levy or tax. In spite of these policies, the British were keenly interested in developing trade relations with Nepal and other trans-Himalayan regions which they regarded as a veritable traders paradise.[246]

The residents and non-residents or itinerant traders paid taxes at different rates. The resident traders were taxed at higher rates than non-residents. According to one report, the residents of the rich traders was rather enforced by official pressures than tempted by benefits to compensate for the trouble and expenses.[247]

Table-3.5
Duties Levied on Various Items

	Items	*Rate of Duties*
1.	Cattle	1–8 annas
2.	Buffaloes	8 annas
3.	Coarse cloth	Per *than* 6 pies
4.	Rice, *Dal,* salt, and butta	One anna per one mound load
5.	Oil and ghee	Eight annas per mound

The resident traders were subject to pay commission called *Arhat* at the rate of 1.5 annas per maund for all goods except cardamom. The rate of *Arhat* on cardamom was 2.25 annas.[248] The resident traders also paid taxes called *hath* and *gathi*. The first one, *i.e., hath* was a market cess usually levied at the rate of 12 annas per one hundred pieces of cloth whether coarse or fine. The second one, *i.e., gathi* was levied on imports at the rate of 7.5 annas per score of fine cloth and in case of coarse cloth the rate was 2.5 annas per score.[249]

The most distinguishing feature of the commercial taxation in Nepal was that the articles exempted in one place were dutiable in other places. Items could be exported freely from Sheoraj which were subjected to duty elsewhere, while those that were dutiable here were abolished elsewhere.[250] In the same way, the rates on *sair* and other duties on goods imported from India were different in Kathmandu valley and the Golas of Eastern Nepal.[251]

3.5 Toll Stations

According to the reports prepared by the local officials of Bengal from time to time, there were no custom houses on Indian side of the border.[252] Even in Nepal there were no regular stations for the collection of taxes. In

Eastern Terai region, seven districts namely Morang, Saptari, Mahottari, Sarlahi, Bara, Parsa and Rautahat collected their taxes through contractors. Within the stipulated time, the contractors had to pay a certain amount to the government. In the above mentioned districts, Dittha Singh Bir and Captain Bishnu Bir were given the contract for Rs. 118,859.13 for 1885 to 1886.[253]

In 1884, on the northern frontier of Bengal, there were thirty-five toll stations at which imports were levied by the Nepal Darbar.[254] There were four toll stations for imposts on the frontier of Darjeeling. They were Froontgar, Dhulabari, Dohungiri and Baradaso. In addition there were five stations in the hills : Mamringtar, Bundooka, Gurkhajagat, Feekul and Monglong. A new outpost, Ghylodooba, was created in 1884-85 and two new outposts were created at the hills one at Teringdobhan and the other at Amjana in 1885-86. In 1884, on the frontier of Bhagalpur district, the farmer of *Sair Mahal* of four Pergunnahs in Nepal had collecting stations at Bishnupur, Chel Pahari, Nurha, etc. There were five *ghats* namely Bashitaghat, Banarpattighat, Sabaila, Bungwanpur and Jamuni on the frontier of Darbhanga District. In 1884-85, there were seventeen stations on the border of Champaran. On the border of Muzaffurpur, the imposts were levied at the ghats situated in Nepal on the path leading from the interior of Nepal to the markets on the border of Muzaffurpur district in India.[255]

The farming system of imposts tax was prevalent in the Darjeeling frontier. In some stations there were two or three contractors, one for collecting imposts on cattle, another on rice and the third on milk, and so on. Direct management was introduced during 1885-86 and the farming system was abolished.

The border between Eastern Nepal and Purnea district in India was divided into certain number of portions known as *sair mahals* which were farmed out for a term of certain years to contractors called *chaudhuries*.

Farmers were responsible for collection of imposts on Bhagalpur frontier. They had to pay certain amount to the government within a stipulated time. Farmers made exactions as much as they could on the border of Darbhanga district.[256]

3.6 British Objections to the Nepalese Taxation System

The British Government opined that the Nepalese Government is a great impediment to the growth of Indo-Nepal trade. According to G. Ramsay, the British Resident in Nepal, taxes imposed by Nepal greatly exceeded the amount fixed by the treaty of 1839.[257] According to Markhan Clement, an itinerant trader, the export and import duties levied by the Nepalese Government were ruinous to the Indo-Nepal and Tibet trade.[258]

Charles Girdlestone asserted that there was no obstructiveness or undue taxation to complain against Nepal.[259] The Deputy Commissioner of Gonda also clarified that there were no exactions imposed by the Nepalese authorities.[260]

Girdlestone, the British Resident in Nepal, argued that the customs duties levied by Nepal were justified on the same reason which justified the duties levied by the British Government. Nepalese taxes were the same for both the Nepalese subjects as well as British subjects.[261]

Rate of taxes in Nepal were seldom heavy in comparison to those prevailing in British India.[262] The Deputy Commissioner of Kheri had compared the *ad valorem* rates of the octroi levied in Nepal with those in Lucknow. For this purpose he prepared the following tables.[263]

Comparison between the *ad valorem* rates of octroi levied on exports in Nepal with those in an Indian town (Lucknow).

Table 3.6
Ad Valorem Rates of Octroi on Exports in Nepal and Lucknow (An Indian Town)

Articles	*Exports from Nepal*					
	Nepal			*Lucknow*		
	Rs.	*a*	*p*	*Rs.*	*a*	*p*
Spices	6	0	0	3	0	0
Edible grains	9	8	0	9	4	0
Oil seeds		Not	known	4	9	10
Ghee	12	8	0	3	4	6
Wax	9	0	0	4	0	0
Country cloth	0	12	0	1	8	0

Girdlestone refused to press the Nepalese Government to reduce the rate of taxation because he thought that the British Government had no right to interfere with the commercial policy of Nepal. The system of levying taxes in Nepal was complicated only from the British point of view.[264] Girdlestone's main objection was against the farming system of taxation in Nepal. Girdlestone opined that such a contractor, in order to make money quickly, was apt to demand more than the authorised tariff allowed. If the Nepalese Government could collect taxes through its own responsible officials these evils could be avoided.[265]

On this the Nepalese Prime Minister also agreed and promised to remove the contract system in phased maimer and replace it with *amanat* system. It was remarked by the Commander in Chief, who was present at the meeting between Girdlestone and the Prime Minister, that if there was any oppression, the courts were there to listen TO their complaints.[266] Nepalese Government warned the contractors against collecting unauthorised duties.

According to G. Ramsay, goods which could pass from the plain of India to Tibet for 6 to 8 per cent levy in 1864, after ten days had to pay 10 to 14

Table 3.7
Ad Velorem Rates of Octroi on Imports in Nepal and Lucknow (An Indian Town)

Articles	*Imports into Nepal*					
	Nepal			*Lucknow*		
	Rs.	*a*	*p*	*Rs.*	*a*	*p*
Cotton	6	4	0	1	8	0
Sweetmeat	1	9	0	4	11	0
Spices	6	0	0	3	0	0
Edible grains	9	8	0	9	4	0
Salt	4	13	0	Not indicated		
Country cloth	0	12	0	1	8	0
European	3	2	0	1	8	0
Refined sugar	3	2	0	3	12	0
Unrefined sugar	4	13	0	1	7	2
Fruits	6	4	0	Not indicated		
Wheat	9	6	0	9	11	0
Tobacco	4	13	0	6	4	0
Fish	0	5	0	2	1	8
Metal	7	2	3	1	8	0
Ghee	12	8	0	3	4	6

per cent. At the instance of British Government, an investigation was conducted which concluded that the taxes imposed by the Nepal were not high and were in conformity with the duty levied by the British Government.[267] In April 1908, the British Government in India requested the Nepalese Government to revise the duties on goods imported to and exported from Nepal.[268] The Nepalese Government informed that some corrective measures had been taken in the schedules of 1909. These schedules were not applicable to the bazars at Brahamadeo Mandi, Morang and Birgung until after the expiry of the periods of contracts.[269]

In the Western Nepal taxes were heavy but the Nepalese Government had withdrawn these taxes in 1896. In the case of necessary goods, taxes were low while the taxes were heavy in case of luxurious goods.[270]

The question of customs duties remained unsettled during the entire period of British India. There was no other option for the Government of Nepal but to impose taxes to generate revenues. It was also realised by the British Government in India that the Nepalese Government imposed tariff for revenue and not for protection.[271]

NOTES AND REFERENCES

1. D.R. Regmi, *Modern Nepal*, Firma K.L. Mukhopadhyaya Pvt. Ltd., Calcutta, 1961, p. 100.

2. Jahar Sen, *Indo Nepal Trade in the Nineteenth Century*, Firma K.L. Mukhopadhyaya Pvt. Ltd., Calcutta, 1977, p. 136.
3. Ramakant, *Indo Nepal Relations 1916-17.* S. Chand & Co., Delhi, 1968, p. 356.
4. Ludwig F. S J. Stiller, "A Note on Himalayan Trade". *Journal of the Tribhuvan University. Kirtipur,* Nepal, Vol. 4, No. 1. November 1972, Kathmandu, p. 25.
5. Foreign Department Political A. October 1873. No. 134. Secretary of the Society for the Encouragement of Arts, Manufacturers and Commerce to the Secretary of State for India, Indian Office, London, dated 4 June 1873, No. 10. (N.A.I.).
6. Foreign Department Political A. August,1864, No. 51. Colonel G. Ramsay, British Resident in Nepal to Colonel H. M. Durand, C.B. Secretary to the Government of India in the Foreign Department, with the Governor General, Simla, No. 1, dated 6 July 1864. (N.A.I.).
7. Ludwig F. S J. Stiller, *op.cit.* p. 25.
8. Jahar Sen, *Essay in Indo –Nepal Trade : A Nineteenth Century Study.* K.P. Bachi & Co., Calcutta, 1990, pp. 3-4.
9. Daniel Wright, *Nepal, History of the Country and People,* K.P. Bagchi & Co., Delhi, 1983, p. 69.
10. Foreign Department Revenue A. June 1879. No. 1-2. Secretary of State for India. London Office to Government of India, dated 13 Febiuary 1879. (N.A.I.).
11. *Ibid,.* July 1880. Nos 194-95. A Note of the Revenue Secretary to the Government of India, Foreign Department. (N.A.I.)
12. Foreign Department Revenue A. August 1877, No. 22.
13. Political A. February 1875. No. 30.
    Revenue A. August 1877. No. 22.
14. Revenue A. June 1879. Nos.1-2.K,W. Note by H.M.D. dated 17.4.1879. (N.A.I).
15. Political A. March 1880. Nos. 298-306. K.W.4. Note by H.S. Barnes dated 6.1.1880. K.W.5 Lyall to Girdlestone dated 8.1.1880.
16. Political A. Feb.1875. No. 30.K.W Note by C.U. Aitchison, dated 26.8.1874.
17. Revenue A. June 1879. Nos.1-2. K.W.7 Note by H. Barnes dated 29.1.1880.
18. Political A. July 1880. Nos. 194-99. K.W.
19. C.U. Aitchison, A collection of Treaties, Engagement Sanads....1892. Vol.1 Part IV. No. LVI. p. 165.
20. Foreign Department Political A. July 1880 Nos.196.
21. Political A. July 1880. No. 196. Proceedings of a Conference assembled at Fyzabad on January 26, 1880 to discuss matters connected with the existing trade between Nepal and the districts adjoining it in the North-Western Provinces and Oudh. (N.A.I.).
22. Political A. July 1880. Nos. 194-99. K.W.I. Note by H.S.B. dated June 16,1880 and by A.C.I. dated June 17,1880.
23. Political A. July 1880. Nos. 194-99. K.W. Note by H.S.B. dated June 3,1880 and by H.M.D. dated June 5,1880.

24. Political A. July 1880. No. 197. Lyall to Girdlestone No. 589-I-P dated, Simla, June 22,1880.
25. Political A. July 1880. No. 198. The Government of India to the Secretary of State. No. 76 dated July 13,1880.
26. Political A. December 1880. No. 46. English version of a Yaddasht from the Resident in Nepal to the Prime Minister and Commander-in-Chief of Nepal dated July 12,1880.
27. Political A. December 1880. No. 47. Abstract translation of a Yaddasht from the Prime Minister and Commander- in-Chief of Nepal dated August 7,1880.
28. Jahar Sen, Essay in Indo –Nepal Trade : *op cit.*p. 10.
29. Political A. December 1880. No. 49. Abstract transaltion of a Yaddasht from the Prime Minister of Nepal to the Resident dated August 31,1880.
30. Political A. December 1880. No. 38, Girdlestone to Lyall No. 32P dated September 25,1880.
31. Ramakant, *op. cit.* p. 316-17.
32. Rishikesh Shaha,*Essays in the Practice of Government of Nepal,* Manohar Publishers, Delhi, 1982, p. 87.
33. *Ibid.*
34. M.H. Ansari, *Nepal in World Affairs,* (unpublished Ph.D. Thesis), Vikram University, Ujjain, 1974, p. 13.
35. Political A. August, 1864, No. 51. Colonel G. Ramsay, Resident in Nepal to Colonel H.M. Durand, C.B. Secretary to Government of India, in the Foreign Department with the Governor General, Simla. No. 1, dated 6 July 1864.
36. *Ibid.*
37. Jang Bahadur supplied the following statement showing the length, breadth, the thickness and price of timber.

No. of Timber	*Length of Timber (in feet)*	*Breadth of Timber (in inches)*	*Thickness of Timber (in inches)*	*Price (Rs.)*
200 (Beams)	32 to 33	15	12	40 each
400 (Beams)	27	12	9	30 each
800 (Beams)	22	11	8	15 each
5000 (Beams)	12	8	5	5 each
15,000 (Poles)	20 to 40	8	2 to $3^1/_2$ In dimension	6 each

Foreign consultation 31 December 1858. No. 1717. F.B. Norris to L. Bouring, Private Secretary to the Governor General, 8 April 1858: Ibid No. 17-25. Khareeta from Jang Bahadur to Lord Canning, Viceroy of India dated (4 Jesth 1915) 31 May 1858 (N.A.I.).

38. Abrol Mridula, *British Relations with Frontier States (1863-1873),* New Delhi, 1974, pp. 46-47.

39. M. H. Ansari, *op. cit.*
40. Leo E. Rose, *Nepal Strategy for Survival,* Oxford University Press, Bombay, 1971, p.132.
41. Political A. December 1862. Nos. 398-402. Ramsay to Durand. No.30 dated November 28,1862.
42. Foreign Department Consultation, August 13,1858. Nos. 98-100. Captain C.H. Bayers, Assistant Resident in Nepal to the Seceretary, Government of India, Foreign Department No. 33 dated June 19,1858.
43. Foreign Department Consultation, May 20, 1859. Nos. 260-62. Bayers to Edmonstone. No. 56 dated August 24,1858.
44. *Ibid.*, Bayers to Edmonstone. No. 57 dated August 26,1858.
45. The Assistant Resident in Nepal reported that the Muchulka did not include Kashmiri and Newar merchants, the former as well as the latter being subjects of Nepal Foreign Consultation. 20 May 1859. No. 260-262. Captain C. H. Byers, Assistant British Resident in Nepal to G. F. Edmonstone. Foreign Department, Allahabad dated 24 August 1858 (N.A.I.).
46. Foreign Deptt. Consultation, Political. Letter to Charles Wood, Secretary of State. No. 159 dated Septemeber 8,1859.
47. *Ibid.*, Letter from the Secretary of State No. 68 dated December 8,1859.
48. Political A. December 1862. Nos. 398-402.
49. *Ibid,* Revenue A. August 1877. Nos. 1-31. K.W.I.
50. Foreign Department, Political A. August 1864, No. 51.
51. Krishna Kant Adhikari, *op. cit. p.* 190. Cited from the Register kept in Kausi Tosa Khana, Nepal, dated (Bikram Sambat 1920) 1863-64. An Order from Jang Bahadur to Lieutenant Buddhinath Upadhyaya regarding the opening of market in the Kanchanpur district.
52. *Ibid.*
53. *Ibid.*
54. *Ibid.*, Cited from the Register kept in Kauri Tosa Khana, Nepal, dated (Bikram Sambat 1920) 1863-64. An order issued by Prime minister Jang Bahadur to the people of Jagarkol, Salyan, Dang, Phalabang, Piuthan and Udayapur.
55. *Ibid.*
56. Political A. August, 1864, No. 51.
57. Foreign Consultation, 26 August 1859. No. 213.
58. Political A. August 1864, No. 51.
59. *Ibid.*
60. *Ibid.*, Jang Bahadur made it clear that similar restrictions were placed on the British subjects by their Government.
61. *Ibid.*
62. Ramakant, *op. cit,* p. 321.
63. Political A. August 1964, No. 51.
64. *!bid.*
65. Foreign Department Political A, November 1862, No. 103-104. Colonel G. Ramsay, the British Resident in Nepal to Colonel H.M. Durand, Secretary to

the Government of India in the Foreign Department. Fort William dated 16 October 1862. No. 24. (N.A I.).

66. From speech at banquet held in honour of Mr. Tanka Prasad, New Delhi, December 4, 1956. India's Foreign Policy, Jawahar Lal Nehru, op. cit., p. 437.
67. *Ibid.* Secretary to the Government of India, Fort William, Foreign Department to the British Resident in Nepal, dated 19 November 1862. No. 1079. (N A.I.).
68. Revenue A. August 1877. Nos 1-4. K.W. Vol. Office notes. (N.A.I.).
69. *Ibid.*
70. Political A. August 1864, No. 51.
71. *Ibid.*
72. Revenue A. February 1879 No.1, Department of Revenue, Agriculture and Commerce No. 328. dated 11 September 1978, K.W. No. 2. (N.A.I.)
73. Ramakant, *op. cit.* pp. 320-21.
74. *Ibid.*
75. Political A, August 1864. No. 51.
76. Ramakant, *op. cit.* pp. 321-22.
77. Shushila Tyagi, *Indo-Nepalese Relations.* (1858-1914), D.K. Publishing House, Delhi, 1974, p. 103.
78. Revenue A. August 1877, No. 22.
79. *Ibid.*
80. Extra Supplement of Gazetteer of India, August 14th 1875, p. 2. Cited in Asad Husain, p. 128.
81. Political A. October 1879, No. 134. Girdlestone to Lyall. No. 22 P dated June 30,1879.
82. Foreign Department Revenue A. August 1877. Nos 1-4. K.W. No. 1. Office note.
83. Asad Husain, op. *cit.* p. 123.
84. Kanchanmoy Majumdar, *op. cit.* p. 240.
85. *Ibid.*
86. *Ibid., Anglo-Nepalese Relations in the Nineteenth Century.* Calcutta, 1973, p. 8.
87. S.K. Jha, *Indo -Nepal Relation*, Archives Books, Delhi, p. 215.
88. According to the law of succession the ruling Prime minister would be succeeded first by all his brothers (or cousin) successively in order of seniority of age and then in the same manner by all his sons (or nephews). Cited from Satis Kumar, *Rana Polity in Nepal, Origin and Growth, Asia Publishing House,* Delhi, 1967, p. 64.
89. *Ibid.*
90. S.K. Jha, *op. cit.*
91. Jahar Sen, *Essay in Indo-Nepal Trade : A Nineteenth Century Study,* K.P. Bagchi & Co., Calcutta,1991, pp. 6-7.
92. Perceval London, *Nepal,* Vol. II, London, 1928, p. 64. Reprint Ratna Pustak Bhandar, Kathmandu, 1976.

93. Foreign Department Political A. 1879. No. 134. Charles Girdlestone, the British Resident in Nepal to A.C. Lyall, the Secretary to the Government of India, dated 30 June 1879. No. 22. (N.A.I.).
94. *Ibid.*, December 1880. No. 38. G. E. R. Girdlestone, Resident in Nepal to A. C. Lyall, Secretary to the Govt. of India, dated 25 September 1880. No. 32 p. (N.A.I.).
95. Revenue A. June 1879. No. 1. The Secretary of State for India to the Government of India. No. 13 (Commercial and Statistics) dated February 13,1879.
96. Revenue A. June 1879. No. 2. T.C. Plowden, Under Secretary to the Government of India, Foreign Department. No. 25 ER & No. 27 ER dated May 1,1879.
97. Political A. October 1879. No.132. H.L. Harrison, offg. Secretary to Government of Bengal to the Secretary Government of India, Foreign Department and Finance Department, Statistics. No. 351 dated June 7,1879.
98. Political A. October 1879. No. 134. Girdlestone to Lyall. No. 22P dated June 30,1879.
99. Political A. March 1880. No. 301.
100. Political A. March 1880. No. 300. The Director of the Department of Agriculture and Commerce, North-West Provinces and Oudh to C. Robertson, Secretary to Government of North-West Provinces and Oudh. No. 1252 C.C.S.V. dated October 11,1879.
101. *The Times Weekly* Edition, August 13,1880, cited in *Ibid.*
102. *Ibid.*, Memorandum of Verbal Representation, put in writing at the request of the Prime minister of Nepal. Nepal Residency, dated 18 July 1879. No.136. (N.A.I.).
103. *Ibid.*, Translation of a memorandum from Prime Minister of Nepal, dated 12 August 1879. No. 139.
104. *Ibid.*
105. *Ibid.*
106. Political A. July 1880. No. 196. Proceedings of the Fyzabad Conference dated January 26,1880.
107. Political A. July 1880. No. 195. The Secretary to Government of N.W. Provinces and Oudh to the Secretary, Government of India, Department of Finance and Commerce No. 752 dated May 6,1880.
108. Political A. July 1880. No. 197. Layall to Girdlestone. No. 589-1-P dated June 22,1880.
109. Political A. July 1880. Nos. 194-99. K.W. Note by D.C. dated June 29,1880.
110. Political A. July 1888. No. 198. The Government of India to the Secretary of State. No. 76 dated July 13,1880.
111. Revenue A. August 1877. No. 22.
112. The second generation of the Ranas was called Shamsher, the first being Jang Bahadur and his six brothers who staged the coup d'eat in 1846.
113. Asad Husain, *op. cit.* pp. 131-33.

114. Kanchanmoy Majumdar, *Political Relations Between India and Nepal* 1877-1923, Munshi Ram Manohar Lal Publishers Pvt. Ltd., Delhi, 1973, pp. 32-33.
115. Asad Husain, *op. cit.* p. 135.
116. Foreign Department, Secret E. June 1893. No. 389. Lieutenant Colonel H. Wylie, C.S.I. Officiating Resident in Nepal to the Secretary to the Secretary to the Government of India, dated 27 May 1893. No. 35 p. (N.A.I.).
117. *Ibid.*, June 1884. No. 460. Government of India, Foreign Department Secret to the Right Honorable, the Earl of Kimberly,
118. *Ibid.*
119. Secret F. November 1884. No. 234 K.W. 3. Cited in Jahar Sen *op. cit.* p. 140.
120. Asad Husain, *British Relations with Nepal 1857-1947. cp. oit.* p. 138.
121. *Ibid.*
122. *Ibid.*
123. Ghyana Mani Nepal. "Nepal Ka Dhan Videshi Bank me" (Nepali) (Nepal's wealth in Foreign Bank). *Arthik Nepal,* Kathmandu. November 1982, pp. 18-19.
124. *Ibid.* pp. 21-22.
125. Ghyan Mani Nepal, *op. cit.* p. 20.
126. *Ibid.* p. 22.
127. *Ibid.*
128. External. B. October 1897. No. 156. H. Wylie, The British Resident in Nepal to John Lang, Assistant Secretary to Foreign Department dated 11 August 1897. (N.A.I.).
129. *Ibid,* John Lang, Assistant Secretary to Foreign Department, Government of India to H. Wylie, the British Resident in Nepal dated 22 September 1897. (N.A.I.).
130. Col. G.H.D. Gimlette, *Nepal and the Nepalese,* H. F. and G. Witherby, London,(n.d.), p. 81.
131. Bhuwan Singh, "*Maharg Niwaran.*" (Nepali) (Price Control Measure) edited by Devi Chandra Shrestha, Kathmandu (2030 Kartik) 1973, p. 29.
132. External A. November 1897. No. 153. Colonel H. Wylie, Resident in Nepal to Captain H. Doly, Deputy Secretary to the Foreign Department Government of India, dated 17 May 1897. (N.A.I.).
133. *Ibid.*, No. 156 (Demi Official) C.W. Balton, the Chief Secretary, Government of Bengal Darjeeling to Captain H. Daly, Deputy Secretary to the Government of India. Foreign Department, dated 17 July 1897. (N.A.I.).
134. *Ibid.*, No. 157. Report of Northwestern Provinces and Oudh, W. G. Jackson, Commissioner of Excise North Western Province to the Deputy Secretary to the Government of India. Foreign Department, dated 21 September, 1897. (N.A.I.).
135. *Ibid. No.* 156. (Demi-Official) Secretary to the Government of the North Western Provinces and Oudh to Captain H. Daly. Deputy Secretary to the Government of India, Foreign Department dated October 1897. (N.A.I).
136. He was imprisoned at that time. Bhuwan Singh, *op. cit.* p. 23.

137. *Ibid.* p. 19.
138. *Ibid.*
139. Political A. July 1881. No. 372-376.
140. Asad Husain, *op. cit.* p. 139.
141. *Ibid.*,
142. Asad Husain, *op. cit.* p. 149.
143. Prem R.Uprety, *Nepal Tibet Relations 1850-1950 Years of Hopes, Challenge and Frustration*, Common Wealth Publishers, Kathmandu, 1980, p. 123.
144. Foreign Department Secret E. Proceedings No. 197 of 1903.
145. "Nepal-Tibet Negotiations" Under Secretary, Government of India. Foreign Affairs, to the Military Department. September 26, 1903. p. 25. Cited in Uprety *op. cit.*
146. Foreign Ministry Nepal, Cha Poka No. 104 Maharaja Chandra to Colonel Harka Jung Thapa, Bada Hakim. Cited in *Ibid.*
147. Foreign Ministry of Nepal, Cha Poka No. 104. A conversatian between Col. Harka Jang Thapa and Col Younghusband at Ghoom Undated; Major Tek Bahadur Khatri to Maharaja Chardra, Kartik 4, 1961 (October 1904) cited in *Ibid.*
148. *Ibid.*, Foreign Department, Secret E. Proceeding No. 147. of 1903 "Tibet Negotiations". Maharaj Chandra to the Four Kazis of Kasyal. Cited in *Ibid.* p. 124.
149. *Ibid.*, p. 125.
150. *Ibid.*, pp. 125-26.
151. Foreign Department Secret E, Proceeding No. 999 of February 1905. Assistant Secretary. Government of India, Foreign Department to Lt. Colonel C. W. Ravenshaw, October 20,1904. p.35 cited in *Ibid.* p. 125.
152. Foreign Department Secret E. February 1903. Nos 93-107, Cited in Niranjan Sharma, *op. cit.* p. 67.
153. Foreign Department, Secret External B, pro. No. 188 of February 1904, Maharaja Chandra to C. W. Ravenshaw, January 25, 1905. Cited in Prem R. Upreti. *op. cit.* p. 151.
154. Ludwig F.S.J. Stiller, *op. cit.* p. 29.
155. Prem R. Upreti, *op. cit.* p. 121.
156. *Ibid*, p. 122.
157. Ludwig F. S. J. Stiller, *op. cit.* p. 30.
158. Foreign Department. External B. March 1905. No. 1. Enclose 2. Translation of an extract from "Moniteur Official du Commerce" article for M. Raoul Bloch, page 17. (N.A.I.).
159. Kanchanmoy Majumdar, "British Impact on Nepal", Firma K.L.M., Calcutta, 1972. pp. 19-20.
160. Foreign Department External B. March 1905. No. 3. encloser 1652-1.2.5. Lieutenant Colonel C.W. Ravenshaw, the British Resident in Nepal to S.M.

Fraser, Esquire, C. I. E. Officiating Secretary to the Government of India, Foreign Department, Calcutta, dated 30 January 1905. No. 19. (N.A.I.).

161. Foreign Department External A. October, 1908. No. 18-21. J.M. Holms, Chief Secretary to the Government of United Provinces to the Secretary to the Government of India, Finance Department, dated 28 February 1908. No. 104 (N.A.I.).

162. Foreign Department External A. October 1908. Pro. No. 20. Lieutenant Colonel F.W.P. Macdonald, officiating Resident in Nepal to the Secretary to the Government of India in the Foreign Department. 24 August 1908 No. 109. (N.A.I.).

163. Kanchanmoy Majumdar, op. *cit.* p. 8.

164. Foreign Department Secret E. December 1207, Nos 121-123. Annual General Report on Nepal for the year 1906-7. (N.A.I.).

165. Foreign Department Secret E. August 1912. Pro. No. 23. Lieutenant Colonel H. L. Showers, Officiating Resident in Nepal to the Secretary to Government of India Foreign Department (Confidential) dated 11 July 1912. No. 88 (N.A.I.).

166. Foreign Department Secret E. December, 1907. Nos 121-123.

167. Niranjan Sharma, *Nepal Foreign Trade* (unpublished Ph. D. Thesis) University of Delhi, 1968. p. 46.

168. *Ibid.* p. 45.

169. *Ibid.* p. 52.

170. P.C.Rawat, *Indo-Nepal Economic Relations,* National Publishing House, Delhi, 1974. p. 58.

171. *Ibid.*, p. 264.

172. Nepal Residency Record Register No. 10, pp. 41-42.

173. *Ibid.*, Resister No. 13, Lawrence to Aitichison dated January 18,1870, pp. 77-78.

174. *The Gazetteer of the Provinces of Oudh 1877.* Vol. I, p. 137.

175. Nepal Residency records Sl. No. 78. F.No. 1023- G. Part III, 1878.

176. Jahar Sen, *Essay in Indo-Nepal Trade: A Nineteenth Century Study, op. cit.* pp. 4-5.

177. Jahar Sen, *Indo Nepal Trade in the Nineteenth Century, op.cit.* p. 104.

178. Foreign Department Political A. October 1864, Nos 63 Colonel Ramsay, Resident in Nepal to Colonel H. M. Durand, C.B., Secretary to Government of India, Foreign Department, dated 21 July 1864, No. 63. (N.A.I.).

179. *Ibid.*

180. Political A. October 1864. No. 64. Under-Secretary to the Government of India, Foreign Department with the Governor General to the Resident in Nepal, dated 13 September 1864. No. 483. (N.A.I.).

181. *Ibid.*

182. Revenue A. August 1877. No. 22.

183. *Ibid.*, Political A. August 1864. No. 51.

184. *Ibid.,* Foreign Consultant. 26, August 1859. No. 211.
185. *Ibid.,* Political A. June 1864. No. 203. Colonel G. Ramsay, British Resident in Nepal to Colonel H.M. Durand, C.B. Secretary to the Government of India, dated 24 June 1864, No. 19.
186. Foreign Department Political A. October 1864. No. 63.
187. Nepal Residency Records Register No. 10. pp. 41-42. Cited in Jahar Sen. "The Tune of Timber in Indo-Nepal Relations". *The Calcutta Historical Journal.* Vol. VII. No. 1. July-December 1982. p. 57.
188. *Ibid.*, Register No. 13, Lawrence to Aitchison. dated 18 July 1870, pp. 77-78. Cited in *Ibid.*
189. *The Gazetteer of the Provinces of Oudh 1877. Vol. I.* p. 137.
190. *Ibid.*
191. Indian Embassy, Nepal Pre 1872 Records. Register No. 11, p. 94. Ramsay to Major Pearre. No. 30. dated 16 May 1861. Cited in Jahar Sen, *op. cit.* p. 58.
192. Foreign Department Foreign Consultation, 26 August 1859, No. 211.
193. M.C. Regmi, Thatched Huts and Stucco Palaces: *Peasants and Landlords in the 19th Century Nepal*, Manjusri Publishing House, New Delhi, 1979, pp. 18-19.
194. Jahar Sen, Indo-Nepal Trade in the Nineteenth Century, *op. cit.* p. 104.
195. Foreign Department, Foreign Consultation, 26 August 1859, No. 211.
196. M.C. Regmi, "Supply of firewood from Bulu" *Regmi Research Series.* Year 13, No. 3,1 March 1981, pp. 44-45.
197. The paper manufacture of Nepal was incomparable to that of India. It was strong and durable as leather and quite smooth to write on. See Brain H Hodgson "On the Native method of Making the paper, denominated in Hindustan, Nepalese" *Journal of the Royal Asiatic Society of Bengal.* Vol. 1, No. 1 January 1832. p. 11.
198. M.C. Regmi, "The Wax and Paper Monopolies" *Regmi Research Series.* Kathmandu. year 13, No. 11, November 1, 1981, p. 162.
199. *Ibid.*
200. *Ibid.* "The copper monopoly. A.D. 1900, *Regmi Research Series.* Kathmandu Year 14. No. 1-2. January -February, 1982, p. 20.
201. *Ibid.*
202. *Ibid.,* "Monoply for Export of Goat and sheep skins". *Regmi Research Series.* Kathmandu, year 13, No. 7, 1 July 1981, p. 101.
203. *Ibid.* p. 102.

The procurement prices were fixed as follows :

Size	*Price*
less than 30 inches in length	8 annas each
Damaged skins	8 annas each
More than 30 inches in length	12 annas each

204. *Ibid.*
205. *Ibid.* "Monoply trade in Cigarettes" *Regmi Research Series.* Kathmandu, Year 12, No. 11, 1 November 1980. pp. 162-63.
206. Triratna Manandhar, "Rana Kalin Pancba Estihar", *Voice of History.* Journal of History Instruction Committee, Kathmandu, Vol. Ill.1976, p. 71.
207. M. C. Regmi, "Cardamom Farming in Nepal." *Regmi Research Series,* Year 15, No. 4, April 1983, p. 54.
208. *Ibid.,* p. 55.
209. *Ibid.,* "Sale of Cardamom in Nepalgunj". *Regmi Research Series,* p. 140.
210. *lbid.,* "Stare Trading at Brahmadeo Mandi". *Regmi Research Series.* Kathmandu, year 13, No. 10.1 October 1981, pp. 145-46.
211. *Ibid.,* "Export of Hides from Dang District" *Regmi Research Series,* Kathmandu, year 12, No. 10; 10 October, 1980, pp. 154-55.
212. Shushila Tyagi, *Indo- Nepalese Relation (1858-1914),* D.K. Publishing House, Delhi, 1972, p. 100.
213. Foreign Department Political A. May 1877, No. 55. Z. Henrey, Officiation British Resident in Nepal to T.H. Thornton, Officiating Secretary to the Government of India, dated 26 March 1877. No. 12, A.P. (N.A.I.).
214. *Ibid.*
215. M. C. Regmi, "Smuggling of Cardamom". *Regmi Research Series.* Year 13, No. 5, May 1981, p. 76.
216. The Sardars were dead against the Nepalese Prime Minister Chandra Shamsher when their commercial interests in Tibet were ignored by him in 1903-4.
217. P.C. Rawat. *op. cit.*, p. 37.
218. M.C. Regmi, "Sair Duties". *Regmi Research Series.* Kathmandu, 1 Oct. 1979, Year 11, No. 10, p. 161.
219. P.C. Rawat. *op.cit.*, p. 60.
220. The term used for import duty was "Chadhati Sair" and export was known as "Nimati Nikasi".
    Foreign Department, Genl. A. March 1882, No. 60, British Resident in Nepal to the Govt of India Foreign Department dated 14 *February* 1882, No. 13 p. (N.A.I.).
221. P.C. Rawat : *op.cit.*, p. 61.
222. Jahar Sen, *Essay in Indo-Nepal Trade: A Nineteenth Century Study, op.cit.* p. 45.
223. Revenue A. August 1870. No. 22.
224. Revenue A. August 1877. No. 16. The Deputy Commissioner, Gonda to the Commissioner, Fyzabad division. No. 964 dated April 15,1876.
225. Report on the External Trade of Bengal with Nepal, Sikkim, Bhutan, Tibet 1890-91 to 1893-94.
226. Revenue A. August 1877. No. 22.
227. *Ibid.*
228. This estimate was based on the rate of about 7 2/3 per cent on the average of the known transactions for the four years 1871-72 to 1874-75. Foreign Department Rev. A. August 1877. No. 15.

229. Revenue A. August 1877. No. 14. The Deputy Commissioner, Kheri to the Commissioner, Sitapur Division. No. 681A dated April 6, 1876.
230. Revenue A. August 1877. No. 13. Captain A. Murray, offg. Personal Assistant to the Chief Comm. of Oudh to T.H. Thornton, offg. Secretary to the Govt. of India, Foreign Deptt. No. 2489 dated May 31, 1867.
231. Report on the Foreign Trade of the North Western Provinces and Oudh, during the Year 1877-78, N.W.P. and Oudh Govt. Allahabad, 1878, p.11.
232. Annual General Administration Report of Patna Division for 1882-83, from F.M. Halliday, Commissioner, No. 514G dated July 7, 1883.
233. P.C. Rawat, *op.cit.*, p. 61.
234. Revenue A. August 1877, No. 22.
235. Annual General Administration Report of Patna Division for 1884-85. No. 4470 dated June 27, 1885, p. 67, Para 12.
236. *Ibid.*, for 1886-87, p. 15 Para 38.
237. Report on External Trade of Bengal with Nepal, Sikkim and Bhutan, Calcutta, p.10.
238. Revenue A. August 1877, No. 22.
239. Report on the External Trade of Bengal for 1880-81, p. 3, para 6.
240. Report on the External Trade of Bengal for 1880-81, p. 3, para 7.
241. Revenue A. August 1877, No. 22.
242. General A. March 1882. No. 60-61. Report on the External Trade of Bengal... for 1883-84. p.8, para 18.
243. *Ibid.*, for 1881-82, p. 3, para 11.
244. Jahar Sen, *Essay in Indo-Nepal Trade : A Nineteenth Century Study, op.cit.*, p. 28.
245. Report on the External Trade of Bengal for 1884-85, p. 9, para 8.
246. P.C. Rawat, *op.cit.*, p. 62.
247. Report on the Foreign trade of the North Western Provinces and Oudh. 1877-78. p. 10.
248. *Ibid.* p. 15.
249. Foreign Department, Revenue A. October 1879. No. 18. G.E.R. Girdlestone, the British Resident in Nepal O. A: C. Lyall, Secretary to the Government of India. Foreign Department, dated 11 July 1879. No 24. p. (N.A.I.).
250. *Ibid,* "Duties on Food Exports". *Regmi Research Series,* April 1984. Year 16, No. l. p. 51.
251. *Ibid.* "Sair dutess", p. 161.
252. *Annual General Administration Report of Patna Division for* 1875-76. From C.T. Metcalfe, Officiating Commissioner of Patna division. No. 292, dated July 21,1876.
253. M.C. Regmi , "Revenue from Customs and Pasturage in the Eastern Terai Region". *Regmi Research Series,* April 1981, Year 13, No. p. 59.
254. *Report on the External Trade of Bengal* for 1883-84, p. 2, para 6.
255. Jahar Sen, *Essay in Indo-Nepal Trade : A Nineteenth Century Study. op.cit.*, p. 23.

256. *Ibid.*, p. 24.
257. Foreign Department Political A. August 1864, No. 51.
258. R. Clements Markham, *Journey of Thomas Manning to Lhasa.* First edition 1876, Trumber & Co London, Reprint 1971, New Delhi, p. xcix.
259. Foreign Department Political A. October 1879, No. 134.
260. Revenue A. August 1877, No. 16.
261. *Ibid.* February 1875. No. 30. G.E.R. Girdlestone, British Resident in Nepal to H. Le Poer Wynne, Officiating Secretary, to the Government of India, dated 9 June 1874.
262. Memorandum on some of the Results of Indian Administration During the Past fifty years of British Rule in India, Calcutta. 1911. p. 31.
263. Revenue A. August 1877, No. 22.
264. *Ibid.*
265. Political A. October 1879, No. 136. Memorandum of Verbal Representation put in writing at the request of the Nepalese Prime Minister. (N.A.I.).
266. *Ibid.*
267. Foreign Department Political A. February 1875, No. 30.
268. Ibid., May 1908, No. 104. Lieutenant Colonel F.W.P. Mac Donald, Officiating British Resident in Nepal to the Secretary to the Government of India, Foreign Department dated 6 May, 1908. No. 67.
269. Ministry of External Affairs, Nepal, Register. Letter of the Nepalese Prime Minister Chandra Shamsher to the British Resident in Nepal Colonel Manner Smith, dated 4 September 1914.
270. William Digby, 1857: A Friend in Need, 1887, Friendship Forgotten. An episode in the Indian foreign office administration, London, Indian Political Agency, 1890.
271. Foreign Department, Revenue A. February 1879, K.W. No. 2.

29. [illegible]
33. [illegible] [illegible] 1880 [illegible]
34. [illegible] 1884 [illegible]

4

Volume of Trade and Trade Registration Stations

4.1 Volume of Trade

Nepal had a direct trade relation with India from time immemorial. The volume of trade between India and Nepal was always on a large scale due to easily accessible trade routes. Before the 19th century, imports from India to Nepal consisted of a few items like scrap metals, precious stones, spices, tobacco etc. Export from Nepal to India, during the same period consisted not only the goods of Nepalese origin but also the goods of Tibetan origin. Among the goods of Nepalese origin, rice, timber, hides, honey, wax, ghee and some artistic metals were the principal items. Among the goods of Tibetan origin, musk, borax, quick silver, was exported to India.

During the 19th and early 20th centuries, the composition of imports from India underwent some changes, but the composition of exports remained, by and large, the same.[1]

In the year 1877-78, the total trade (taking import and export together) with India was valued at Rs. 1,687,000. Out of this, more than two thirds was conducted through Bengal. Exports from Nepal stood at Rs. 1,054,000 and imports into Nepal at Rs. 633,000.[2] The registered trade of Nepal with India increased tremendously in the next year and valued at Rs. 22,322,457 of which exports and imports were Rs.13,968,953 and Rs. 8,355,504 respectively. But in the year 1879-80, the volume of trade of Nepal with India decreased from Rs. 22,322,457 to Rs.14,059,492. However, Nepal's trade with North-Western Provinces increased as compared to the preceding year and valued at Rs. 1,699,330. In that year exports from and imports into Nepal were Rs. 7,834,770 and Rs. 6,224,722 respectively. In all these years exports from Nepal exceeded imports as shown in the following table.[3]

Table-4.1
Comparison between the value of commodities exported from and imported to Nepal through Bengal and North Western Provinces during 1878-79 and 1879-80

	1878-79		*1879-80*	
	Export from Nepal (Rs.)	*Imports to Nepal (Rs.)*	*Exports from Nepal (Rs.)*	*Imports to Nepal (Rs.)*
Bengal	9,862,800	6,437,479	2,892,566	3,445,418
N.W.P. & Oudh.	4,106,153	1,916,025	4,942,204	2,779,304
	13,968,953	**8,353,504**	**7,834,770**	**6,224,722**

	1878-79 (Rs.)	***1879-80 (Rs.)***
Total registered trade with Bengal	16,300,279	6,337,984
Total registered trade with N.W.P and Oudh	6,022,178	7,721,508
	22,322,457	14,059,492

Restrictive trade policy of the Nepalese Government was the main reason of downward trend in the Indo-Nepal trade in1879-80.[4]

However, Nepal's trade with British India increased in the year 1880-81 and valued at 2 crores, 48 lakh, 78 thousand and 16 hundred 29 rupees of which export valued at 1 crore, 60 lakh, 40 thousand, 5 hundred and 60 rupees and import at Rs. 8,838,069. Most of the trade was conducted through Bengal.

In 1881-82, the value of trade between Nepal and India stood at about Rs. 216 lakh. Out of this volume, export from and import to Nepal constituted Rs.13, 457,436 and Rs. 8,133,468 respectively. There was a decline of Rs. 3,287,725 in that year as compared to the preceding year. This trend of declining trade between India and Nepal continued till 1882-83. According to the Collector of Champaran, the reason of this trend was the shortness of the *aghani* harvest and conflicting relation with Tibet (the export of grain from Nepal was stopped for some time). A *chainpatia mahajan* cultivating land in Nepal made complaint to SDOs of the Bttiah District that he was not allowed exporting his grains to India.[6]

In comparision to the preceding two years (1881-82 and 1883-84), the Indo-Nepal trade increased during 1883-84 by Rs. 2,630,126 and Rs. 2,490,275 respectively.[7]

Table-4.2
Value of Indo Nepalese Trade (1880-81 to 1889-90)

Years	*Exports to British India from Nepal (Rs.)*	*Imports into Nepal from British India (Rs.)*	*Total (Rs.)*
1880-81	16,040,560	8,838,069	24,878,629
1881-82	13,457,436	8,133,468	21,590,904
1882-83	13,326, 704	8,124,349	21,451,053
1883-84	14,694,763	9,386,416	24,081,179
1884-85	14,055,191	9,573,645	23,628,836
1885-86	16,633,552	8,391,077	25,024,629
1886-87	17,993,354	8,533,715	26,527,069
1887-88	17,872,111	11,110,714	28,982,825
1888-89	15,097,010	10,652,568	26,049,578
1889-90	1 5,406,349	11,530,656	26,937,005

*(Report on the External Trade of Bengal with Nepal, Sikkim, Bhutan and Tibet 1880-81 to 1889-90. Note on the Trade of the North Western Provinces and Oudh for the year ending 31 March 1879; Annual Report of the Foreign Trade of North Western Provinces and Oudh for the year 1880-90.)

As compared with all the previous years, the value of import from India to Nepal was the highest in 1883-84. The Indo-Nepalese trade again decreased by Rs. 352, 343 in 1884-85 from Rs. 24,081,179 in 1883-84. Between 1885-86 and 1887-88, Nepal's trade with India gradually increased. The total trade in 1885-86 increased by Rs. 1,395,793 against Rs. 23,628,836 in 1884-85.[8]

The total value of trade of Nepal with India increased by Rs. 1,402,440 from Rs. 25,024,629 in 1885-86 and to Rs. 26,427,069 in 1886-87. The value of trade however, decreased by Rs. 2,933,247 from Rs. 28,982,825 in 1887-88 to Rs. 26,049,578 in 1888-89. All through 1880s, the highest volume of trade was recorded in 1887-88. Nepal's imports were the highest in 1889-90 in the entire decade of 1880. As against the total value of export of Rs.15, 406,349, the imports were worth Rs. 11,530,656.[9]

In 1890-91, the value of Indo-Nepal trade was recorded at Rs. 301 lakh which further increased to Rs. 399 lakh in 1900-01. This improvement in the value of trade was accompanied by the expansion of trade of forest produce in Nepal.[10]

Colenel Wylie, a British Resident in Nepal, gave statistics about Indo-Nepal trade as follow:[11]

With the turn of the twentieth century, the Indo-Nepal trade witnessed rapid increased till the First World War. Nepal had a favourable balance of trade with India as in the earlier years.

Table 4.3

Years	*Exports Rs.*	*Dollars (Million)*	*Imports Rs.*	*Dollars (Million)*
1895-96	1,83,36,959	2-1/2	1,36,23,888	2-1/4
1896-97	1,89,30,554	2-2/3	1,53,67,519	2-1/3
1897-98	2,05,65,292	4	1,82,88,103	2-1/2
1898-99	2,14,09,805	4-1/8	1,60,63,496	2-1/3
1899-1900	2,09,34,621	5	1,37,44,745	2-1/4

It was reported by the Director General of statistics of Bengal, J.E O'Coner. "There was an exceptional increase in the export of treasure, caused by a demand for gold in connection with the construction of a temple by the Nepalese Durbar."[12]

There was no significant change in the value and composition of exports from Nepal during 1900-01 to 1904-05 owing to good harvest in India during these years.[13] In the year 1906-07, there as some setbacks in Indo-Nepal trade. Total value of trade declined by about 48 percent. Both the exports and imports decreased. According to the Annual General Report, "This is the result of a partial failure of the autumn crops in the terai. As regards exports from Nepal, the most remarkable decline appears in grain and jute. The principal imports that were affected included cotton piece goods, twist and yarn, and

Table 4.4
Value of Indo-Nepal Trade 1900-01 to 1913-14 (In million rupees)

Year	*Exports from Nepal to British India*	*Imports into Nepal from British India*	*Trade balance*
1900-01	24.4	22.7	+ 1.7
1901-02	27.4	16.5	+10.9
1902-03	26.2	14.3	+11.9
1903-04	26.7	13.7	+13.0
1904-05	26.4	15.0	+11.4
1905-06	35.3	16.1	+19.1
1906-07	22.4	12.0	+10.4
1907-08	35.5	15.7	+19.8
1908-09	35.5	17.3	+18.2
1909-10	32.9	16.1	+16.8
1910-11	37.3	17.2	+20.1
1911-12	45.4	22.6	+22.8
1912-13	46.5	22.2	+24.3
1913-14	38.3	19.2	+19.1

salt. The fall in the value of the first two imported articles was thought to be due partly to the fact that prices ruled high during the year which tended to reduce importation, and partly to depression of trade owing to bad harvest. The decrease in the value of the imported salt was partly accounted for by the reduction in the duties charged and the consequent reduction in price."[14] It was also a result of sluggishness in India's exports and imports in this period.[15] After a quick recovery in 1907-08, there was again stagnation in Nepalese exports during 1908-09 because of bad harvests and rising prices of foodgrains in Nepal. Despite these setbacks, Nepal had favourable balance of trade and surplus amounted to one third of the total Indo-Nepalese trade.[16]

Nepal's exports to India in 1911-12 amounted to Rs. 43,676 thousands which rose to Rs. 58,200 thousands in 1924-25. The value of import amounted to Rs. 2,21,32 thousands in 1911-12 which increased to Rs. 279,43 thousands in 1924-25.[17]

Table 4.5

Value of Registered Exports from and Imports into British India

(in'000 Rupees)

Year	Export		Imports	
	Treasure	Merchandise	Treasure	Merchandise
1911-12	475	2,21,32	1738	4,36,76
1912-13	568	2,16,58	1144	4,53,55
1913-14	626	2,04,80	1547	4,32,75
1914-15	609	1,91,40	1102	3,84,82
1915-16	1565	2,06,95	977	3,94,89
1916-17	382	2,04,31	6379	3,96,90
1917-18	1732	2,10,81	1318	3,84,41
1918-19	640	2,28,07	4368	4,77,13
1919-20	452	2,90,46	2770	5,20,13
1920-21	495	2,82,03	1985	5,96,93
1921-22	370	2,49,27	2298	5,91,42
1922-23	471	2,75,36	604	5,08,03
1923-24	300	2,80,88	2003	6,07,21
1924-25	466	2,79,43	1858	5,82,00

The total trade between India and Nepal rose to the peak figure of Rs. 68.7 million in 1912-13. Out of this, commodities worth Rs. 4.65 crore were exported. However, imports from India into Nepal decreased to Rs. 2.22 crore from Rs. 2.26 crore in 1911-12. The surplus in balance of trade of Nepal increased to its peak figure of Rs. 2.43 crore in 1912-13. But the value of Indo-Nepal trade declined by nearly 20 per cent in 1913-14. The value of exports from

Nepal recorded at Rs. 3.83 crore and that of imports amounted to Rs.1.92 crore in that year. There was decline of 21 percent and 13 per cent in export and import respectively. The Indo-Nepal trade remained stagnant during the First World War. But First World War affected the Indo-Nepalese trade. In the later period, Indo-Nepalese trade increased due to the lifting of wartime controls, improvement in freight position, resumption of trade with some of the enemy countries etc.[18]

In comparision to the Second World War period, the quantum of exports during the decade of 1950s recorded on an average a substantial fall. The high level of exports during the war period (1942-45) was due to an abnormal situation created by war. Demand for food and raw materials in India were high during the war period. Despite some erratic changes, the overall trade was on the whole towards a decline, more so in the case of major items of export.[19]

4.2 COMPOSITION OF INDO-NEPALESE TRADE

Major imports of Nepal from India constituted of cotton piece goods, sugar, salt and provisions. Nepal's major exports to India consisted of grains, some forest products like timber, ginger, tejpat, ghee, honey, fruits, hides and elephants and a few manufactures kike cutlery and war-like instruments, metal utensils and a superior quality of indigenous paper.[20]

4.2.1 Composition of Nepal's Export to India

In the earlier decades of the 19th century, forest products and herbal plants dominated the overall exports of Nepal. These items were replaced by food grains at the end of the century.[21] Among various items of food grains, rice emerged as the major export commodity of Nepal in the 20th century. Food grains constituted approximately half of Nepal's total exports.[22] Rice was Nepal's most voluminous export item of which more than 200,000 maunds entered the Gorakhpur District in a single year.[23] The other food grains which were exported to India were wheat, gram and pulse. Nepal exported 661,986 maunds of food grains to North-Western Provinces and Oudh during 1877-78. Out of this, 501,340 maunds consisted of rice 20,494 maunds of wheat, 71,070 maunds of gram and pulse and other miscellaneous items.[25]

As compared to other food grains exported from Nepal through Bengal, exports of rice was the highest. During 1878-79, 1,997,114 maunds of food grains were exported through Bengal of which rice constituted 1,607,882 maunds. This trend continued in the entire period under review, though the absolute amount of export of rice was on declining trend after 1878-79, because of good harvest and low price in India.[26] But in 1887-88, the export of rice again increased to 999,770 maunds from 990,644 maunds in 1878-79 registering an increase of 9,126 maunds. After declining in the next two years, the export of rice greatly increased in 1899-1900.[27]

Table- 4.6
Food grains exported from Nepal to India through Bengal 1878-79 to 1889-90

(in mds)

Years	Wheat	Gram & Pulse	Other spring crops	Rice (husked)	Rice (Un-husked)	other Rain Crops	Total
			Description of food-grains				
1878-79	9,467	31,415	25,730	990,644	617,238	322,620	1,997,114
1879-80	7,606	54,089	23,019	811,105	665,457	244,039	1,805,315
1880-81	13,556	78,209	74,530	791,191	495,772	187,020	1,640,278
1881-82	8,360	64,762	43,162	747,268	640,690	173,415	1,677,657
1882-83	12,890	58,258	58,164	832,516	758,458	228,069	1,948,355
1883-84	16,455	63,842	37,526	508,288	644,137	275,142	1,545,390
1884-85	7,432	43,300	27,920	361,560	541,118	213,995	1,195,325
1885-86	9,375	30,937	33,157	613,117	649,504	293,849	1,629,939
1886-87	39,618	95,790	53,626	786,411	811,946	201,778	1,989,169
1887-88	69,979	113,501	50,546	999,770	1,184,152	333,926	2,751,874

(Contd.)

(Contd. Table 4.6)

(in mds)

Years	Description of Food-grains						
	Wheat	Gram & Pulse	Other spring crops	Rice (husked)	Rice (Un-husked)	Other Rain Crops	Total
1888-89	22,903	40,127	38,460	376,922	632,623	152,745	1,263,780
1889-90	7,272	23,496	14,179	704,401	977,587	276,019	2,002,954
1890-91	29,112	122,955	43,301	879,926	1,296,506	235,754	2,607,554
1891-92	43,813	81,247	45,113	441,520	700,887	142,508	1,455,088
1892-93	6,878	70,705	11,605	460,539	857,579	309,066	1,716,372
1893-94	7,558	84,298	20,107	582,219	909,282	162,132	1,765,596
1894-95	28,199	143,671	86,905	659,651	1,009,555	886,595	2,814,576
1895-96	56,293	179,414	131,100	761,696	991,522	279,951	2,399,982
1896-97	44,111	158,919	113,184	690,970	709,656	570,946	1,987,786
1897-98	17,083	160,298	59,739	737,316	893,881	361,831	2,230,148
1898-99	31,471	145,267	95,137	634,598	1,032,352	287,977	2,226,802
1899-1900	34,808	162,477	89,575	1,136,688	1,520,563	498,779	3,442,890

Upto 1882-83 the export of husked rice was higher than unhusked rice (paddy) but afterwards the amount of unhusked rice exceeded that of husked rice. 1899-1900 was the highest rice exporting year. Since 1884, the Nepal Government imposed restrictions on the rice export due to the scanty produce of grain in terai, and the necessity of collecting rised for the Tibet expedition. Hence the lowest amount of rice was exported during 1883-84.[28]

The British Resident in Nepal was informed by the Prime Minister of Nepal that the Nepalese officers in Terai were given instructions to direct the *zamindars* and tenants to store up the grain for the whole year consumption before selling any part of it.[29]

In comparision to other foodgrains, wheat was exported in small quantities because Nepal did not produce much wheat. Wheat was not a favourite food article and was used only for manufacturing coarse beer and spirit.[30]

Timber was the second most important article of export after foodgrains.[31] Most of the timber was exported through North Western Provinces and Oudh. For example, in 1878-79, total export of timber was 569,409 maunds of which 48,373 maunds were exported through Bengal and the rest through North Western Provinces and Oudh.[32] But in respect of rice, the position was just opposite. Larger amount of rice was exported through Bengal than North Western Provinces and Oudh because during the 19th century, Western Nepal adjoining North Western Provinces and Oudh was a vast tract of forest lands, whereas cultivated tracts were few and scattered.[33]

Eastern Terai of Nepal adjoining Bangal and Bihar was more suitable for the cultivation of foodgrains especially rice.[34]

It is clear from Table 4.7 that the total exports of timber during 1879-80, increased by 109,826 maunds from the previous year, though the export of timber through North Western Provinces and Oudh decreased by 74,874 maunds as compared with total export of 521,036 maunds in the preceding year. Even the timber exports through Bengal were 213,089 maunds as compared to North Western Provinces though 446,162 maunds timber were exported. Due to the heavy construction of railway lines in North Western Provinces, the export of timber through that region remained always high.[35]

During 1880-81, the export of timber from Nepal was 1,492,721 maunds which was more than double as compared to the preceding year. It was the highest timber exporting year till 1883-84. In 1884-85, Nepal exported 3,517,341 maunds of timber amounted to Rs. 3,634,130, which was the highest export of timber from Nepal. About 38 per cent of the total value was exported through North Western Provinces and Oudh. This high value of timber export in 1884-85 was due to heavy rain which washed down a large amount of timber in India.[36]

The timber export in 1889-90 fell greatly. In the year, Nepal exported only 451,001 maunds of timber that was worth Rs. 699,206. It was less by 118,408

Table 4.7
Export of timber from Nepal to India (1878-79 to 1889-1900)

Years	*Quantity (Mds)*	*Value (Rs)*
1878-79	569,409	845,110
1879-80	679,235	1,489,994
1880-81	1,492,721	3,110,042
1881-82	1,290,623	1,891,194
1882-83	1,763,097	2,635,669
1883-84	1,850,276	2,536,662
1884-85	2,517,341	3,634,130
1885-86	2,110,105	2,930,375
1886-87	2,222,383	3,024,613
1887-88	2,430,756	2,350,040
1888-89	1,423,007	2,054,123
1889-90	451,001	699,206

maunds as compared to the total export of 48,373 maunds during 1878-79. Due to some misunderstanding between the merchants of India and Nepalese officials, the Nepalese Government prohibited the exports of timber.[37] Internal disturbance were another reason for the decrease of timber export.[38]

Another important article of export from Nepal to India was animal skin.Through North Western Provinces and Oudh, 2047 maunds of hides (animal skin) valued at Rs. 32,723 were exported in 1877-78.[39]

Nepal exported hides through Bengal in 1878-79 amounting to Rs. 39,527. If we consider the entire period of decade starting from 1878-79 to 1889-90, the highest quantity of hides were exported during 1879-80. During the year, Nepal exported 70, 706 pieces of hides which were valued at Rs. 167, 927. On the basis of value, the year 1882-83 was the highest exporting year for hides. During 1882-83, Nepal exported 64,969 pieces of hides valued at Rs. 178, 665. Districtwise, Muzaffarpur received the largest amount of hides. In 1879-80,out of 70, 706 pieces of hides 31, 879 pieces were exported through Muzaffarpur.[40]

One of the most important commodities exported from Nepal to India was ghee. According to the Deputy Commissioner of Kheri, in 1875-76,111 maunds and 32 seers of ghee valued at 2,898 rupees, 3 anna and 9 paisa only was through Singhai and Ramnagar post.[41]

It was informed by the Director of Agriculture and Commerce of North Western provinces and Oudh on November 4,1877 that ghee worth Rs.126,350 was exported by Nepal which was 4.5 per cent of the total amount of exports.[42]

Table-4.8
Exports of Ghee from Nepal to India through Bengal (1880-81 to 1889-90)

Years	*Quantity* *(Mds)*	*Value* *(Rs)*
1880-81	4,284	138,083
1881-82	5,881	188,192
1882-83	10,352	300,208
1883-84	7,239	209,931
1884-85	7,244	211,558
1885-86	5,640	168, 810
1886-87	3,460	111,975
1887-88	5,127	171,397
1888-89	9,075	289,021
1889-90	11,295	349,636

In 1877-78, 11, 933 maunds of ghee (worth Rs. 260,055) were exported through North Western Provinces. In addition, some ghee was exported from Dang and Deokhuri of Nepal by the Dara Pass, which was not registered on its entry, a few quantity might have been caught at Matariaghat. The 3,037 maunds from Butwal were registered at Lotan and 5,875 from Banke were registered at Babaganj.[43]

The main centre of ghee export from Nepal was Butwal. As compared to the preceding year, the export of ghee had declined by 2,589 maunds in 1879-80.

Table 4.8 shows that after 1880-81 ghee export increased gradually with exception of one year, i.e.1886-87, and reached its peak in 1889-90. In 1889-90, Nepal exported 11,295 maunds of ghee worth Rs. 349,63, an increase of 3,220 maunds from 1888-89. Out of 11,295 maunds, the amount of 2,843 maunds valued at Rs. 87,982 were recorded through Muzaffarpur post. Through Sukiapokhari and Goompahar in Darjeeling district, 2,672 maunds of ghee worth Rs. 82,706 were exported.[44]

4.2.2 Composition of Imports from India into Nepal

Cotton, salt, sugar and tobacco were the principal imports of Nepal. Nepal imported large amount of raw cotton, yarn and Indian as well as European piece-goods from British India. In 1873 and 1874, Nepal Imported cotton goods worth Rs. 248, 045 and Rs. 285, 398 respectively.[45] According to the report of a special committee on Statistics (1874), only a small quantity of cotton was imported by Nepal from Oudh.[46] However, it was also mentioned in that report that the figures related to foreign trade of Oudh were not accurate.[47]

Table-4.9
Exports To India From Nepal (Tibet, Sikkim & Bhutan)

(Qty : in'000 md.)

Year (April-March)	*Rice**	*Wheat*	*Gram & Pulses*	*Hides & Skins*	*Ghee*	*Oilseeds (b)*	*Raw Jute*	*Raw Wool*	*Tobacco*
					(b)	(p)			
1942-43	1343.3	50.3	536.5	24.9	45.3	428.8	96.6	60.7	5.9
1943-44	1025.5	58.3	242.7	23.5	56.4	238.4	71.0	32.1	6.1
1944-45	1134.4	53.6	206.1	19.7	48.9	325.0	110.9	61.0	4.8
1945-46	811.1	61.1	245.9	27.4	41.9	540.2	144.8	75.2	3.5
1946-47	1072.5	34.7	292.4	32.5	29.4	257.0	188.6	72.4	5.5
1647-48	544.1	13.4	225.3	12.1	22.8	220.1	249.6	71.1	5.2
1948-49	828.5	15.5	232.6	11.9	24.0	184.9	127.6	86.8	7.6
1949-50	602.2	4.1	149.1	16.3	26.7	236.0	70.4	77.1	7.8
1950-51	529.1	7.0	150.0	16.1	24.8	197.1	168.9	72.2	5.3

(Contd.)

(Contd. Table 4.9)

Qty : in 000 md.)

Year (April-March)	Rice*	Wheat	Gram & Pulses	Hides & Skins	Ghee	Oilseeds (b)	Raw Jute	Raw Wool	Tobacco
1951-52	259.2	12.4	61.2	19.7	33.4	258.9	193.3	24.2	4.2
1952-53	1075.5	4.5	152.2	18.9	44.3	00.0	141.5	13.2	2.2
1953-54	1080.1	21.7	167.0	17.4	38.2	307.9	111.8	9.4	0.4
1954-55	906.5	56.3	139.7	17.7	38.9	130.8	28.7	17.9	2.6
1955-56	819.9	49.9	202.6	21.5	40.3	172.1	125.5	20.2	0.6
1956-57	1180.3	25.0	278.2	18.9	41.2	169.5	156.4	23.8	1.4
1957-58	756.2	9.5	190.3	16.3	32.2	253.0	95.0	46.1	4.0
1958-59 $	515.6	26.0	211.5	16.5	40.2	242.5	92.8	0.5	2.2
1959-60 $	62.7	2.8	111.6	12.6	45.2	278.8	76.9	0.4	0.03

* - Husked and unhusked;

b - Mustard, Rape and Linseeds;

Table 4.10[48] indicates the accurate figures of the different types of articles imported from North Western Provinces and Oudh into Nepal.

Table-4.10
Imports of Commodities from North Western Provinces and Oudh into Nepal 1877

Name of Articles	*Total Value Imported (Rs.)*	*Percentage of the total Value of Imports (the total value of each article to)*
Raw cotton	14,820	1.4
Yarn and piece goods (European)	219,160	21.5
Yarn and piece goods (Indian)	437,534	42.9
Salt	97,178	7.8
Sugar	44,205	4.4
Others	224,130	22.0
Total	1,019,027	100.0

It is clear from the above table that imports of Nepal from North Western Provinces and Oudh comprised 88 per cent of cotton and cotton manufactures. More of cotton goods were imported into Nepal than raw cotton. The goods made of cotton sent to Nepal were by far the most important feature in the export trade.[49] 23,406 maunds of cotton goods were imported by Nepal from North Western Provinces and Oudh in 1877-78. The share of Indian spuntwist, European piece goods and Indian piece goods were 363 maunds (worth Rs. 12,407), 4,643 maunds (worth Rs. 427,987) and 18,400 maunds (worth Rs. 772,266) respectively. The total value of imports of cotton goods were Rs. 1,212,660. Of the Indian cloth imported to Nepal, 1,164 maunds were imported through Nautanwa, 4, 157 maunds through Marni and 4,579 maunds through Babaganj. Out of 4,643 maunds of European piece goods, 1,132 maunds were imported through Thunthibari and 789 maunds through Babaganj.[50]

It is clear from Table 4.11 that cotton piece goods were imported more than raw cotton by Nepal. The import of raw cotton through Bengal was highest during 1882-83. The total import in that year was 8,154 maunds of raw cotton valued at Rs. 138,618. The import of raw cotton started declining after 1882-83. In 1886-87, Nepal imported the lowest quantity of raw cotton. The fall of imported quantity of cotton was due to initiative taken by the Nepalese Government to start cultivation in their own country. Cotton plantation was

Table-4.11

Imports of Cotton and Cotton Goods from Bengal into Nepal 1878-79 to 1887-88

Years	*Raw Mds*	*Cotton Rs*	*Piece goods (European) Value (Rs)*	*Piece goods (India) Value (Rs)*	*Total Value (Rs)*
1878-79	6,511	104,176	1,887,996	259,842	2,252,014
1879-80	7,011	119,187	1,724,118	297,426	2,140,731
1880-81	5,721	96,306	2,174,290	184,979	2.455,575
1881-82	5,623	95,591	1,834,818	232,693	2,162,102
1882-83	8,154	138,618	1,819,592	178,058	2,136,268
1883-84	8,069	132,750	2,135,246	247,540	2,515,536
1884-85	5,849	88,264	1,864,682	336,557	2,289,503
1885-86	7,198	99,123	1,557,508	162,654	1,819,285
1886-87	5,454	86,072	1,646,437	173,627	1,906,136
1887-88	5,836	87,768	1,927,111	307,190	2,322.060

started in Nuwakot district in Nepal in 1897 under the auspices of the Government. The responsibility to administer the project was on the Lt. Colonel, Devi Bahadur Sijapati. Thirty-four labourers were employed on pay roll on 13 April 1897 to start plantation.[51]

European piece goods were in greater demand than Indian piece goods in Nepal. As compared to Indian piece-goods worth Rs. 259,892, European piece-goods worth Rs. 1,887,996 were imported during 1878-79. But in 1879-80 the import of Indian piece-goods increased to Rs. 297,426 from Rs. 259,842 in 1878-79, whereas the import of European piece goods decreased by Rs. 163,878 in the same year as compared to the previous year. During 1879-80 to 1884-85, the imports of Indian cotton piece goods fell continuously. Indian piece goods imported to Nepal reached its peak during 1884-85. Again after 1884-85, import decreased drastically in 1885-86,1886-87 and 1887-88 by Rs. 173,903, Rs. 162,930 and Rs. 29,367 respectively in 1880-81 and 1885-86, the highest and lowest amount of European cotton piece goods were imported respectively. During 1885-86, the import of Indian piece goods as well as the total value of cotton goods also decreased due to internal disturbances in Nepal[53] and also owing to the fact that prices were high owing to bad harvest.[54]

The import of cotton twist and yarn to Nepal from India was 23.9 thousand maunds in 1942-43 which decreased to 5.4 thousand maunds but again increased to 23.8 thousand maunds during 1949-50. The import of cotton piece goods from India into Nepal was 66.1 thousand maunds in 1942-43 which reached its peak during 1944-45. The total import of cotton piece-goods in that year was 115.2 thousand maunds. But the import of cotton piece goods decreased to 99.4 thousand maunds in 1949-50.[55]

The most important import of Nepal was salt. The people of Nepal, particularly of eastern Nepal, almost entirely depended either on Bristish India[56] or on Tibet. In comparision to the Indian salt, the Tibetan salt was cheaper because, " the salt of Tibet cost little on the bank of lakes where it was collected, and was carried on sheep and goats, which graze their way and realized something as butcher's meat at the end."[57] Whereas, the Sambhar salt in India was sold at 10 annas per maund on the spot with addition of customs duty at Rs. three per maund in Nepal. The people of Terai area used Indian salt but in the hill, Lahori rock salt was used only in times of mourning when Tibetan salt was forbidden.[58]

In 1877, Nepal imported salt worth Rs. 97,178 from North Western Provinces and Oudh, which was 7.8 per cent of total imports of Nepal from that region.[59] Total 29,191 maunds of salt was imported by Nepal in 1877-88 as against 14,509 maunds in the preceding year.[60] During 1879-80, the imports of salt to Nepal from India through Bengal reached its peak of 87,510 maunds worth Rs. 393,777 as against 80,708 maunds worth Rs. 363,186 the previous year.[61] After 1879-80, the value of salt imported by Nepal decreased gradually but due to reduced customs duty as uniform[62] at Rs. two per maund all over India in 1882 ,the volume of salt imported to Nepal increased after 1883-84. The inland customs line was also abolished. As a result of these two measures, salt became cheaper in India as " a whole than it was fifty years ago, or at any earlier stage of Indian history."[63]

In 1942-43, the import of Indian salt in Nepal was 646.6 maunds which increased to 648.9 maunds in 1949-50.[64]

Sugar was also an important article of import to Nepal. Nepal imported sugar worth Rs. 44,205 in 1877, which was 4.4 per cent of total import to Nepal from India.[65] It was reported by the Deputy Commissioner of Kheri that 19 maunds and 7 seers of sugar worth Rs.118 annas 8 and 334 maunds 27 seers of molasses worth Rs.1746 were imported by Nepal through Singhai and Ramnagar.[66] A total of 430 maunds of Shira worth Rs.784 was also imported through that route.[67] Nepal imported 791 maunds and 25,347 maunds of refined and unrefined sugar (including Shira and molasses) respectively during 1877-78. None of the registration posts in North Western Provinces registered more than 3,000 maunds of sugar import.[68]

A total of 10,662 maunds worth Rs. 170,592 of refined sugar and 20,847 maunds worth Rs. 145,929 unrefined sugar were imported by Nepal through Bengal. Refined sugar imported to Nepal gradually decreased by 1887[69] but the import of unrefined sugar was stagnant. Unrefined sugar particularly molasses was in great demand in Nepal.

In the 19th century, import of molasses was the Government monopoly in Nepal. The instruction was given to the agent of Government to purchase molasses at reasonable prices, and collect fines from any person who sold the commodity to others. The agent was warned not to harass traders by purchasing molasses from them at unduly low prices.[70]

The import of sugar (refined as well as unrefined) reached its peak in 1887-88. In that year Nepal imported 12,486 maunds worth Rs 134,545 of refined sugar and 46,854 maund worth Rs. 215,450[71] of unrefined sugar.

Another article of import to Nepal was tobacco. It was considered as a luxurious item.[72] The cultivation of tobacco was lately started in Nepal.[73] Land under tobacco cultivation was the most heavily taxed.[74]

The 4,735 maunds of tobacco worth Rs. 34,288 was imported by Nepal during 1877-78 through North Western Provinces and Oudh. Out of 4,735 maunds of tobacco, 2,294 maunds were imported through the Babaganj post,[75] whereas 12,642 maunds of tobacco valued at Rs. 75,852 was imported through Bengal in 1878-79.[76] The import of tobacco increased to 78,480 maunds valued at Rs. 286,551 in 1887-88 from 12,642 maunds worth Rs. 75,852 in 1878-79 and 19,276 maunds worth Rs. 125,314 in 1879-80.[77] Tobacco grown in Bengal was "uncommonly good" and this was the reason that the Eastern Terai region of Nepal imported larger amount of tobacco.[78]

During 1879-80 to 1942-43 26.9 thousand maunds of tobacco was imported from India to Nepal (including Tibet, Sikkim and Bhutan) in 1943-44. The

Table -4.12
Imports from India into Nepal (Tibet, Sikkim and Bhutan)

(Qty : in '000' md.)

Year (April to March)	*Husked Rice*	*Wheat*	*Gram & Pulses*	*Iron & Steel Sections**	*Brass & Copper (*)*	*Kerosene & other Oil and Products*	*Salt*	*Betel-nuts (*)*	*Sugar*	*Tea*	*Cotton twist & yarn*	*Cotton Piece goods (a)*	*Tobacco (β)*
1942-43	172.7	32.0	174.0	13.1	0.9	73.8	646.6	9.2	62.0.	1.2	23.9	66. 7	55.0
1943-44	103.0	25.0	202.2	12.0	0.3	79.4	717.2	13.9	78.7	3.8	46.3	113.4	26.9
1944-45	27.9	12.1	169.0	15.8	1.3	29.0	712.9	13.6	64.0	2.5	41.7	115.2	23.0
1945-46	49.7	15.0	280.8	33.6	5.8	66.6	937.8	25.1	62.3	2.3	8.0	34.7	36.9
1946-47	66.2	10.6	268.8	29.0	11.6	59.7	629.5	11.0	51.2	3.1	15.6	68.4	27.9
1947-48	64.0	5.3	149.9	16.9	6.9	62.4	680.0	11.8	31.9	13.3	8.4	84.4	18.3
1948-49	84.1	15.1	127.4	13.2	3.5	64.2	851.2	19.5	51.8	4.1	5.4	64.8	13.6
1949-50	95.5	35.0	89.6	25.3	17.6	62.4	648.9	18.8	31.3	1.2	23.8	99.4	24.4
1950-51	74 .1	8.2	200.5	51.7	7.8	70.5	748.6	22.6	49.2	1.6	10.2	133.5	26.0
1951-52	16.5	41.2	33.6	47.7	4.1	100.0	795.0	20.8	47.7	9.4	6.6	126.3	19.5

(Contd.)

(Contd. Table 4.12)

(Qty : in '000' md.)

Year (April to March)	Husked Rice	Wheat	Gram & Pulses	Iron & Steel Secti-ons*	Brass & Copper (*)	Kerosene & other Oil and Products	Salt	Betel-nuts (*)	Sugar	Tea	Cotton twist & yarn	Cotton Piece goods (a)	Tobacco (β)
1952-53	3.8	6.1	89.7	24.9	2.3	59.9	802.3	10.2	37.7	2.1	8.2	120.3	17.4
1953-54	0.3	7.2	33.4	28.6	3.1	83.1	430.9	10.6	38.8	1.0	12.5	90.2	12.9
1954-55	1.1	4.7	38.2	23.3	3.7	76.1	588.3	4.8	43.3	0.4	4.4	82.4	15.5
1955-56	21.1	12.6	39.4	29.7	3.7	118.8	773.4	3.9	49.0	0.6	9.9	120.5	19.3
1956-57	34.1	8.5	91.0	36.1	3.6	232.4	516.7	4.6	56.1	1.3	13.4	110.7	8.7
1957-58	197.1	23.8	65.1	72.4	11.3	403.1	742.4	10.3	74.1	1.9	16.7	121.9	51.9
1958- 59$	30.2	518.5	85.4	41.25	11.0	325.1	830.8	4.8	84.3	1.8	12.4	92.0	45.8
1959-60$	10.9	29.8	20.4	27.0	4.7	245.2	581.6	0.6	14.2	0.8	24.0	120.9	48.6

* - Imported by Nepal only

a - Indian and Foreign Cotton piece goods;

ß - Raw and Manufactured Tobacco;

import of tobacco by Nepal reached its peak in 1945-46 (Table 4.12). In that year, 36.9 thousand maunds of tobacco was imported from India to Nepal. However, the import of tobacco by Nepal gradually declined to 13.6 thousand maunds in 1948-49, and yet it again rose to 24.4 thousand maunds in the next year.[79]

To sum up, Nepalese import from and export to India fluctuated over the years in all the commodities mentioned above. According to the collectors of Bhagalpur, the difference in the rates of duty had very little impact on the fluctuation of volume of trade. The volume of trade was dependent more on the demand for different commodities in different places.[80]

The salient features of Indo–Nepal trade in late 1940s were as follows:

(a) Due to its backwardness and agricultural economy Nepal had very few items for export to India. Items of export comprised paddy, raw jute, timber, mustard oil seeds, ghee etc. On the other hand, India supplied a large variety of agricultural products as well as manufactured goods to Nepal, which included tea, tobacco, refined and unrefined sugar, pulses, wheat, cotton textiles, machinery, dyes and dying materials, metal articles, cigarettes, hardware and basic materials like iron and steel, cement, kerosene, petroleum and salt.[81]

(b) On account of this wide gap of export and import, the balance of trade was in favour of India.[82]

(c) With the passage of time Nepal's imports from India kept on increasing whereas its exports to India remained constant. This created severe imbalance of trade for Nepal.[83]

(d) Nepal did not possess a stable currency and that necessitated payment in Indian currency.

(e) There was warm welcome of Indian currency in Nepal. Hence, it circulated freely throughout Nepal alongwith Nepalese currency, i.e. Nepalese rupee.

(f) The Indo–Nepalese border was naturally open which led to free movement of people from both sides and they sold and bought goods to fulfill their needs without any hindrance.

On 31st July, 1950, India signed a treaty of trade and transit with Nepal for the regulation of trade and granting Nepal certain transit facilities.

On the same date, another treaty was also signed between both countries. This was the treaty of Trade and commerce.[84] Under this treaty, the two governments agreed to "assist each other, by making available, to the maximum extent possible, commodities which were essential to the economy of the other.

Steps were also taken to curb the abuse of mutually conceded trading facilities by preventing the smuggling of goods from one country to another.

4.3 Smuggling

Between India and Nepal, smuggling was a common phenomenon. The main items of smuggling from Nepal to India were opium,[85] cardamoms,[86] and timber.[87] From India arms and ammunition[88] were smuggled to Nepal.

4.3.1 Opium

A large amount of opium was brought to Nepal from India to smuggle into China during 1851 and 1852. In 1852, the export of opium was prohibited from Nepal to India by Nepal Durbar because they wanted to send it to China with the quiquennial mission.[89]

The cultivators of opium in the terai region in Nepal in concert with the headmen of their villages and the agents of its receivers in Calcutta and Chandernagore were the principal smugglers of opium. The smugglers from Punjab and Assam were also involved in this illegal trade. The main centres were Baidyanath and a place in the terai near the Gorakhpur frontier, where the smuggled opium was deposited *en route* to Calcutta and Chandernagore before its shipment to foreign ports. The Nepalese *kothis* or godowns at Govindganj, Patna and Calcutta were also involved in this illegal trafficking.[90]

A large quantity of opium from Nepal was smuggled to India every year. At Chandernagore, a monopoly of the sale of the drug was enjoyed by Bengali businessman. To assist him, about twenty-five Chinese were involved in the retail distribution of this commodity. French steamers shipped off the greater portion of the smuggled opium to the port of Macao at the mouth of the canton river.[91]

The smuggling of opium was started in Punjab in 1886. Some persons smuggled opium on their own account and sold it to the contractors of Patiala. State officials did not oppose this illegal trade. Some contractors in Patiala were natives of some Punjab districts, and so they used to smuggle opium into those districts as well.[92]

Opium was smuggled into India from Nepal because Indian Government prohibited its import.[93]

To escape registration and customs duty, timber and cardamoms were also smuggled from Nepal to India.

Arms and ammunition were also smuggled from India to Nepal. Generally, these items were taken from India to Kathmandu without license. The consignment under various passes and through different routes was collected at Patna. As opportunity occurred, the consignments were despatched from Patna to Nepal. Some of the consignments were sent to Nepal through Muzaffarpur and Darbhanga. There were various routes from where goods found their way to Nepal. Of all these routes, the route via Patna was most frequently used. The contraband arms and ammunition concealed in small quantities in boxes containing other legitimate articles of trade were sent to Nepal by this route.[94]

During the Nepal conflict with Tibet, Tibetan salt was smuggled.[95] If smuggling was detected the trader was fined with double duty and confiscation of goods.

4.3.2 Slave Trade

Prior to the regime of Jang Bahadur, private sale of children was a common practice among parents belonging to the lower castes of Newars and other hill tribes.[96] But this practice was banned by the Prime Minister Jang Bahadur.

In India, slave trafficking was a penal offence.[97] British officials tried their best to check slave trafficking on the Indo-Nepal border but it remained unchecked. The British officials blamed Nepalese officials who were posted near the border for the illegal activities.[98]

The purchase of slaves were made from the poverty stricken people of Bihar and North Western Provinces in India at the rate of four or five rupees and they were sold in Nepal for Rs. 30 or 40 per slave.[99] As on December 1, 1836, the cost of a full grown-up male slave was eighty rupees and for a full grown female slave hundred rupees. Boy and girl slaves were sold at Rs. 40 and Rs. 50 each.[100] In 1877, the price charged for male slaves ranged between Rs. 100 and Rs. 150 and that for female slaves between Rs. 150 and Rs. 200.[101] Due to famine in Champaran and other districts, the slave trade increased tremendously in 1866-67. During the famine of 1866–67, several people from affected areas in Bihar went to Nepal to get food which was then distributed as charity in Nepal. These people started selling their children when they did not obtain sufficient food.[102] According to the Officiating Commissioner of Patna, during periods of scarcity, parents sold their children to Nepal in large numbers to obtain food, shelter and other necessities for their children.[103]

British-Indian Government found it very difficult to check slave traffic in such a wide open frontier. Slaves were generally taken to Nepal one by one and not in batches. On the part of Indian officials, it would be a blunder to arrest persons walking into Nepal with children who went willingly and seemed to be their own. Hence, the Indian Government could not stop the slave traffic.[104] Jang Bahadur,the Nepalese Prime Minister, ordered his officials that, "although they were not to encourage the sellers, they were not to prohibit any one from purchasing children."[105]

British officials opined that if the slavery was treated as criminal in Nepal it would die out.[106] Ultimately, Chandra Shamsher, the Prime Minister of Nepal, made an appeal to abolish slavery on 28th November 1924. To make slavery a penal offence, a new law was passed in Nepal. Out of 59,875 slaves, 51,782 slaves were liberated by the Nepalese Government by paying compensation, 4,651 slaves liberated by their masters without compensation, 1984 slaves died, 134 fled and 114 paid for their own release.[107]

4.4 Entrepot Trade

The bulk of Nepal's trade with Tibet was entrepot trade.[108] But it was not so profitable as a whole because it enriched only some persons involved in this trade.[109]

The Newars of the Kathmandu Valley and Kashmiri and Gosain traders from India were involved in entrepot trade and specialised in articles of great value and small bulk. With the coming of foreign traders, the Newars lost their monopoly and their activities became limited. The role of Newar merchants in Nepal-Tibet trade was confined to the export of commodities brought by Indian traders to Kathmandu and retail trade in Tibet. Some goods are imported to Nepal from India for the sake of re-export to Tibet. [110]

The towns of Kathmandu Valley and Patna were the main links in the trade that was conducted along the Kerung and Kuti routes, which were the shortest and the most [111] convenient between Northern India and Tibet.

European commodities and products of Bengal were carried to Tibet through Nepal.[112] There was a great demand of broad cloth in Tibet. Broad cloth worth Rs. 300,000 was sold every year. There was also great demand for coral among the army and Sardars of China and in some parts of Tibet.[113] Tibetans exported Pashmina or shawl wool, salt, borax, musk, quicksilver and gold dust in exchange for Nepalese metal wares, European cotton piece goods, Indian cotton goods and spices.[114]

Indo-Tibetan trade through Nepal dwindled to a negligible quantity due to the opening of trade route between Tibet at Kalimpong in North East Bengal and also because of Younghusband mission of 1904-05. Indo-Tibet trade through Nepal was again affected by the political change that occurred in Tibet in 1959. Nepalese and Tibetan traders were prohibited in border trade, which had a great impact on the life of the people living in northern border area of Nepal. [115]

4.5 Trade Registration Stations

Despite old commercial traffics there were no custom houses along the long-open border between India and Nepal in the Indian districts. Prior to 1875, the British Government in India had not made any attempt to register the amount of trade traffic passing through the different routes on the Indo-Nepal border. Though the Nepalese side had custom houses set up by the Government of Nepal, it did not attempt to register its Trade with British India.[116]

A conference held at Allahabad in 1857 had taken the decision for registration of provincial traffic. The delegates from Bengal, North-Western provinces, Oudh, Panjab and Central Province had attended the conference. The Collectors of Bhagalpur, Darbhanga, Muzaffarpur and Champaran were also consulted. [117] On 23rd August 1875, the financial department of the Government of Bengal passed a resolution sanctioning certain arrangements for the registration of traffic between Bengal and Nepal with effect from the first day of September. The resolution mentioned that until now there was no organized attempt to register the amount of traffic between India and Nepal. It was also mentioned that, as the boundary line was extensive and the trade passed through numerous channels, there was great difficulty in organizing a complete system of registration. The arrangements were experimental only and liable to modifications. In addition, it was also resolved that a copy of daily returns of each registering centre would be submitted every week by the registering *Mohurir* to the district headquarters in prescribed performa for the purpose of analysis and preparation of monthly returns. It was desirable to bring to the notice of Government all the most important markets and the amount of their traffic.[118]

The British Government in India sanctioned the establishment registration posts at Khandauli and Birpur in Bhagalpur district, Sitamarhi and Pupri in Muzaffarpur district Jaynagar, Kamtaul and Madhubani in Darbhanga district and Katkana, Raxaul and Ghorasahan in Champaran district on August 28, 1875.[119] On September 4, 1875, the Government had sanctioned the establishment of registration centres at Amona, Sikti, and Kalughat in Purnea district.[120] Trade registration centres at Kunjulio, Ghoompahar, Adhikari and Naxalbari were approved and sanctioned on October 2, 1875 to register the frontier traffic between Darjeeling and Nepal.[121] The registration of traffic at Naxalbari was discontinued with effect from June 1, 1885. In place of it, an arrangement was made with the traffic Superintendent of Northern Bengal State Railway for the registration at Siliguri.[122]

There were three trade registration posts at Sukhiapokri, Kunjulia, and Siliguri in the last decade of the nineteenth century for the registration of the traffic with Nepal. By 1898-99 only two posts were retained which continued to register the trade with Nepal till 1907.These two posts were Sukhiapokri and Kunjulia.[123]

In 1883 the Purnea district had six trade registration posts at Kalughat, Degalbank, Byreah, Sikti, Megahat and Mirganj.[124] On 16 June 1884 the Megahat centre was shifted to Nawabganj.

Byreah post was shifted to Teragach in October 1884 and Kalughat and Degalbank posts were shifted to Panthamari and Doorsa respectively in September 1884.[125]

On the suggestion of the Commissioner of the Bhagalpur Division, the Government of Bengal sanctioned the establishment of the five new registration centres at Bansgaon, Bhatgaon, Geendharoadanga in Kisanganj Sub Division and Kuari and Kusumba in the Araria Sub-Division with effect from December 1887. From December 1887 to January 1888, Bansgaon centre was kept open and thereafter it was shifted to Kohabari hat through which much traffic passed to and from Nepal.[126] The trade registration post at Bhatgaon was shifted to Korlekote on 1 May1888.[127]

The trade registration centre at Sikti was transfered to Paharia from 1 April 1899. Through Paharia the bulk of traffic was passed. The Pathardena centre was abolished and later on registered at Sonap[128] Kuari, Kusumbee, Mirganj, Panthamari in Araria Sub Division and Bhatgaon, Dharsa, Gandharbadanga, Karabari, Pahora and Teragach in Kishanganj Sub Division were the trade centres in the first decade of the twentieth century.[129] In the

Bhagalpur District, there were originally two trade registration centres. They were at Khandauli and Birpur.[130]

Another centre in Panchpararia occurred in the reports of 1882-83.[131] In the Darbhanga District there were five trade registration centers in 1882-83. They were at Madhwapur, Hatwari, Jainagar, Mirzapur and Pipraghat.[132]

The opening of Bengal and North-Western Railway and several new roads which crossed the frontier of Darbhanga into Nepal compelled to readjust the location of the registration centres. Accordingly three new centres were opened at Khajauli, Phulparas and Jhitpi and the Mirzapur centre was shifted two miles away to the north-east. Pipraghat centre was abolished.[133]

Consequently, there were seven trade registration centers established in the Darbhnga District towards the end of nineteenth century.

No major change occured in the location of registration centers in the Muzaffarpur and Champaran districts during the last two decades of the nineteenth century. In Bhagalpur there were five registration centres at Bairagnia. Majorganj, Sonbarsa, Bela and Sursand. Champaran too had five registration centres at Tribenighat. Raxoul, Adapore, Katkana and Ghorasan. When the trade registration system first started in1875, there were 17 centres in Bengal which increased to 27 ports in 1882-83 and further to 34 ports in 1898-99. Trade registration centre at Tribenighat in Champaran was closed for two months (September and October) and registration posts at Naxalbari, Ghoom, Pahar and Kunjulia were closed for three months i.e. from16 June to 15 September on account of rains.[134]

Trade registration post at Pathardena in the Purnea District remained closed for six months from June to November on account of rains. Similarly, Seekhipokri and Kunjulia posts in the Darjeeling District remain closed for three months from 16 June to 15 September each year from1895 to 1899 for the same reason.[135]

To obtain complete information about the traffic passing along all the important trade routes on the northern frontier of British India, a common system of traffic registration was adopted in Bengal and North-Western Provinces from June 1879.[136]

Initially registration post at Kakrahighat registered road traffic crossing the Banganga by ferry. The registration of river traffic on the Banganga by Kakrahighat post was arranged in 1880-81.[137]

In 1883-84 the registration post at Barmdeo was shifted to Tanakpur due to change in the course of river Sarda. When the river again changed its course, a great portion of the traffic was diverted to Mundiaghat, and a new post was diverted to Mundiaghat, therefore a new post was created at this point.[138] Due to insignificant registration of traffic, the Jhulaghat post in the Kumaun District and Sehas in the Barti District were discontinued in July 1885.[139]

Later, it was found that the working of the trade registration system was not very satisfactory. It was noticed by the Government of Bengal that statistics supplied by the trade registration centres were incorrect and the whole system was useless. It was advocated that it might be expedient to confine the registration to the marts in India from where traffic flowed into Nepal, and to those points in Bengal and North-Western Provinces, directly opposite to the Nepal marts, from where the trade flowed into India.[140] To measure the extent of the trade and to determine its capablity to increase was the main objective of registration of the traffic.[141] But the objective was not fully realized. It was argued that to register the import and export traffic, registration clerks would visit the Nepalese marts. According to most of the Divisional Commissioners of Bengal and North-West Provinces and Oudh, the system of trade registration was "very imperfect", "completely untrust worthy", "inaccurate", and "completely a failure".[142]

The list of import from Nepal prepared by the commissioner of Kumaun omitted tea for which there was an increasing demand from Darjeeling and Kumaun. The statistics from Bengal did not include the river traffic, tea from Darjeeling, the export of musk, silver, gold and furs from Nepal and the return trade in coral and precious stones and also in personal clothing. Musk was sent from Nepal mostly by the Resident's part and by the same means much personal clothing was sent to Nepal. So these things were not registered by the registering clerks.[143]

In his report for the 1881-82 to the commissioner of Bhagalpur Division, the SubDivisional officer of Kishanganj asserted "I know personally that several elephants and horses, and large quantities of gold and silver, and at least 20,000 pigs are taken to Nepal every year; but theses never pass the registration office. Large quantities of timber and musk and almost all the plywood for this sub-division are imported from Nepal, and these are never registered. There are only three registration offices, while there are about 200 routes. Consequently, every body chooses the easiest route for himself and will not take the trouble to pass by a circuitous route to have the articles registered."[144]

The commissioner of Bhagalpur N.S. Alexander complained in his report on Annual General Administration for 1885-86 that trade in cattle and livestock was centred at Hirampore market in Pakour but there was no supervision and sales were not registered.[145] As reported by the SDO of Madhubani in 1881-82, fifteen merchants left the area of Mirzapur by road with many carts and visited a fair held at Janakpur in Nepal and did large business. Their transactions were not registered.[146]

For a frontier of 700 miles, there were only 52 registration centres in 1878-79, i.e. on an average one post for every 13.5 miles.[147] There were twenty trade registration centre in 1877-78 over 330 miles of border along the North-Western Provinces, i.e. on an average one post for every 16.5 miles.[148] The number of these registration stations were inadequate and left undue gaps. Most of the traffic passed the border by roads and foot paths not commanded by the registration stations 100 of roads by the merchandise trade was recorded in arbitrarily by value was overestimated. [149]

The deputy Commissioner of Darjeeling, Edger, stated in August 1876 that the staff of the registration centres in Darjeeling district had confusions regarding the classification and columns of the registration forms. He also made suggestion that clerks well acquainted with the languages spoken by the frontier traders and Hindi should be appointed. [150]

In 1877-78, the District Magistrate of the Bhagalpur Division reported that the people were against the system and they were hesitant to furnish information to the clerks of the registration centres. [151]

In his annual report for 1884-85, the Commissioner of the Bhagalpur Division, O.N. Barlow complained that the unsuitability of police agency for trade enquiries had become so obvious that it should have been abandoned. It was very difficult task to collect statistics from about five lakhs people scattered in about seven hundred villages. A single officer could not be able to collect exhaustive information, even if he gave the whole time in this matter. If an officer could confine himself to one bazaar only, even then the result would not be trustworthy.[152]

The weight of timber was guessed by the registration clerks. They calculated the value of timber on the basis of such guess, as the value of timber in Nepal depended on size, length and quality.[153]

The Indian traders, particularly of Muzaffarpur District often confused registration with license tax and thus avoided registration.[154]

The Sub-Divisional Officer of Sitamarhi reported in 1879-80 that all the former registeration clerks were careless in noting whether the traffic passing their stations was actually from Nepal or going to Nepal.[155]

The registration clerks used to get mere 3 ½ rupees per month as salary which was quite low.[156] This left room for petty exaction on the traders.

In 1887, Rs. 2,744 was spent on the registration arrangements in the North-Western Provinces. This amount was insufficient for registration arrangements and for increasing the salary of the registration clerks. Charles Girdlestone, the then British Resident in Nepal, suggested that providing them better salaries could increase the efficiency of clerks. The remedies lay in better salary, close supervision and intermittent enquiries.[157]

Though the registration system had many drawbacks, the system had some tangible utility. The statistics provided by these registration stations related to the main trading routes and the articles forming chief staples of trade were of very considerable service.[158] A fair basis for a comparison of fluctuations in trade from year to year was made available by the registration of the trade.[159] The returns filled by the registration centres showed both volume and direction trade.[160] The trade statistics contained two useful formations, first as giving a minimum limit, and second as furnishing a standard for improvement in future years.[161]

There were frequent lines of communication between India and Nepal. Also, there were numerous marts for the exchange of commodities. Thus, the complete registration of the trade was not possible. But, according to Girdlestone, "the very fact of their number implied facilities rather than obstacles.[162]

Notes and References

1. B.P. Shreshtha, *An Introduction to Nepalese Economy,* Ratna Pustak Bhandar, Kathmandu,1974 p. 177.
2. W.W. Hunter, *The Indian Empire, Its people and products.* Reprint Concept Publishing.Co., New Delhi,1976, London, 1892, p. 691.
3. This chart was supplied by British Resident in Nepal to the British Indian Government for the year 1878-79 to 1879-80. Political A. December 1880, No. 38. (N.A.I.).
4. W.W. Hunter, *op. cit.,* p. 691.
5. Report on the External Trade of Bengal with Nepal, Sikkim, Bhutan and Tibet 1880-81. (N.A.I.).
6. Report on the External Trade of Bengal with Nepal, Sikkim, Bhutan and Tibet 1882-83. (N.A.I.).
7. In 1883 Nepal-Tibet conflict reached its climax, when Nepalese shops at Lhasa were looted by Tibetan monks, see, Kanchanmoy Majumdar, *Anglo-Nepalese Relations in the Nineteenth Century,* Firma K.L.M. Pvt. Ltd., Calcutta, 1973. p. 118.
8. Report on the External Trade of Bengal with Nepal, Sikkim, Bhutan, Tibet 1883-84 to 1885-86.
9. *Ibid.,* for 1886-87 to 1889-90.
10. Satish Kumar, Rana *Policy in Nepal,* Asia Publishing House, Bombay, Calcutta, New Delhi, 1967, p. 135.
11. Asad Hussain, *British India's Relations with the Kingdom of Nepal (1857-1947)*, Geogre Allen and Unwin Ltd. London, 1970, p. 136.
12. The trade of Bangal with Nepal, Tibet, etc. for the year ending March 31, 1901, Calcutta. September 11, 1901. (N.A.I.).
13. Foreign Department Secret E. December 1907, Nos 121. Annual General Report on Nepal for the year 1906-07 (N.A.I.).
14. Parimal Roy, *India's Foreign Trade since 1870,* London, 1934, p. 52.
15. B.P. Shrestha , *op. cit*, p. 158.
16. *Ibid.,* The annual confidential dispatch of the British Resident in Nepal to the British India. British Residency Record. (N.A. I.).
17. N.P. Banskota, *Indo-Nepal Trade and Economic Relations*, B.R. Publishing Corporation, Delhi, 1981, p. 23.
18. *Ibid.,* p. 24.

19. B.P. Shreshtha, *op. cit.*, p. 185.
20. P.C. Rawat, *Indo-Nepal Economic Relations,* National Publishing House, Delhi, 1974, p. 58.
21. "As development proceeds, increased availability of capital and skilled labour broadens the product range over which a country can effectively compete in the international market." See Vijaya Katti, "Commodity and geographic concentration in Indo-Nepalese Trade". *Foreign Trade Review* (18) (3). October-December 1983, p. 322.
22. *District Gazetteers of U.P., Gorakhpur District* Vol. xxxi. pp. 78-79.
23. Report on the Foreign Trade of North Western Provinces and Oudh during the year 1877-78. (N.A.I.).
24. *Ibid.*
25. Report on the External Trade of Bengal with Nepal, Sikkim and Bhutan 1880 81. (N.A.I.).
26. *Ibid,* for 1899-1900.
27. A General E. March 1884. No. 3. Extract from the Nepal Diary for the week ending the 1884. (N.A.I.), Report on the external trade of Bengal with Nepal Sikkim and Bhutan 1878-79 to1899-2000 .
28. *Ibid.*
29. *Imperial Gazetteer of India, Afghanistan and Nepal,* Calcutta, 1908, p. 115.
30. M.C. Regmi, *The State and Economic Surplus Products,Trade and Resource Mobiliation in Early 19th Century in Nepal, Varanasi,1984.op. cit.* The exports of salwood was one of the principal sources of income to the Nepalese Government; also see Lt.Col. Eden Vansittart '*The Gurkhas*: Reprint of ed. 1890, New Delhi, 1980. p. 6.
31. Report on the Foreign Trade of North Western Provinces and Oudh, 1877-78. (N.A.I.).
32. M.C. Regmi, *Thatched Huts and Stucco Palaces, Peasants and Land- lords in 19th century Nepal, Vikas Publisher*, New Delhi, 1978, pp 5-6.
33. *Ibid.* p. 5.
34. External B. September 1906. No. 50. Annual Report on the Foreign Trade of the United Province with Nepal. (N.A.I.).
    Report on the external trade of Bengal with Nepal Sikkim and Bhutan 1878-79 to 1899-1900.
35. Jahar Sen, "The Tune of timber in Indo-Nepal Relation". *Calcutta Historical Journal.* Vol. VII. No. 7, July-December 1982, p. 64.
36. Report on the Administration of the North Western Provinces and Oudh for the year ending 31 March 1899. Allahabad, 1900.
37. Jahar Sen, *op. cit.* p. 64.
38. Report on the Foreign Trade of North Western Provinces and Oudh. 1877-78. (N.A.I.).

39. Report of N.W.P. and Oudh recorded exports of hide in maund whereas all other documents mention it in number.
40. Revenue A. August 1877, No. 14.
41. *Ibid.* December 1877. No. 2.
42. Report on Foreign Trade of North Western Provinces and Oudh 1877-78. (N.A.I.).
43. *Ibid.*
44. Revenue A. August 1877, No. 13. Captain A. Murray, Officiating Personal Assistant to the Chief Commissioner of Oudh to T.H. Thornton, Officiating Secretary to the Government of India, dated 31 May 1876. No. 2489. (N.A.I.).
45. Ibid., No. 3. Extract paragraph 6 from a report by a Special Committee on Statistics relating to India, dated 10 December 1874, No. 73. (N.A.I.).
46. *Ibid.*
47. *Ibid.* No. 2.
48. Report on the Foreign Trade of North Western Provinces and Oudh. 1877-78. (N.A.I.).
49. *Ibid.*
50. Report on the External Trade of Bengal with Nepal, Sikkim and Bhutan. 1878-79 to 1887-88. (N.A.I.), M.C. Regmi, "Cotton Cultivation in Nuwakot." *Regmi Research Series,* Year 12, No. 2. February 1980, p. 23.
51. Report on the External Trade of Bengal with Nepal, Sikkim and Bhutan. 1878-88.
52. Yagya Acharya, *Nepal Ka Itihas.* Kathmandu, (2039 v.s.) pp. 4-15.
53. Foreign Department, Secret E. December 1907 No. 121-123. Annual General Report on Nepal for the year 1906-7. (N.A.I.).
54. G.H.D. Gimlette, *Nepal and the Nepalese,* London, H.F. and G wither by ,1928 p. 81.
55. B.P. Shreshtha, *op .cit.,* p. 187.
56. Report on the Foreign Trade of North Western Provinces and Oudh, 1877-78. (N.A.I.)
57. *Ibid.*
58. Revenue A. August 1877. No. 2.
59. Report on the Foreign Trade of North Western Provinces and Oudh 1878. (N.A.I.).
60. Report on the External Trade of Bengal with Nepal, Sikkim and Bhutan 1877-78. (N.A.I.).
61. *Ibid,* for 1878-79.
62. Before 1882 customs duty was not uniform in India. From times immemorial a tax on salt was a source of revenue in India. In 1858 the salt tax was Rs. 2.5 a maund (about 82 lbs) in Bengal, Rs. 1 maund (including cost of manufacture) in Madras, 12 annas in Bombay, and

Rs. 2 a maund in North India. In 1859 the rates were raised to Rs. 3, Rs. l, and Rs. 2.5 respectively and in 1861 they were again raised to Rs. 3.25 in Bengal, Rs. 3 in Madras and in North India. In 1878 the salt duty was raised in Madras and Bombay and reduced over the rest of India and ultimately in 1882 it was fixed and made uniform all over India. See, Memorandum on Some of the Results of Indian Administration. During the Past Fifth Years of British Rule in India. Calcutta, 1911, pp. 2-3.

63. *Ibid.*
64. B.P. Shreshtha, *op .cit.,* p. 187.
65. Revenue A. August 1877. No. 14.
66. *Ibid.*
67. Report on the Foreign Trade of North Western Provinces and Oudh. 1877-78. (N.A.I.).
68. Report on the External Trade of Bengal with Nepal, Sikkim and Bhutan. 1878-79 & 1886-87.
69. M.C. Regmi, "Monopoly Trade in Gur". *Regmi Research Series.* Year 14 No. 9. September 1982, p. 138.
70. Report on the External Trade of Bengal with Nepal, Sikkim and Bhutan. 1887-88. (N.A.I.).
71. Revenue A. August 1877. No. 14.
72. Tobacco had been introduced in India by the Portugese during the early seventeenth century and later on its cultivation started in the eastern Terai region of Nepal. See M.C. Regmi, *The State & Economic Surplus,* p. 46.
73. *Ibid.*
74. Report on the Foreign Trade of North Western Provinces and Oudh 1877-78. (N.A.I.).
75. Report on the External Trade of Bengal with Nepal, Sikkim and Bhutan. 1878-79.
76. *Ibid.* for 1887-88.
77. Francis Hamilton, *An Account of the Kingdom of Nepal.* Reprint of 1819 ed. New Delhi ,1971, p. 62.
78. Report on the External Trade of Bengal with Nepal, Sikkim and Bhutan. 1882-83. (N.A.I.).
79. B.P. Shreshtha, *op. cit.,* p. 187.
80. Finance B. February 1882. No. 40 G.E.R. Girdlestone. the British Resident in Nepal to the Officiating Lieutenant to the Government of India in the Foreign Department, Calcutta dated 27 January 1882. No. 4 p. (N.A.I.).
81. For a list of the items along with the quantity in maunds exported to Nepal in 1947-48, 1948-49 and April-December 1949. See India, *Parliamentary Debates,* Appendix Vll, Annexure No. 15 (February-April 1950).

82. For instance imports from and exports to Nepal in November-December 1948-49 were estimated at Rs. 2,92,92,000 and Rs. 3,25,50,000 respectively. See reply to starred question no. 1970, *Parliamentary Debates,* India, Pt. I, Cols. 1998-99, 8 March, 1951.
83. P.P. Karan and William M. Jenkins, Jr., *The Himalayan Kingdoms: Bhutan, Sikkim and Nepal* (D. Van Nostrand Company, Inc. : London, 1963), pp. 111-12.
84. See Appendix VII, For the text of the treaty see India, *Parliamentary-Debates,* Appendix I, Annexure 25: Second Session, July-August 1950, pp.198-201.
85. M C. Regmi, Smuggling of Cardamom *Regmi Research Series.* 1 May 1981, p. 75.
86. External A. November 1889. No. 51. Major E.L. Durand, the British Resident in Nepal to the Secretary to the Government of India. Foreign Department dated 12 October 1889. No. 92 (N.A.I.).
87. The British Government blamed the Nepalese Government for the smuggling of arms and ammunition. See Secret E. June 1884. No. 438. Departmental Note by the Secretary to the Government of India dated 20 February 1884. (N.A.I.).
88. Ibid. 1890. No. 529. Note in the Foreign Department dated 3 May 1890. (N.A.I.).
89. September 1852, Nos. 12-14. F. C. Ramsay to Charles Allen, No. 20 dated August 25, 1852.
90. Nepal Residency Records. SI. No. 4. File No. 13G. Part II of 1872. K.G.Gupta, offg. Secy, to the Board of Revenue, L.P. to the Secy. Govt, of Bengal, Finance Department. No. 349B dated April 27, 1888.
91. *Ibid.*, Excerpts from the Reports of Jogendra Mitter, quoted in the Consultations mentioned above.
92. *Ibid.,* Serial No. 524. File No. G 4215 of 1900.
93. Salt was smuggled from Tibet during the Nepal-Tibet Conflict which led to the shortage of this commodity in Kathmandu and elsewhere. The traders who smuggled salt from Tibet without paying customs duties were punished with a fine amounting to half the value of the smuggled salt.

    M.C. Regmi, *Regmi Research Series.* "The Salt Trade during the Nepal-Tibet War." p. 18.
94. Political B. January 1880, Nos. 210-225, Special Inspector Degan Lal's Final Report.
95. Political A. November 1867. No. 84 Abstract translation of a *yaddasht* from Jang Bahadur Rana to the British Resident in Nepal dated 28 October 1867. (N.A.I).
96. *Ibid.*

97. Political A. November 1867. No. 83. An English version of *yaddasht* from Colonel G. Ramsay British Resident in Nepal to Jang Bahadur Rana, Prime Minister of Nepal dated 3 October 1867. (N.A.I.).
98. Kanchanmoy Majumdar, "British Impact on Nepal." *Bengal Past and Present.* January -June, 1971, p. 140.
99. A. Campbell, *Notes on the Agriculture and Rural Economy of the Valley of Nepal.* Kathmandu, 1836, p. 32.
100 Daniel Wright, *Nepal : History of the Country and People, Cambridge University Press,* 1877, reprint, Delhi , 1983., p. 45.
101. Political A. November 1867. No. 82. Colonel G. Ramsay, British Resident in Nepal to the Secretary to the Government of India. Foreign Department. Viceregal Camp at Lucknow dated 8 November 1867. No. 35. (N.A.I.).
102. Proceedings of the Government in the Political Department for August 1867. No. 27. Jekins, the Officiating Commissioner of Patna division to the Secretary to the Government of Bengal. No. 28 dated 29 July 1867. (NA.I.).
103. The number of Musalmans were increasing in Nepal. They were zealous in purchasing girls, and in propagating their sect. Similarly Musalmans and Syyed women were taken by the Rajput and were turned into slave girls in India. They were taught the art of dancing also. Brahman and Rajput were also enslaved forcefully in the region between the Bheri and Mahakali river in Western Nepal. Therefore, the Government of Nepal proclaimed, 'no Brahman or Rajput shall be enslaved except with their consent in presence of the respectable person of the village, not through the use of force.' See, Hamilton, *op. cit.* p. 88; Srivastava, *op. cit.* p. 241. M. C. Regmi, "Documents on Slavery". *Regmi Research Series.* Year 1 No. 2. December 1, 1969. p. 44.
104. Political A. November 1867. No. 84.
105. Political A. October 1867. No. 225. G. Ramsay, the British Resident in Nepal to J.W.S. Wyllie, Under-Secretary to the Government of India in foreign Department No. 29. dated 23 September 1867. (N.A.I.).
106. Proceedings of the Bengal Government in the Political Department for August 1867. No. 32. H.A. Cockerel Officiating Magistrate at Tirhut to the Commissioner of the Division. No. 120 dated 21 July 1867. (N.A.I.).
107. The reshipment of imported goods, i.e., entrepot is not as much profitable as brisk indigenous trade. Almost the whole prices of the object sold comes back to enrich the exporting country incase of latter but a few persons get profit from the former. See F. Stiller S.J. Ludwig, "A Note on Himalayan Trade". *Journal of Tribhuvan University.* Kirtipur, Nepal, Vol. VII, No 1, November 972. p. 1.
108. *Ibid., A Study in Nepali Economic History.* New Delhi, 1971. p. 24.

109. M.C. Regmi, "The Kathmandu Valley Entrepot Trade". *Regmi Research Series.* Year 12, No. 1, 1 January 1980, p. 185.
110. K.C. Chaudhury, *Anglo-Nepalese Relations from the Earliest Times of British Rule in India Till the Gorkha War,* Modern Book Agency Pvt. Ltd., Calcutta, 1960, p. 91.
111. *Regmi Research Series. op. cit.* pp. 187-88.
112. K.C. Chaudhury, *op. cit.*
113. William Digby, 1857: *A Friend in Need 1887, Friendship Forgotten.* An episode in the Indian Foreign office Administration, London, Indian Political Agency,1890, pp. 20-21.
114. Report on the Foreign Trade of North Western Provinces and Oudh. 1877-78. (N.A.I.).
115. Shreeram Upadhyaya, *Indo-Nepal Trade Relations*, Nirala Publication, Jaipur, 1992, p.181
116. K.K. Adhikari, "A Brief Survey of Nepal's Trade with British India During the latter Half of the Nineteenth Century". *Contribution to Nepalese Studies.* No. 1 February, 1975, p. 187.
117. Revenue A. August 1877. No. 7.
118. *Ibid.*
119. Revenue A. August 1877, No. 2. K.W.
120. *Ibid.,* No. 8.
121. Progs. of the Bengal Government. Gen. Mis. August, 1876. File No. 190. S. No. 1-2.
122. *Report on the External Trade of Bengal with Nepal, Sikkim and Bhutan* for 1884-85. p. 12.
Ibid., for 1885-86. p. 1 ; for 1893-94. p. 1.
123. L.S.S. O'Malley, *Bengal District Gazetteer,* Darjeeling, 1907.
124. *Report on the External Trade of Bengal...* for 1882-88. p. 7.
125. *Ibid.,* for 1883-84. p. 14 ; for 1884-85. p. 12.
126. *Ibid.,* for 1887-88. p. 2.
127. *Ibid.,* for 1888-89. p. 2.
128. Progs. of the Bengal Government. Gen. Mis. December 1899. File 5R/17. S. No. 12-14.
129. L.S.S . O'Malley, *Bengal District Gazetteer Purnea,* 1911, p. 123.
130. W.W. Hunter, *Statistical Account of Bengal Vol. XIV, Bhagalpur.* 1877, p. 191.
131. *Report on the External Trade of Bengal for* 1882-83, p. 7, Progs, of the Bengal Government. Gen. Mis. December 1892. File 5R/29. S. No. 18-19.
132. *Annual General Administration Report of the Patna Division ; Report on the External Trade of Bengal for* 1882-83. p. 7.
133. *Report on the External Trade of Bengal for* 1895-96. p. 1.
134. *Ibid.,* for 1883-84. p. 14 ; for 1884-85. p. 12.

135. *Ibid.*, for 1893-94. p. 2; for 1894-95. p. 2; 1896-97 p. 2; for 1897-98. p. 2; for 1898-99. p. 2.
136. *Ibid.*, for 1881-82. p. 1.
137. *Annual Report of the Foreign Trade of North-West Provinces and Oudh for the year ending* 31st March 1881. p.3
138. *Ibid.*, for the year ending 31st March 1885. p. 3
139. *Ibid.*, for the year ending 31st March 1886. p. 1
140. Political A. October 1879. No. 133
141. Foreign Department, Political A. October 1879, No. 134, Girdlestonc to Lyall, Secretary to the Government of India No. 22, p. dated 30 June 1879.
142. Jahar Sen, *Indo-Nepal Trade in the Nineteenth Century.* Firma K.L.M. Pvt. Ltd., Calcutta, 1977, p. 88.
143. Revenue A. August 1877. No. 22.
144. Progs, of the Bengal Government A .for September 1882. File No. 101. Serial No. 1-3.
145. Progs. of the Bengal Government. Gen. Mis. September 1886. File No. 15. S. No. 6-10.
146. *Annual General Report of Administration, Patna Division for* 1881-82.
147. Foreign Department Political A. December 1880, No. 38. Girdlestone to Lyall No. 32 p. dated 25 September 1880.
148. *Ibid.*, October 1879, No. 124.
149. *Imperial Gazetteer of India* 1908. Vol. III. pp. 298-300.
150. Progs. of the Bengal Government. Gen. Mis. August 1876 Colln. 9-148. No. 212, dated, Darjeeling, 2 August 1876.
151. Progs. of the Bengal Government, Gen. September 1878, File No. 62. S.No. 4-6.
152. Progs. of the Bengal Government, Gen. Mis. January 1886, File No. 151/2.
153. Political A. October 1879. No. 134, Girdlestone to Lyall, Secretary, to the Government of India, Foreign Department, No. 22P dated 30 June 1879.
154. *Annual General Administration Report of the Patna Division* for 1879-80.
155. *Ibid.*
156. Foreign Department Political A.October 1879. No. 132.
157. *Ibid.*
158. *Report on the Trade of the North-West Province Oudh for the year ending* 31st March 1879. p. 9.
159. Progs. of Bengal Government, Gen. Mis. January, 1886. File 15. S. No. 1-2. Revenue A. August 1877. No. 16. *Annual General Administration Report of Patna Division for* 1892-93.p. 23.

160. *Gazetteer of the North-West Province,* 1881, Vol. VI p.300.
161. *Annual General Administration Report of the Patna Division for* 1882-83.
162. Revenue A. August 1877. No. 22.

5

Currency and Prices of Commodities

5.1.1 The Evolution of the Nepalese Currency System

It was the Fifth century A.D. when the first Nepalese coins were found and since then several kings issued coins. Most of these coins bear images of animals and other religious symbols like those of Indian coins. However, the denomination, and dates of these coins are not known.[1] King Amsuvarman and then Jisnugupta of the Gupta dynasty issued coins in early 600A.D.[2] By issuing new copper and silver coins and adjusting the deficiency of the previously issued debased gold coins, he reformed the Nepalese monetary system.[3] Nepal did not strike her own coins from about 800 A.D. onwards, and thus it remained as part of the Indian Empire upto Mughal days.[4] According to Wright, during the times of Raja Ratna Malla, *sukichas* (a quarter of rupee) were circulated. The king Mahendra Malla (1566A.D) issued '*Mohar*', a silver coin of 84 grams. Since, this Nepalese half rupee coin bore the seal of the king , it was given the name of '*Mohar*'. Raja Ranjit Malla introduced a copper coin, called '*Paisa*' in 1722. Coins issued by Bhupabindra Malla circulated freely, even in Tibet. Jaya Prakesh Malla issued gold as well as silver coins named '*Asharfi*'. One rupee of India was equal to two *Mohars* of Nepal. During the period of Prithvinarayan Shah, rupee coins were introduced and known as 'double Mohar. Later on 25 '*ganda system*' was introduced in Nepal . To stabilize the Nepalese currency, the Prime Minister Ranodip Rana took the necessary legal steps by passing an act blocking the value of Mohar at 50 pice and making criminal all attempts to change in the coin at a value greater or less than the declared one or to sell or purchase it or melt it.[5]

Nepal is in close proximity of India and it has wider interaction between people of both the countries. The people purchase and sell in both Indian and Nepalese currencies respectively. Not only in the bordering areas, but also in some far off areas the people do the commercial business and always involve the common currencies of India and Nepal. Several times, people of Nepal were found collecting the Nepalese currencies for its contrast and beauty. But on the Nepalese side, Indian currencies were in circulation only in the limited area of Kathmandu and in the Terai. This was not in use or circulation in mountains or hills and at distance of a few miles from the British Residency in the Kathmandu Valley.[6] Similarly some of the coins minted in Nepal were in circulation in Indian districts adjoing the Nepalese border. Nepalese Government gave importance to the Indian currency as it gave much value, though official accounts were kept in Nepalese currency.[7] This can be reflected if we consider the duty of 24 per cent levied on the exportation of Indian currency from Kathmandu but there was no such charge on the export of Nepalese coins. In the mind of the people, the Indian currency had much importance. In the Terai, people preferred Indian currencies. In the western Terai of Nepal, traders hesitated to accept the currency of Nepal. The main reason for this was the prevalence of base counterfeit coins of copper coated with silver.

A new copper coin was issued by Jang Bahadur in 1865 because of the anticipated scarcity of old coinage. The supply of old pice was, in fact, abundant. In Champaran and Tirhut, where the supply of old pice was abundant, it had the same rate (27 gundas) instead of, 25 and 26 gundas as earlier.[8] The Indian traders complained that neither the new silver, nor the new copper coins would replace the old coins. Since the new *Mohars* (half rupee coins) were so soft that they would soon be entirely defaced and useless because it could be mixed with the old ones. They also complained that the new copper coins were made entirely to supply the Nepal Darbar, through Dhurmnarayan Sahoo, to whom the agency of supply was given, by means of carrying on extensive speculation in old copper currency in India where it was in great demand.[9] In weight a *mohari* rupee was 96 Lals (8 pice = I ruttee; 8 rutters = I masha ;12 mashas = I tola). A lal was less than a ruttee). Two *Mohars* in one single piece (A mohari rupee) was rarely issued . The exchange rate of Nepalese rupee (mohair rupee) with the Indian rupee varied from 119 to 122 for 100. On an average, the value of *mohari* rupee was equivalent to 13 *annas.* one pice 11/3 dams of the Indian rupee.[10]

There was no fixed policy with regard to the amount of coinage to be issued annually. The amount of coinage depended on the market price of silver and copper. The amount of coins issued in1872-76 in Nepal is shown in Table 5.1.

The mohari rupee had already been less in demand since there was greater circulation of Indian rupee in all parts of Nepal. Therefore, mohars were issued in less amount.[12]

Table-5.1
Statement showing the amount of coins in Nepal during 1872-1876[11]

Years rupee	*Mohar Pice*		*Black Pice*		*Gorakhpure Pice*		*Thin or New Pice*			*Purokalam*	
	Rs	*A*	*Rs*	*A*	*Rs*	*A*	*Rs*	*A*	*P*	*Rs*	*A*
1872-73	276,900	9	47,021	8	257,832	11	58,669	2	3	1,662	8
1873-74	296,000	10	46,389	9	135,755	7	218,110	0	2	1,127	14
1874-75	105,400	13	35,700	3	194,028	8	132,800	0	0	280	0
1875-76	179,063	8	42,624	9	156,922	5	633,16	14	0	213	8
Total	857,365	3	171,735	13	744,538	15	472,896	0	1	3,283	14
Average	214,340		42,933		186,134		118,223				

In Golamandi and Banke, the payments were made either in Indian currency or in kinds. This is very clear from the remark of Captain A. Murray, Officiating Personal Assistant to the Chief Commissioner of Oudh, "the Nepalese will really accept rupees in exchange for goods and our money is received into Durbar treasury, but Nepal coinage is so debased and there is so much counterfeit coins that merchants from British territories now refuse to receive payment other than in goods or in Indian currency. Currency notes are not accepted in payments by the Nepalese.[13] The Officiating Deputy Conservator, Oudh Forest, was of the opinion that currency notes fetched rupees 99 per 100 notes of Calcutta and Northern Circles. Apart from these, there were plenty of evidence which proved that Nepalese and Indian counterfeit coins were minted and circulated in both the countries. There were several places where the Indian counterfeit coins were minted but the Gonda district of India and the Nepalese district of Butwal were the main districts where the coinages were being minted in large quantities.

The people also indulged in counterfeiting of the currency and wanted to acquire the wealth in such currency. The Nepal Government resorted to punish for such offences. In 1874, Jang Bahadur Rana, the Nepalese Prime Minister, informed Girdlestone that he had Rs. 450 worth British Indian counterfeit coins in his camp in the last cold weather and that he had two men in confinement charged with this offence.[14] In 1914, there were two establishments at Kanpur where Nepalese counterfeit coins were made.[15] British Indian coins were also not standard unit.[16] Only on the Indo-Nepal border, Indian currency notes were slightly demanded. Nepal made paper currency only in 1945-46.[17] There was a talk between the Nepalese and British Indian Governments regarding the circulation of Indian paper currency in Nepal. After the talk, it was made a rule that paper currency note of India would be received only when the dues were heavy for the sale of timber. It was done for helping the merchants and for removing the risk of carrying Indian currency from one place to another. According to the law prevailing in Nepal, the Nepalese treasures were not allowed to make payments in Indian currency notes. This could be done only when they were asked to collect Indian currency notes and when the amounts were small.[18]

The Nepalese Government refused to accept the British Indian Government proposal of reciprocal arrangements made in 1873 for manufacturing coins. The Nepalese Government had stated that if it allowed the striking of the currencies, its economy would be affected and old custom of this country would stop. The Nepalese Government was not able to agree to the proposed value of the coinage in the English language because the Government of this country professes the Hindu religion and that the Nagri character should remain on its coins. Nepalese Government also thought that if the coins be minted as mentioned in the proposal, it would become mandatory for the Nepalese Government to shut the mint of Nepal. They preferred to carry their old usage. The traders of Nepal while trading in British India received British coins as legal tender.[19] It was further stated that the Nepalese coinage was minted not only for the use in the country but also for Tibet.[20] The Prime Minister did not accept the proposal. The main reason attributed to it was that it would have bad effect on the Nepal's Commercial Policy and its trade relations with other neighbouring countries, especially Tibet.

Much profit for the Nepal Government was generated due to minting of coins for Tibet. The circulation of the Nepalese currency in Tibet gave a strong leverage to Nepal in the Tibetan economy.[21]

5.1.2 Minting of Coins

Before 1866, the minting activity in Nepal was insignificant but after 1866, there was a significant change in the history of Nepalese taksal i.e. mint. In that year minting machine was established and consequently hand made coins were replaced by machine made coins.[22] Jang Bahadur opened *Saraf Khana*, an office for the exchange of Nepalese and Indian rupees.[23]

There were several mints located at Banglung, Beni, WamiTansen, Samakot in the west[24] and Khika Maccha in the east[25] besides Kathmandu Valley. According to the report of Charles Girdlestone in September 1876, Khika Maccha mint was the most famous of all the mints located in the eastern hills of Nepal.[26] The main reason for the establishment of mint outside the capital was to use mineral resources lying in other parts of the country.[27] The Nepalese Government did not want to bring new metals in the capital for minting coins due to the difficult physiography and system of transport. There was no fixed policy as to the amount of coinage to be issued annually.

The Gold coins called Asharfi[28] were also struck but in small quantity in Nepalese mints though, and this currency was neither a legal tender,[29] nor legally enforceable, but they were minted for giving presentation.[30]

According to Colonel G. Ramsay, British Resident in Nepal, "gold coins were very rarely used in currency and consequent to the small number coined they can be but little hoarded as a reserve for value. I was told that Gold mohars were only coined on the Nepalese mint in sufficient numbers to supply the requirements of the Sirdars and the wealthier merchants of Kathmandu, who purchased them to offer as *nuzzur* to the King, the Minister, and other high functionaries, or to make gold ornaments, Some of the Sirdars occasionally received a portion of their pay in gold, but only some enough for these purposes.[31]

The use of silver coins though much in circulation, decreased on account of the greater circulation of the Indian currency. The export of Indian rupees from Nepal was subject to duty of 2 per cent, while there was no such duty on

Surendra Vikram (1847-1873), Gold Coin 1 Tola

Prithvi Vir Vikram (1892-1907), Copper Coin

Tribhuwan Vir Vikram (1911-1920), Back 1 Paisa

Tribhuwan Bir Vikram, Gold Coin 1 Tola

Tribhuwan Bir Vikram, 5 Paisa Copper Coin

Tribhuwan Bir Vikram, 5 Paisa Coin Nickel-Zink

the export of Nepalese mohars. This showed that the Indian rupees had value in Nepal. In Kathmandu and surrounding areas, currency notes were prized as a means of remittance and fetched a premium of three to five per cent depending on the state of the market.[32]

Several Indian coins were in circulation in areas close to the Indian border. These were Patna rupee, the Kaldar rupee,[33] the Farrukhabadi rupee,[34] the Sicca rupee.[35] Lathsahi rupee[36] or the Kampani rupee, the Rikabi rupee[37] and Murshidabadi coins.[38] Since Patna was connected with the Kathmandu valley and the eastern terai region, it witnessed the bulk of trade, and so the Patna rupee was in the widest circulation. The actual market value of each of these Indian rupee units was different in terms of the Mohar rupee. The exchange rate between Patna rupee officially fixed at 1000 : 123 during the early years of the Rana regime.[39] In 1865, a new copper currency-the thin new pice was introduced by Jang Bahadur in Nepal. Its exchange rate was fixed at 27 ganda for an Indian rupees.[40] In Champaran[41] and Tirhut, it had the same rate (27 gandas). Previously its rate was different at 25 and 26 gandas.[42] In both the districts, the coinage had great influx.

Introduction of new copper currency was caused due to the anticipated scarcity of old coinage. But there were conflicting arguments from the British Resident. The British Resident categorically told that supply of old pice was abundant.

This new currency caused wide dissatisfaction among the Indian merchants. They always lodged complaint that neither the new silver nor the new copper currency would replace the old ones. They often argued at the futility of the new coins. They were of the opinion that even if the new Mohars would be mixed with the old ones, they would entirely be defaced and useless.[43] But their thinking was not genuine and they were not correct in evaluating the impact of the introduction of new currency. Because the new silver coinage was of the same average weight as the old one, their intrinsic value was also the same. The new copper pice was not more than twice as much pure copper as the old one. The value of the old and new copper pice was at par. But the fluctuation in the price of the exchange rate did not discontinue and people always made frequent complaints with regard to fluctuations in the price. Therefore, considering the complaints of the people against the proposed increased rate of the new coins, the relative value with new mohar rupee (silver coin) of the new copper pice was fixed at 8 gandas instead of 11 at the old rates. Later the machine made gold coins were issued which were heavier and purer than the old one. The relative value new gold coins were against that of the old ones. The intrinsic values were found out by means of assay at Calcutta Mint.[44]

The Gorakhpuri pice was very helpful and advantageous and the Nepalese Government extensively issued it for carrying out the trade.

During the scarcity of 1873-74, there was an extraordinary demand of this pice[45] in order to pay the labourers employed in the relief work.

On March 22, 1908, a regulation was promulgated by the Nepalese Prime Minister, Chandra Shamsher and so the conversion was made at the rate of thirty gandas (120 paise) for each Kampani rupee and twenty five gandas (100 paise) for each Mohar rupee. Thus, the Government fiat was also used to control the exchange rate of the currency in Nepal from time to time. It clearly indicates that currency always fluctuated and its fixation was done in general interest and if it could not be controlled it could harm the economic prospects of Nepal.

Nepalese officials responded quickly to the demand at Butwal. The New coin (thin pice) was prevalent in the Kathmandu valley and the adjacent hills and also in Hetowar in the Terai.[46]

The *rikabi* rupee of Lucknow was also found at Butwal which was equal to 14 annas of Indian rupes. The Indian pice was current in Kumaun from where it was taken to Dottee in Nepal. In the market of Pilibhit, the Jhardar pice was in use on an average the value of the coin was equal to that of the Indian pice. The Indian pice was passed into Nepal by the merchants of Bahraich at rate of nine for two annas.[47]

The fluctuation in the value of the Indian currency against the value of the Nepalese currency caused much instablity and it was a source of difficulty among all classes of people and business community. Loss of value caused indebtedness, recession in the asset value and widespread resentment among the general mass. The increase in the price of essential commodities also caused increase in the poverty of the people. The permanent solution for solving to this problem was the use of single currency either Indian or the Nepalese currency throughout the country[48] but it was never done during the period under review.

5.1.3 Dual Currency System

There were two currency areas prevalent in Nepal : (i) the Indian currency area (ICA), and (ii) the Nepalese currency area (NCA). The Nepalese currency area included the whole of Kathmandu Valley and its surrounding hills. In this area Nepalese currency was the main medium of exchange. The Indian currency was used almost exclusively as the circulating medium and measure of value in the Terai region and in the border areas of the Eastern and Western Hills. Thus, these areas may be designated as the Indian currency area.[49]

There was always a surplus in Indian currency account, but this surplus was not sufficient to meet the demand of Indian currency in the Nepalese currency area. Therefore, mostly the demands for Indian currency were being met in the free exchange markets.[50]

5.1.4 The Exchange Rate between Nepalese Currency (NC) and Indian Currency (IC)

The Government had very little capacity to regulate the market rate of exchange between the two currencies, i.e., NC and IC. The official rate of exchange between these two currencies was fixed for the first time in and around 1876 by the Rana Prime Minister. At that time the rate was Rs.128.12 NC per Rs. 100 IC. This rate was fixed on basis of two factors, firstly, the then prevailing rate of Nepalese silver coins and British Indian silver coins containing different quantities of silver. Secondly, the rate was also based on the cost of remittance of transport of coins from one part of the country to another. This official rate was quite stable for the period of 57 years from 1876 to 1933.[51]

5.1.5 Currency System At the Time of Independence

The price of the silver became abnormally high during the Second World War. Consequently, in order to make profit, the people started melting the Nepalese silver coins. Silver coins worth Rs nine crores disappeared from the market.[52] For meeting the scarcity of coins and to check the malpractices, HMG Treasury known as '*Mulki Khana*' issued one rupee note in 1945. These Nepalese currency notes bore the signature of the treasurer. Till 1950s, their currencies were in circulations. But the Nepal Rastra Bank notes replaced these notes in 1960.[53]

5.2 Barter System

Barter is the oldest mode of transaction and it is the exchange of goods for goods without any use of currency. It suffers from several drawbacks including the lack of double coincidence, proper ascertaining of value, etc. Barter was common along the Indo-Nepal border. It was mostly restricted to the exchange of local products such as dried fish, coarse sugar, earthen vessels and more rarely tobacco, cotton and salt for vegetables, rice and ghee. A report of 15 April 1876, by the Deputy Commissioner of Gonda said that Nepalese exchanged Tagans (horse) for European fabrics and country stuffs and dried fish.[54]

Barter system was prevalent in Kheri district, which was based on the multiple value of each and every article. If the products of the country were not sufficient for such barter then the difference was paid in cash. The hill traders always accepted the current rupee. A trader named Abdur Razazak sold goods worth Rs. 900 to Jang Bahadur and received payment in standard rupees.[55] Even the Nepalese traders themselves refused to receive payment in Nepalese currency because their coins were so much debased and counterfeit. The Deputy Commissioner of Kheri reported, "for it is devious that if, as most often be the case, the Nepalese cannot purchase with the standard currency of their territories, transactions will be limited to the quality of goods which each side can barter."[56] It was arranged by the Indian Government to turn out from its oun mint coins for the different native protected states of the same value as those of British India. The Deputy Commissioner of Kheri suggested, "there seems to be no reason why both the executives and traders of that country should not accept as a boon such an offer on the part of our authorities".[57]

The use of currency notes was not prevalent between the Indian and Nepalese traders.[58] Actually, Nepalese traders did not accept currency notes for payments and the credit transactions were very rare.[59] In Oudh district, iron, spices and musk were exchanged for salt, coloured cloths and piece – goods. Currency notes were exchanged at the rate of Rs. 99 per 100. The value of copper coins (Gorkhali or Nepali, thick pieces) changed considerably within a few miles. The possessors of Indian pice desired to go to annas and the receivers required 9 to equal two annas in value. This was the most common rate and also the customs of the Terai of Oudh.[60]

5.3 Credit and Payment of Debt

Historically, the maximum ceiling or annual interest rate was fixed at 10 per cent by the Gorkhali rulers, since the time of King Ram Shah. British officials denied that the frontier districts in India were agreed to the fact that credit contracts were usually respected in Nepal and there was no any difficulty between the parties in contract. Contracts were fulfilled even when export of grains was prohibited due to scarcity. In this case, money was returned with interest. In Purnea district, a few and small transactions were carried on credit.[61] According to the collector of Bhagalpur, there were no civil cases between the traders of India and Nepal regarding the credit and payment of debt.[62] According to the collector of Darbhanga, the recovery of payment was easier in Nepal than India.[63] Collectors of Champaran and Muzaffarpur were of the similar view and stated that there was no difficulty in realizing debts or enforcing contracts in the courts of Nepal.[64] Officials of Gorakhpur stated that with regard to payments of debts, there was no complaint and suits were rarely filed in Nepalese courts by Indian traders. In case a suit was filed in Nepalese courts by Indian traders, the court immediately appropriated 10 per cent of the claim from the plaintiff and five per cent from the dependent. The orders of the courts were executed in a summary manner.[65] However, the collector of Gorakhpur, Lumsaden stated that he had received repeated complaints from Indian traders regarding the difficult credit contracts.[66] From Basti it was reported that debt were recovered with difficulty. Before the plaintiff was allowed a hearing by the Nepalese court, he had to deposit 25 per cent of the value of his claim.[67] The claim of the plaintiff was realised from the sale of the defendants property if the plaintiff proved his case before the court.[68] The first legal code of Nepal of 1854 stated in this regard.

"In case any one has borrowed money from the government or from any individual, with or without any bond, he shall repay the loan from this wealth or through the sale of his houses, lands, cattle, and other property. If he has no such property, he shall sign a bond stipulating repayment of the loan in installments'.[69] In case of not proving his suit, the plaintiff had to pay thrice the amount of the claim. For the compromise settlement of a suit, a fee of rupees five from each party was demanded for the compromise settlement of a suit.[70]

According to the British Resident, Charles Girdlestone, "my own experience during a residency of four and a half years in Nepal was that there was no evasion in the courts of Kathmandu of the obligation incurred in 1839, by which the Nepalese Government enjoyed that 'British subjects shall hereafter be regarded as per own subjects in regard to access to the courts of law, and that the cases of the former shall be heard and decided without denial or delay, according to the usages of Nepal.' I have also to remark that during this period I have never received from any British official any reference concerning exactions or denial or miscarriage of justice in matters of trade as might have been expected from district Gorakhpur for instance, with respect to the traders of which the Collector now submits that difficulties exist. I have never had a single complaint against the Durbar or any of its officials of oppression or restriction. I can only recall two occasions on which my good offices as the representative of the British Government have been invoked and there were cases in which British subjects trading in the capital with Newar subjects of the Durbar wanted a settlement of accounts. In both cases the Durbar gave the necessary orders for the attainment of petitioner's object, and saw that they were carried out. In one of the two cases in which the accounts were intricate and extensive, a special court composed of some of the highest officers in the country was entrusted with the duty of effecting the desired adjustment."[71]

According to the Deputy Commissioner of Gonda, the credit transactions were made to a limited extent and the rate of interest was generally two annas per rupee. He further stated that there was not any evidence regarding the enforcement of the payment of debts, that Nepalese traders appeared in Indian courts.[72]

5.4 Prices of Commodities

If we look at the rise in the prices during the reign of Jang Bahadur (1846-77), it rose to 200 per cent. The price rose rapidly and it doubled in every ten years. After the death of Jang Bahadur, the price index increased by 381 per cent within fifteen years. The prices of all the articles rose rapidly but in the case of rice and paddy it was more rapid. For e.g., the cost of paddy was one rupee per 6 pathi (1 pathi = 8 Mana) in 1875-76 which rose to one rupee per 1.5 pathi. Thus, the price of 1 murii[73] (20 pathi) increased by Rs. 3.5 to 13.33 in 1889.[74]

The British Resident in Nepal reported on 19 September, 1876, that the price of rice depended on the season and places. In distant places from the place of production, the price of rice was more. It ranged from 64 to 10 seers per rupee.[75] In comparison to the average rates in the plains, the prices of rice were always high in the hills.[76] The traders always resorted to raise the prices and thus gained by the earning profits and they did not believe in lowering the sale prices and making maximum sales. According to the British Resident, paddy was dearer than rice in Nepal. The price of rice in the Nepalese Terai was three times greater than the price in Pilibhit. The British Resident in Nepal once wrote regarding the prices of commodities imported from Nepal, "Catechu, which was manufactured in large quantities on the Dhundwa hill, was found to be worth rupees 6 a maund in Gonda after payment of an *ad valorem*[77] duty of 13 per cent."[78] The *ad valorem* duty was imposed on the proportion of the prices and was different from the specific taxes. The prices of ghee was Rs. 25 per maund in Kathmandu, Rs. 20 at Sugauli and Calcutta, Rs. 16 in Kumaon, Rs. 12 in Gonda, Rs. 27 in Gorakhpur and Rs. 32-12 in Pilibhit. The price of borax was Rs. 17 a maund in Kathmandu, Rs. 8 in Kumaun Rs. 2-4 annas in Pilibhit and Rs. 11 in Calcutta. Similarly the cost of large cardamom in the Kathmandu valley was Rs. 14 per maund.[79] But at Brahmdeo mandi, the cost of the cardamom was Rs. 30 per maund.[80] It was sold at the rate of Rs. 23 per maund in Nepalgunj.[81] One maund and 7.5 seers of cardamom was smuggled to Singahi in India and was sold at the rate of Rs one per seer.[82] There was widespread smuggling of goods as the control over the goods and services were little due to absence of the efficient officers. The Administrative machinery could not provide adequate check posts and safeguards. People used several tactics to evade the investigation, the smugglers often liased with the officers and often passed through different routes to evade the custom duty.

The prices of gold, silver and copper were Rs. 10, 12 and 2 annas per tola respectively during 1874-75.[83] The elephant was sold at the rate of Rs. 25 per head and horse at Rs. 7 per head. The goat and the ram were of the low status and they were sold at Rs. 1 per head.

There were different kinds of sweets found in the market. Among them a few can be mentioned as follows-Barfi, Gulabjamun, Jalebi and Peda. These items were sold at the same price *i.e.* Rs. 1 anna 8 paise 3 per dharni. The two other kinds of sweets which had the same price were—Balushahi and Malpuwa. Both of them cost Rs. 1 anna 4 per dharni. The price of swari was one rupee per dharni which was relatively cheaper.[84] During 1880-90, near Indo -Nepal border, 13 seers of rice, 23 seers of paddy, 15 seers of millet, 13

Table -5.2

Comparison between the New and Old Rate of Timber Sold During 1870-71 and 1875-76

Girth feet	*Length feet*	*Old rate*			*New rate*			*Drawbacks* [89]		
	Sal wood	Rs	A	P	Rs	A	P	Rs	A	P
4.5	24 to 27	18	9	0	20	14	0	6	8	0
5	”	22	7	0	25	3	0	7	4	0
6	”	28	12	0	32	5	6	9	4	6
7	”	50	7	6	56	12	0	16	5	0
4.5	30 and 31	20	1	0	22	9	0	6	8	0
5.5	”	28	14	6	32	8	0	9	8	0
6.5	”	45	0	0	50	10	0	14	12	0
7	”	52	3	9	58	11	3	16	14	0
5.5	15 and 16	17	4	9	19	7	0	5	9	6

(Contd. 5.2)

(Contd. Table 5.2)

Girth feet	Length feet	Old rate			New rate			Drawbacks [89]		
6	15 to 16	18	4	6	20	9	0	5	14	6
6.25	15 and 16	22	3	9	25	0	3	2	1	0
6.5	15 to 16	29	15	6	33	11	3	9	11	0
7	"	31	14	0	35	14	0	10	5	0
7.25	"	33	15	0	38	2	6	10	15	6
Shisham wood										
3.25	24 to 27	10	13	3	12	2	6	3	15	0
4	"	11	8	6	12	15	6	4	0	0
5.25	"	21	9	0	24	4	0	8	8	0
6.25	"	23	11	0	26	10	3	8	15	0

seers of *urad* (Black grands), 8 seers of flattened rice, 13 seers of potatoes, 12 seers of mustard, 14 seers of salt and 4 seers of oil were available at the same cost of Rs. 1.[85]

The price of timber was rising rapidly as was complained by some British officials . According to the Assistant Collector of Pilibhit, earlier the rate of timber was one rupee per log and if many logs was taken in the price reduced even 12 annas per log. When Oudh province was annexed, the price of timber was raised to rupees 4 per log and subsequently to Rs. 5 and Rs. 7. The price was charged according to measurement.[86]

Cribbon surveyed the forest of Butwal over a period of twenty years. He stated that for over hundred timbers sold a year by the Nepalese before the mutiny. However, the situation changed slightly after the mutiny. After the mutiny even a single log was not sold. He again stated that the price of one log of 20 ft and 24- 28 inch in circumference was Rs. 25, whereas similar timbers were sold at much lower rate in Faizabad and Patna.[87]

According to Peppe, a British Officer, one had to pay Rs. 24 for a sal log of 22 to 18 ft long and 12 to 15" in diameter at Taulihawa in Western Nepal.[88] As the demand for timber was increasing in India, so was also the price of timber increasing. But in course of time, the export of timber from Nepal to India declined because of the large cutting of timber in the most extravagant manner and partly due to misconduct of some Indian traders.[90]

By paying Rs. 30 or more, timber could be cut to any extent. But in1868, the Nepalese Government took control of timber business and hence this practice was stopped. Timber was cut down by officials employed by the Nepalese Government. Timber was sold by auction at different Kathmahals[91] and or Thingurimahal.[92] At the end of 19th century, the total number of Kathmahals were eighteen in the Terai region of Nepal.[93] After 1877, the timber was not sold to contractors in the forest. Indian traders were not allowed to cut timber in the forest. After cutting by the Nepalese officials, timber was carted to the Kathmahals or Thingurimahals to be sold by auction.

Notes and References

1. Nepal's Finances, Ministry of Finance, Kathmandu, 1965, p. 29.
2. These large copper coins give the names of at least four kings, Mananka, Gunanka, Ansuvarman and Jishnugupta. They have the symbols of goddess seated cross-legged and a cow and a winged horse with the King's name on the reverse, C.J. Brown, The Coins of India, *the Heritage of India Series*, p. 38.
3. E. H. Walsh, Coinage of Nepal, *Journal of Royal Asiatic Society of London*, 1908, p. 120.

4. At the close of Karnataka period, we find Nepal imitating the coins of Allauddin Khilji. Then followed a trouble period until stability was restored under Jayasthimalla, KP. Jayaswal, *Chronology and History of Nepal*, 600 B.C. to 800 A.D.
5. Kirkpatrick has given a very comprehensive account of Nepalese currency thus: "The currency of Nepal consists of silver pieces of eight annas and sixteen annas (sicca). The *sicca* indeed has been known in this country only since the time of Prithvinarayan. Sometimes, gold coins are struck for sending occasionally as presents to foreign powers. Kathmandu enjoyed for some time the privilege of supplying Tibet with coins", p. 217.
6. Foreign Department, Political A. April 1866. No. 170. Colonel George Ramsay, the British Resident in Nepal to D.R. Onslow, Secretary to the Currency Commission, the treasury, Calcutta, dated 5 April 1866. No. 20. (N.A.I.).
7. The official accounts were maintained in Mohar rupees, annas, pice and dams, the relative value of which was as follows :

   4 Dams = 1 Pice
   4 Pice = 1 Anna
   16 Annas = 1 Mohar rupee.

   The valuation before the introduction of silver coinage was

   4 dams = 1 pice;
   4 pice = 1 ganda ;
   24 ganda = 1 paisa rupee.
8. Political A. June 1866. No. 177. G. Ramsay to the Secretary, Government of India, Foreign Department, No. 16 dated 13 June 1866.
9. *Ibid.*
10. Jahar Sen, *Indo–Nepal Trade in the Nineteenth Century*, Calcutta, Firma K.L.M., Pvt. Ltd., 1977, p. 96.
11. *Nepal Residency Records.* Sl. No. 32. F. No. 82-G of 1876. Resident to Foreign Secretary, Govt. of India, No. 2 dated 10.8.76.
12. *Ibid.*
13. Foreign Department Revenue A. August 1877. No. 13. Captain A. Murray, Officiating Personal Assistant to the Chief Commissioner of Oudh to T.H. Thorton, Officiating Secretary to the Government of India, Foreign Department. 13 May 1876. (N.A.I.).
14. *Ibid.*, Political B. October 1874.N0.143.G.E.R. Girdlestone, British Resident in Nepal to the Secretary to the Government of India in the Foreign Department at Fort William, 12 September 1874, No. 26p (N.A.I.).
15. Records of Foreign Ministry of Nepal, Chandra Shamsher Jang Bahadur Rana to Colonel Manner Smith, British Resident in Nepal, dated 15 May 1914, p. 71.
16. M.C. Regmi, *The State and Economic Surplus, Production, Trade and Resource Mobilization in Early 19th Century in Nepal.* Varanasi, 1984, p. 224.

17. *Ibid.*, "Introduction of Paper Currency". *Regmi Research Series.* Year 16, No. 3, March 1984. p. 47.
18. Records of Foreign Ministry of Nepal, Marich Man Singh, the Adviser of the Nepalese Prime Minister to Austa Man Singh, Officer of the Nepalese Government, Kathmandu, dated 29 October 1914.
19. Foreign Department, Financial A. April 1873. No. 2. An abstract translation of a memorandum of Prime Minister and Commander in Chief of Nepal to the G.E.R. Girdelstone, the British Resident in Nepal, 15 March 1973 (Chaitra Sambat 1923). (N.A.I).
20. Mahendra Malla, Malla King of Nepal, who reigned in 1560 A.D., made a treaty with Tibet, by which he supplied the Nepalese currency and obtained silver and gold from Tibet to mint coinage. The Tibetans had no knowledge of smelting metals, and hence they had to depend on the Nepalese for minting their coins. This privilege continued to be the source of an extensive annual revenue to Nepal. After the fall of the Malla dynasty and conquest of Shah King Prithvi Narayan Shah in 1768 in the Kathmandu Valley,Tibet refused to accept Nepalese currency. But this practice continued even during the Prime Ministership of Jang Bahadur Rana.
    E. H. Walsh, *The Coinage of Nepal,* Delhi, 1973, pp. 16-17 ; Captain Samuel Turner, *Tibet, An Account of an Embassy to the Court of the Teshoo Lama in Tibet,* Delhi 1971, p. 372.
21. The Nepalese Government made a profit of a lakh of rupees annually in exchange of silver coinage for Tibet, i.e. exchange for his bullion the Tibetan merchant received Nepalese currency. The Nepalese Government derived a profit of twelve per cent from the transaction, four per cent being charged on account of coinage and eight per cent arising from the alloy of the rupee.
    Colonel Kirkpatrick, *An Account of the Kingdom of Nepal,* Miller, London, 1801, Reprint, Manjusri Publishers, Delhi, 1969, p. 211.
    Ravuri Dhanalaxmi, *British Attitude to Nepal Relation with Tibet and China 1814-1914,* Bahari Publication, New Delhi, 1981, p. 8 ; D.R. Regmi, *Medieval Nepal op. cit.* part II, Calcutta ,1966, pp. 43-44 ; Leo Rose, *Nepal Strategy of Survival*, Bombay 1971, pp. 14 ; Ramakant, *Nepal-China and India,* New Delhi, 1976, p. 19.
22. Krishna Kant Adhikari, *Nepal Under Jung Bahadur1877.* (Unpublished Thesis), Nagpur University, 1974, p. 440.
23. Hem Narayan Agrawal, *The Administrative System of Nepal, Vikas Publishers,* New Delhi, 1976, p. 12.
24. Krishna Kant Adhikari, op. *cit.,* p. 440.
25. Revenue A. August 1877. No. 22.
26. *Ibid.*
27. Krishna Kant Adhikari, *op. cit.* p. 348.
28. *Ibid.,* p. 444.

29. Nepal Residency, 10 August 1876, *op. cit.*
30. Foreign Department, Political A. April 1866. No.170. Colonel G. Ramsay, British Resident in Nepal to D.R. Onslow, Secretary to the Currency Commission, the treasury, Calcutta, dated 5 April 1866, No. 20.
31. E.H. Walsh, *op. cit.* p. 48.
32. *Imperial Gazetteer of India.* Vol. VII. 1881. p. 111. *Ibid.,* Vol. XIX 1908. p. 54.
33. The term Kaldar first appeared in the Nepal-Company documents in the Anglo-Nepal trade treaty of 1835. See, Ludwig F. Stiller. S.J. "Currency Confusion". *Journal of the Tribhuvan University,* Vol. VIII, No.1 November 1973, p. 4.
34. It was minted at Farukhabad. See, Krishna Kant Adhikari, *op. cit.* p. 440.
35. It was Mughal currency. The Nepalese king Prithvi Narayan also issued this coin. It consisted of 16 annas and was confined to the Kathmandu Valley. See *Ibid.* p. 444.
36. The British coin issued from Calcutta was called Lath Sahi in Nepal. The term Lath Shahi denoted the Governor General during British rule. Side by side with the Lath Sahi, Company rupee was also commonly circulated in Nepal. Probably the Lath Sahi and Company's rupee were the same coins, only called by two different names. *Ibid.*
37. Rikabi rupee as its name suggests, was round in shape. *Ibid.*
38. The coin minted at Murshidabad. It was issued in the name of the titular Emperor Shah Alam in the nineteenth year of his reign. In 1913 the Nepalese Government had 20 or 30 lakhs of Murshidabadi coins which were not easily exchangeable in British India. Upon the request of Nepalese Government, British Government agreed to exchange their stock of Murshidabadi coins for current British Indian coins at the rate of one rupee a tola. The date of exchange was limited up to 1 July 1913. Foreign Departmrnt. Internal B. April 1913, No. 271. The Assistant Secretary to the Government of India in Foreign Department to Leiutenant Colonel H.L. Showers, British Resident in Nepal dated 7 April 1913. No. 727-1 A. (N. A. I.).
39. M.C. Regmi, *op. cit.* p. 225; Devichandra Shresth *op. cit.* p. 10.
40. Political A. April 1866, No. 170.
41. Two copper coins called Lohia and Gorakhpur pice were current in Champaran district. The latter were largely composed of copper and the former of iron. Both were called Dhebua. These were manufactured in Nepal and United Provinces. They have no fixed value but varied according to the demand in the market and the season of the year. Generally 104 to 128 used to get the rupees but in 1907 their value rose as high as 90 to the rupees, L.S.S. O' Malley, Bihar, Orissa District Gazetteers, Champaran. Patna, 1938, pp. 103-04.
42. The British Resident in Nepal, Charles Girdlestone, argued that the thin or new pice were in circulation in Kathmandu and adjacent hill districts as far as

Hetauda in the Tarai. These circulars and fairly stamped coins had an average value of 29.25 gandas (117 pice) to the Company's rupee. Revenue A. August 1877, No. 27.

43. *Ibid.*
44. Krishna Kant Adhikari, *op. cit.* pp. 440-41.
45. Revenue A. August, 1877, No, 22.
46. *Ibid.,* Reading in *Nepal Economic History*, Varanasi, 1979, p. 57.
47. Jahar Sen, Indo –Nepal Trade in the Nineteenth Century, *op.cit.* p. 99.
48. Barun Shamsher, (ed.), "From the Himalayan Height". *Nepal Guardian,* Kathmandu, n.d. p. 17.
49. B.P. Shreshta, An Introduction to Nepalese Economy, Ratna Pustak Bhandar, 1974, Kathmandu, p. 200.
50. *Ibid.*
51. *Ibid.* p. 201.
52. J.C. Ogha, *Banking and Modern Currency in Nepal*, p. 57.
53. P.C. Rawat, *Indo–Nepal Economic Relations,* National Publishing House, Delhi, 1974, p. 130.
54. Revenue A. August 1877. No. 16. The Deputy Commissioner of Gonda to the Commissioner of Faizabad Division, dated 15 April 1876, No. 964.
55. Revenue A. August 1877. No. 14. Deputy Commissioner, Kheri to the Commissioner, Sitapur Division. No. 681A dated 6 April 1876. Paras 8 & 9.
56. *Ibid*, Para 12.
57. *Ibid.*
58. Revenue A. August 1877. No. 16. The Deputy Commissioner, Gonda to the Commissioner, Fyzabad Division. No. 964 dated 15 April 1876.
59. Revenue A. August 1877. No.13. Captain A. Murray, offg. Personal Assistant to the Chief Commissioner, Oudh to Thornton, Offg. Secretary, Govt, of India, Foreign Deptt.
60. Revenue A. August 1877. No. 17. Offg. Deputy Conservator, Oudh Forests, Bahraich Division to the Conservator of Forests, Oudh. No. 306/303 dated 10 March 1876.
61. Revenue A. August 1877, No. 22.
62. *Ibid.*
63. *Ibid.*
64. *Ibid.*
65. *Ibid.*
66. *Ibid.*
67. *Ibid.*
68. *Ibid.*
69. Ministry of Law and Justice, *Shri 5 Surendra Bikram Shahdeva ka Shasanakalma Baneko Muluki Aio.* (Legal Code enacted during the reign of King Surendra Bikram Shah Dev), Kathmandu. 2022 (1965), p. 90.

70. *Ibid.*
71. Foreign Department. Revenue A. August 1877, No. 22.
72. Ministry of Law and Justice, *op. cit.* pp. 98-99.
73. The traditional dry measures are as follows :
10 muthi = 1 mana
8 mana = 1 pathi
20 pathi = 1 muri
1 muthi is handful.One mana is equal to half a seer or approximately equal to 1 lb. One muri is equal to 160 lb. The mana is the commonest measure used in the hilly regions of Nepal. But in the Terai the measurement and weight are the same as in India. Mana consists of a brass vessel shaped like a cup, the bottom being bulbous and widest than the mouth. There is a stamped seal on the side showing that it is a certified measure. See British Ministry of Defence, *Nepal and the Gurkha,* London, 1965, p. 152.
74. B.P. Shreshtha, *op. cit.*, p. 12.
75. Revenue A. August 1877, No. 22.
76. Political A. February 1875, No. 30.
77. In the ad valorem system of Nepal the valuation depends on the market price both at the place of purchase and the place of sale. Revenue. A. August 1877. No. 22.
78. *Ibid.*
79. *Ibid.*
80. Regmi Research Series, *op. cit.,* p. 145.
81. *Ibid.* p. 75.
82. *Ibid.*
83. Krishna Kant Adhikari *op. cit.* p. 449.
84. The system of weights in Nepal is as follows :

4.5	tolas	=	1 Kanuwa or Chatak
4	Kanuwa	=	1 Pan
4	Pans	=	1 Seer
3	Seers	=	1 Dharni.

85. P.C. Roy Chaudhury, *Bihar District Gazetteer,* Darbhanga, p. 304.
86. Revenue A. August 1877, No. 22.
87. *Ibid.*
88. *Ibid.*
89. Revenue A. August 1877. No. 22.
90. Kathmahal was an establishment for the export of timber of twelve main varieties, including sal and *sisham* with a diameter of more than three feet. See M.C. Regmi, "Kathmahal in the Terai and Inner Terai at the end of the 19th century". *Regmi Research Series.* Year 11, No. 10, October 1979, p. 160.
91. Report on the Administration of N.W. Provinces and Oudh for the year ending 31 March 1899. Allahabad, 1900.
92. The export of timber of smaller sizes was handled by a separate establishment known as Thingurimahal. *Ibid.*

93. Kathmahals in the Terai Region of Nepal.

	Kathmahal	*District*
1.	Kosi-Purwari	Morang
2.	Kosi Pachhuwari	Saptari
3.	Kamala	Saptari
4.	Bhanẁarpura	Mahotari
5.	Tinpatan	Sindhuli
6.	Chhattauna	Rautahat
7.	Jamuni	Bara
8.	Chhapkaiya	Parsa
9.	Reumadi	Chitaun
10.	Tribeni	Butwal
11.	Banganga	Butwal
12.	Dunduwa	Dang
13.	Rapti	Banke
14.	Babai	Bardia
15.	Karnali	Kailali
16.	Mohana	Kailali
17.	Mahakali	Kanchanpur
18.	Gusari	Kanchanpur

See: Appendix VIII, M.C. Regmi, "Kathmahal in the Terai and Inner Terai at the end of the 19th century". *Regmi Research Series.* Year 11, No. 10, October 1979, p. 160.

6

Trade Centres and Markets

6.1 Trade Centres

The word market refers to a place or area where the sellers and buyers meet to sell and buy goods and services. It also refers to business or trade, or the amount of trade in a particular type of good. Market also refers to a particular area, country or section of the population that might buy goods. The trade centre is a special type of market where people from different countries meet to exchange the goods and services with the respective currencies.

Various big and small trade centres were developed along the long open border provinces of Bengal, Tirhut, Bihar, North-Western Provinces and Oudh through which trade traffic passed. The most important among them were Birganj, Raxaul, Sitamarhi, Purnea, Madhubani, Nepalganj, Bhutwal, Hanumannagar and Dhulabari.[1] These markets were of two types: permanent and temporary. *Mandi* or *Golas* constituted permanent markets and *Hat-Bazars* were temporary markets.

At the border of far Western part of Nepal and Kumaun and Bareilly districts of British India, Brahmdeo *Mandi* was the most important trading centre. State trading was prevalent between the *Mandies* of Brahmdeo and Kumaun. The Nepalese Government instructed its officials to purchase cardamom and wax on a monopoly basis.[2] The Nepalese traders were forced to sell their commodities at the *Mandi* of Brahmdeo and were not allowed to cross the border to sell their commodities.[3] The market of Brahmdeo was situated on the bank of river Kali. Nepal was informed by the British Government that the market at Brahmdeo *Mandi* on the British side would be removed and a new market would be established at Tanakpur. Tanakpur was on the high bank of the river Kali and was two miles away from the present market. Nepalese Government was also informed that the ferry carried on the river Kali would be stopped. They argued that this step would cause huge loss to Nepal. Beside the loss of state revenue, the ferry tolls would also be lost.[4] But the British Government in India decided to move the market to Tanakpur from Brahmdeo and asserted that the cause of the removal was that the river Kali, which was also known as Sarda, was dangerous for the safety of the market.[5]

Katema, Sheopur, Muzaffarnagar, Puranpur, Kalinagar and Bhagwantpur on the Indian side and Dhaknabagh and Bilauri on the Nepalese side were the other local marts in this region. Besides these markets, there was a fair held annually at Mandia Ghat on the right bank of the river Kali.[6]

On the border of Western Nepal and Awadh in India, Golamandi and Nepalganj were the biggest marts. Hill traders were forced by the Nepalese Government to sell their products only in these markets. There were British merchants to dispatch the goods according to their will. There were two types of traders in this region : first those who had permanent shops at the market and second itinerant traders. The traders, who had shops at the market, had to pay varied rent of Rs. 1-8 to Rs. 2-8 per month. The traders, without shops, had to pay Rs. 1-8 per annum for the privilege of admission.[7]

Nepalese had established a series of marts in Nepalganj. Various goods from both the countries were exchanged in these markets. Since the Nepalese traders were not allowed to cross the border, Indian traders had to visit Nepalese markets to transact business and in many cases British-Indian traders had settled in Nepal. The traders of North-west provinces carried their products across the border. In case if some quantity could not be sold, traders returned with that quantity. Those articles which were returned unsold were treated as both exports and imports.[8]

The Nepalese Government ordered the Bandabasta Adda of Nepalganj in November 1894, to shift the Golamandi market to a new place in Bardia district. A huge money was spent on the renovation and construction of buildings and shops at Rajapur.[9]

The main marts in Deokhur district in Nepal were Captainganj, Sisewa and Bahadurganj. As the Nepalese traders were not allowed to cross the border, they secretly visited Indian markets. Tulsipur, Punchperia, Utrowala and Balrampur in Gonda district, Biscohar in Basti district and Ekona, Bhinga, Mataganj and Naupara in Bahraich district were the main markets in the Indian side where Nepalese traders visited. There was a fair held at the shrine of Debipatan near Tulsipur where Nepalese traders exchanged hill ponies for European and native piece goods and dried fish.[10] Since the restriction was imposed on the traders by the Nepalese Government, the number of traders visiting the fair was decreasing.[11]

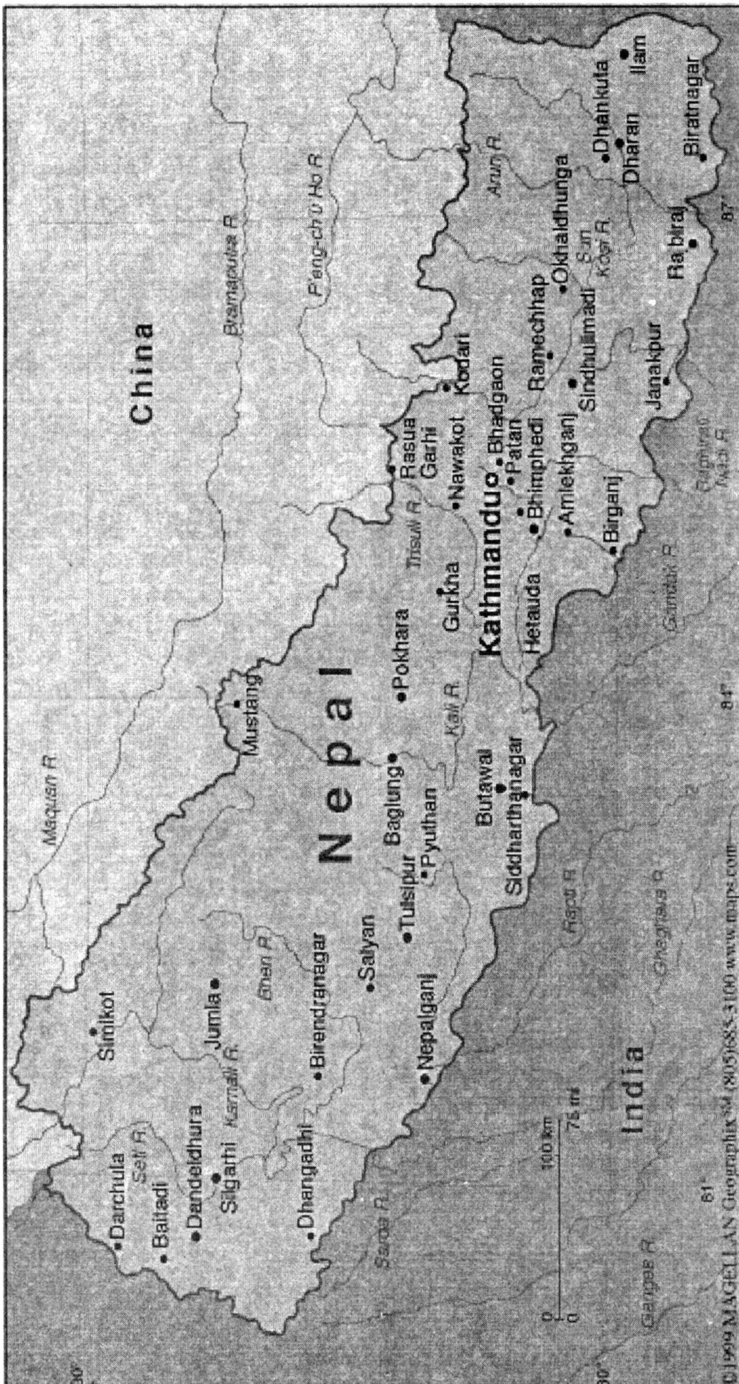

Major Trade - Centres of Nepal

The trade between Butwal and adjoining Indian districts, though small was increasing . Butwal was a great mart in Nepal which was situated between Arrah Naddi and Gandak. Indian traders sold cotton goods both coarse and fine, in this market. In the year 1873 and 1874, cotton goods worth Rs. 248,045 and Rs. 285,398 respectively were brought in this town. Taulihawa, Abiram, Bhagwanpur, Jogia, Sheorajpur, Gulabha, Kussahar and Batisi were other markets in Nepal. In these markets, rice was the chief commodity of trade. Adjoining to Butwal there were local markets in Basti district in India. These were Bhojaha, Uska, Berdpur, Narkul, Mahana, Kakrowah, Mindehwal and Lotan. A few Nepalese traders also brought spades to sell in a fair held annually at Pulta Devi near Birdpur in the month of April.[12]

Bharti, Hathbanwa, Palhi, Amaniganj were the local Nepalese markets adjoining Gorakhpur district in India. The local market on the Indian side were Nautanwa, Deoghat, Thunthibari, Nichloul, Mithanra, Bahwar, Baitanibya, Padrowna, Siswa, Dhani and Lar Bazar. Soap products manufactured from these factories in Lar Bazar were exported to Nepal. To import Kharimitti from Nepal was the main objective of establishing soap factories in Lar Bazar.[13] In the year 1906, total 2,150 maunds of soap were exported to Nepal and in return 2,369 maunds of Kharimitti were imported.[14]

Chapkaiya, Barewah and Simraunghar were the main markets in Bara and Parsa districts of Nepal. A fair was also held at Tribenighat on the Gandak river in Nepal twice a year, one in February and other in March.[15] Another market known as Birganj was also established by Bir Shamsher, the Prime Minister of Nepal.[16] The local traders were not allowed to sell their products elsewhere or to export to India without paying duties at Birgunj Bazar and thus they had to sell their commodities only at Birganj. The authorities of Birganj Bazar Adda were given instruction to seal consignments destined for the Kathmandu Valley and further to Chisapani, where duties were collected at fixed rates.[17] But it was found that consignments were diverted by the traders to other places of Nepal or smuggled to India because the functions were not discharged properly by the Birganj Bazar Adda.

Since the duty was collected only at Chisapani, the traders were able to evade payment. Later on arrangements were made for the collection of customs duties at Birganj itself. Also a State Trading Agency, known as Mahajani Adda was established at Birganj. Another trade agency called Resham Kothi was established in Birganj where silk was accumulated.[18]

Bettiah, Ramnagar, Sugvli, Motihari, Kutkenwa and Raxaul which was adjacent to Birganj were the main local marts in Champaran district in India.[19] European and Indian goods were carried to Kathmandu via Sugauli and Raxaul. There was direct contact between Kathmandu and Calcutta and Patna. A buying agent was appointed in Calcutta by the Nepalese Government in January 1859 for the purchase and supply of goods required by the government from time to time. He was given instruction to purchase articles at lowest possible price. The Nepalese Government provided for this purpose. An instruction was given to the agent in which it was mentioned that he had to maintain accurate accounts of such purchases, rents paid for office, transportation charges, packing charges etc. The agent was also instructed to obtain receipts while making a purchase of gold on behalf of the Government. The receipts should be based on the same weights and units that had been used at the time of the purchase. The Government warned him that he would be subjected to punishment if it was found that he debited amounts in excess of actual expenditure, or amounts, which had actually not been disbursed.[20]

To carry on trade with India, the Nepalese Government had set up a Cardamon Depot in Patna.[21] Several Nepalese gold and silver smiths settled in Patna only with their tools. They had no money with themselves. They were provided materials by the Indian merchants and paid according to their work.[22]

A forwarding agent was appointed by the Nepalese Government in India. He was instructed to forward goods purchased in India by the Government or royal family or by other prominent persons or traders, etc., by railway to Patna on payment of brokerage. A forwarding agent named Biharilal was asked to forward goods to Patna or Motihari by railway and then deliver them to the owner within the stipulated time and charge brokerage at the normal rates. In case of loss of any goods or consignment on which the agent had charged and had been paid brokerage, he was made responsible. If it was found that the agent had not worked in satisfactory manner or he increased the rate of brokerage or had failed to deliver goods within the stipulated time, the agent would be dismissed and be held liable to pay compensation and punished with a fine.[23]

There was a fair held annually at Sonepur in Bihar where different kinds of European and Indian goods were exchanged with Nepalese dogs, skins, forest products, curios and silver work.[24]

In Mahatari district of Nepal there were three important markets: Jaleshower, Dhanukha and Janakpur.[25] Janakpur was the holy place and was popular for its annual fair. The Ramnavami fair of Janakpur was famous for cattle. The local markets on Indian side adjoining Mahotari district of Nepal were Bairagania, Pachlakki, Majorganj, Chapra, Bosahia, Monaha, Belamuchhapakouni, Barahi, Sursand, Bhita and Madhwapur. An annual fair was also held Sitamadhi, Maniari and Marania.[26] For the frontier trade with Nepal Bairayania was an important market.[27] The dealers of plains met the Nepalese hillmen and the Nepalese trade changed hands at Bairagania, where there was a large grain and oilseed depot. Bairagania was the terminus of the branch of the Bengal North Western Railway.[28]

For eastern Nepal, Siraha, Orahi, Sarsowar, Rampur and Hanumannagar in Saptari district were the important markets. At Hanumannagar and Barachatra, a fair was held every year. Other popular markets in this region were Deodha, Lawkaha, Piprahi, Patauli, Khutobawna in Darbhanga district and Kundowli,

Bagjan, Panchpandaria, Silashpur and Birpur in Bhagalpur district.[29] Two and other important trade centres for Nepalese traders were Madhubani and Jayanagar. Generally Nepalese traders brought pack animals with merchandise to the markets on Indian side of the border. Indian traders too brought their own products for export to the same markets. The traders, after selling and purchasing, took away their articles offered by their counterparts.[30]

Vijaypur and Ambarpur were the two famous markets in Saptari and Morang districts respectively. There were six golas in Saptari and four golas in Morang. *Ijara* (contract) system was prevalent for the collection of taxes on golas before 1858. After paying customs duties, traders were allowed to sell the commodities in India if they were permitted by the Goladars to do so. Since funds were not sufficient, traders would generally not like to procure the commodities. This created monopoly which was not favourable to the state revenue. Some traders used to make an attempt to smuggle cardamom and other articles to India because of the difficulties created at the Golas. Consequently there was loss to state revenue. But after 1858, the *Ijara system* was replaced by the *Amanat system* on all the golas. Under the authorities of the Commanding General for southern zone several employees were deputed to different golas. The Commanding General was instructed to take cardamom and other commodities for sale at Ambarpur and Vijaypur. Weights bearing the royal seal were used for taking weight of the commodities. Payment was made at current rates revised from time to time. The commodities of the smugglers were confiscated if detected inside the border. Proceeds were seized if the smugglers were recognised even after the sale of the articles across the border. The traders sold their articles (especially cardamom) at the golas of their majesty's Government. They were the subjects of punishment if they used force and smuggled commodities elsewhere.[31]

This restriction was relaxed after some time. After paying customs duties, traders were made free to sell their articles directly in Indian markets.

At several villages along the Indo-Nepal border, markets were held for the exchange of rural products of daily consumption.[32]

The Nepalese Prime Minister Jang Bahadur also tried to develop markets in Kathmandu and other places of the country. A retail shop was opened by him in Kathmandu. According to G. Ramsay, though it seemed that the shop belonged to Newar merchants but it occupied a public building and a portion of Darbar. Even the Government officials checked its accounts. All these showed that the Prime Minister gained the profit. It was done to control the market price as Prime Minister thought his wives and other prominent people paid high prices for all kinds of European goods. All these goods were held for sale in a building in Prime Minister's own premises. For general public similar other shops were opened in Kathmandu at different places.[33] In these shops there were British and other European goods such as needles, tea pots, empty bottles, powders, various brass and other metal pots, strings of red silk or cotton and other valuables.[34]

To remove the practices of intermediaries and middlemen, the Prime Minister had taken various steps because these intermediaries were real cause for the increase of price of the articles of daily consumption. He had issued an order banning the system of intermediaries. The Prime Minister ordered either consumers would go to the villages to buy the commodities or the producers in the surrounding villages would bring the articles to sell in the city of Kathmandu. The agents of small merchants, who went to the villages to procure goods, were also restricted. According to G. Ramsay, the British Resident in Nepal, prices of every commodity became high because of this strange order, which had opposite effects.[35]

Jang Bahadur wanted to establish a large bazar to be known as Hayat Nagar at Beechakoh. He also planned to construct stores, shops and barracks in this Bazar. He thought that this would encourage the British traders to take resort in the market. But the British Resident in Nepal did not agree with this plan and asserted that Jang Bahadur's intention was to expel the British traders from Kathmandu and to sell their articles in this Bazar.[36]

In the Bhagalpur District, the Nepalese traders used to bring their products mainly grains and seeds to the local marts situated mainly on the Ganges and the Kosi. There were two large Newar firms who transacted their cloth business with Calcutta through Bhagalpur.

The rich merchants like Bunyas, Irakis, Kashmiris, Newars, etc., managed the export trade from Champaran to Nepal but the Indian traders conducted the import trade in Champaran. Much trade in Basti and Gorakhpur was conducted by Indian traders either as principals or as agents at Butwal. At the markets of Gonda districts more trade was managed by Indian traders than by Nepalese traders.[37] Around 114 Indian traders used to go to Nepalganj market for only six month in a year. The number of traders who carried on business at Nanpara and Babaganj permanently settled there.[38]

About one hundred traders frequently visited the mart for six months annually *i.e.,* from November to May when the trade was at its peak. There were two types of Indian traders in the Kheri district : (i) those who had taken shops on lease and resided in the Nepalese marts for the whole of the trading season, and (ii) those traders who resided in Nepal just long enough for their sales and purchases. There were about 50 shops at Golmandi the owners of which were resident of Pilibhit, Bareilly, Shahajanpur, Sitapur, Moradabad, Lucknow and Kanpur, Muslim traders were also there.[39]

The British Resident Charles Girdlestone reported that at Brahmdeo there was a permanent mart and about two hundred shops had been established both sides of the border. Small boats, which were plying backwards and forwards throughout the day were the means of communication. At this mart, the Nepalese Government had collected twenty thousand rupees as duties during one season. According to the Resident, the sum might be approximately taken to represent transactions of some two lakh rupees.[40]

To sum up, it can be said that there were various trade centres in the frontiers through which trade traffic passed. The most important among them were Birganj, Raxaul, Sitamarhi, Purnea, Madhubani, Nepalganj, Butwal, Hanumannagar and Dhulabari.

There was no direct route to Kathmandu in those days. Alexander Powell said that it was not known with certainty as to which was the best route to Kathmandu. The routes for Kathmandu went through Birganj, Bhimpedi, and Thankat.[41]

Due to lack of roads and conveyance, *Melas* (fairs) were very popular way of trading.

6.2 Major Trading Regions

We shall now proceed to discuss in detail the trade performance of each region in Nepal and India in the light of recorded data. Here is described breifly the general features of each region (its topography, population, trade channel and trade centres) in addtion to discussing the value of its trades in the selected commodities.

6.2.1 The Mechi Region

The eastern most region of Nepal is Mechi. It is surrounded by Tibet in the north, Sikkim and West Bengal in the east, Bihar in the south, and Koshi Region on the west. The region contains only four percent of the total population in the country. Nearly four-fifth of the area of total region is mountainous.[42] Nevertheless, the region is the largest surplus producer of foodgrains in the country. This is reflected in the region's trade pattern.

The trade of the region is primarily conducted through the Bhadrapur and Ilam trade centers. It is directed exclusively towards India. Most of the exports from this regions are effected through Bhadrapur, whereas, Ilam serves as the main trade centre for distributing the imports from India as the trails from Ilam run throughout the region and beyond. An important traditional trade route runs from Ilam to Aunbang to Taplejung (the major trade centre in the interior of the region) and hence to Tibet through Olangchung and Khagla Deorali Pass.

The Mechi region is the principle contributor to the Nepal's rice export, which is the leading commodity in Nepal's overall exports. Bulk of the region's imports is accounted for by cotton textile.

6.2.2 The Koshi Region

The Koshi region is situated between the Mechi and Sagarmatha regions with Tibet in the North and Bihar in the south. Nearly three-fifths of the area of the region is mountainous and the rest consists of the alluvial plain of the Terai. Roughly 6 per cent of the total population of the country resides in the region. Koshi is the most industrialized region in the country. The trade of the region is primarily transacted through the Biratnagar trade centre and is directed towards India. A traditional trade route runs from Biratnagar to the interior trade centres of the region i.e Dhankuta, Terathum and Chainpur. This trade channel further connects the 'Dingla-Hatia' trade route to Tibet through the Rakha Pass. Dharan and Dhankuta are thus the principal trade centres of the region.

In this region, paddi, mustard seeds etc., are exported to India from Nepal and cotton textiles, salt, betal nuts and mechinery are exported from India into Nepal.

6.2.3 The Sagarmatha Region

The Sagarmatha regions is situated between the Koshi and Janakpur regions with Tibet to the north and Bihar on the southern border. Nearly 70 per cent of the area of this region consists of mountains and includes the highest peak of the world, the Sagarmatha (Mount Everest) The region contains 12 per cent of the total population of the country. Of this population, more than 50 per cent is concentrated in the alluvial plains of the Terai.

The trade of the region is primarily conducted through the trade centres of Rajbiraj, Siraha, Lahanbazar and is directed towards India. An important trade route runs from the Siraha to the interior centres of the region like, Balsat, Manebhanjang and Okhaldhunga. This route further leads to Namchebazar, *enroute* to Tibet through Nangpala. Another trade channel runs from Lahanbazar to the interior centres of the region, Nepaltar, Udaypur-Garhi and Bhojpur. This route further connects the Hanumannagar-Khotang-Bhojpur route and the Okhaldunga-Namchebazar trail. Thus, Narnchebazar, Udaypur and Bhojpur are the principal trade centres in the interior of the region.

The region's exports of raw jute, hides and skins and raw tobacco contribute significantly to the Nepal exports of these commodity. However, the value of the region's exports of these commodities is small enough not to significatnly affect the region's share in the overall exports of the country. Paddy and rice together contribute to the bulk of the region exports. Cotton textiles, salt, sugar are exported from India into Nepal.

6.2.4 The Janakpur Region

Situated between the Sagarmatha in the east and the Narayana and Baghmati regions in the west, the Janakpur region borders Tibet on North and Bihar on South. Nearly three-fifths of the area of the region consists of mountains. The rest of the region's area is the alluvial plains of the Terai, where approximately three-fifths of the region's population dwells. The Janakpur region is inhabitated by 12 per cent of the total population of the country.

The trade of the region is mostly conducted through the trade centres of Janakpur, Jaleshwar and Malanga and is directed towards India. An important traditional route runs from Jaleshwar to the interior of the regions Sindhuligarhi and Ramechap. The route further leads to the centre of Charikot and Lamabagar *enroute* to Tibet. Another route from Janakpur leads to Ramechap through Chisapani. Ramechap is thus a major trade centre in the interior of the region.

In this region, rice, paddy, maize, mustard seeds are exported to India from Nepal and cotton textiles are exported from India into Nepal.

6.2.5 The Baghmati Region

The Baghmati region is not contiguous to the Indian frontier. It borders Tibet on north and on the remaining three sides, is flanked by the Janakpur, Narayani and Gandaki regions. The whole region is mountainous and inhabited roughly by 15 per cent of the total population of the country.

Kathmandu valley, Trisuli and Banepa are the major trade centres in the region. A major trade channel runs from Kathmandu to Banepa to Kodari enroute to Tibet. While another trade route runs from Kathmandu-Trisuli to Rasua enroute to Tibet. The bulk of the Nepals trade with Tibet is carried through these routes. Another important transport route connects Kathmandu with Birgunj in the Narayani region and almost all the imports of the region are effected through this route.

In this region, rice, cereal products are exported from Nepal into India and cigarettes, sugar, machinary, etc., are exported from India into Nepal from this route.

6.2.6 The Narayani Region

The Narayani region is flanked by Janakpur on east, Baghmati on north, Lumbini and Gandaki on west. The region borders India on south. The Narayani region is unlike other regions, not mountainous and its area consists of only rich alluvial Terai lands. The region is inhabitated by 8 per cent of the total population of the country. It may also be noted that the region is important in so far as the overland access to Kathmandu from India and the rest of the world (excluding Tibets) lies through this region.

The trade of the region is effected mainly through the Birgunj bazar, contiguous to Bihar in India. A major transport route links Birgunj with Kathmandu in the Bagmati region thorough the Taura Bazar. A second route also runs to Narayanaghat bazar connecting the trail to Upperdang-Bandipur trade centres in the Gandaki region. Hetaura and Narayanghat are thus the major trade centres is the interior of the region.

In this region, paddy and rice together contributed to the bulk of the region's trade. Mustard seeds, potatoes, maize and pulse are also exported to India from Nepal. Cotton textiles, cigarette, petrol and sugar are the principle import commodities of the region from India.

6.2.7 The Gandaki Region

The Gandaki region is situated between the Baghmati and Dhaulagiri regions. Lumbini and Narayani lie on its southern side and Tibet on the North. The whole region, on the foothills of the Himalayas, is mountainous. Nevertheless, the region is inhabited by 10 per cent of the total population of the country.

Since the region is not contiguous to the Indian frontier, as noted earlier, its imports come mainly through the adjoining Lumbini region.[44] A traditional trade route runs from the trade centres of Butwal and Tomsen in Lumbini region to Putlikhet and Pokhara centres in the Gandaki region. Another trade channel runs from Tansen to Bandipur, the latter is also connected with the trails from Tribenighat and Narayangat trade centres. The imports into the Gandaki regions are generally passed through these routes. The main trade centres in the region are Putlikhet, Pokhara, Bandipur and Gorkha.

6.2.8 The Lumbini Region

The Lumbini region is flanked by the Narayani, Gandaki, Dhaulagiri and Rapti regions and borders the UP (India) on the south. Roughly 56 per cent of the region's area comprises the alluvial Terai lands. However, approximately 55 per cent of the region's population is concentrated in the mountainous areas of the region. The population in the Lumbini region constitute roughly 10 per cent of the total population in the country.

The trade of the region is conducted through the trade centres of Bhairahawa and Krishnanagar and is directed towards India. Major trade channels run from these trade centres to Palpa in the interior of the region. Palpa further connects Tamghas and Musikot and the route further leads to Beni-Mustang in the Dhaulagiri region. The other routes from the trade centres of Palpa and Tribenighat feed the major trade centres of the Gandaki region. Butwal and Palpa are the major trade centres in the interior of the region, also serving the Dhaulagiri and Gandaki regions.

In this region, paddy and rice together contributed to the bulk of the region's exports. Ghee was also exported to India from this region. Cotton textiles and cigarette were the principal items which were exported from India into Nepal.

6.2.9 The Dhaulagiri Region

The Dhaulagiri region lies on the foothills of the Himalayas. It is hemmed in by the Gandaki and Karnali regions. Lumbini and Rapti lie on its south and Tibet on the north. Only 2 per cent of the total population of the country inhabits the region.

Since the region is contiguous to Tibet and not to the Indian frontier as noted earlier, its basic necessities mostly cotton textiles, kerosene and salt, have to be imported through the adjoining Lumbini region. A major trade channel runs from Palpa in the Lumbini region to the centres of Baglung Beni

Major Trading Regions

and Dara in the Dhaulagiri region. The trade route further leads to centres of Kagbeni and Mustang in the interior of the region. Baglung, Benibazar and Mustang are the major trade centres of the region.

6.2.10 The Rapti Region

The Rapti region is hemmed in between the Lumbini and Bheri regions with the Dhaulagiri and Karnali regions on the north and the UP (India) on the South. Roughly 86 per cent area of the region is mountainous. Nearly 7 per cent of the total population of the country dwells in the Rapti region.

The trade of this region is conducted mainly through Koilabas trade centre and is directed towards India. A traditional trade route runs from Koilabas to Piuthan in the interior of the region. The route further leads to the principal trade centres Salyan in the interior of the region.

In this region, mustard seeds, pulse, herbs and Ghee are major commodities that are exported to India from Nepal. Cotton textiles, salt, kerosene and machine are exported to Nepal from India.

6.2.11 The Karnali Region

The Karnali region also lies on the foothills of the Himalayas, west of the Dhaulagiri region with the Bheri and Seti regions on its south and Tibet in the north. Roughly 2 per cent of the total population of the country dwells in this region.

Since the region is not contiguous to the Indian frontier, its basic necessities (mostly cotton tentiles, kerosene and salt) are imported mostly through the adjoining Bheri region. A major trade channel runs from its trade centre of Surkhet–Dailekh in the Bheri region of the centres of Kalikot, Jumla, and Mugu in the region enroute to Tibet. Humla and Jumla are the major trade centres in the region.

6.2.12 The Bheri Region

The Bheri region is flanked by the Rapti, Karnali and Seti regions and borders the UP (India) on the south. Roughly three-fifths area of the region is mountainous. The region contains 5 per cent of the total population of the country.

The trade of the region is conducted through Nepalgunj and Rajapur trade centres and is directed towards India. Major traditional trade channels run from three centre to the interior centres of Surkhet and Jajarkot. It also connects the Kalikot Jumla-Mugu trade channel in the Karnali-region. Surkhet and Jajarkot are the major trade centres in the interior of the region and they also serve the Karnali region.

In this region, rice and paddy together contributed a significant proposition of the region's exports from Nepal. Ghee, maize, cotton textiles are major commodities that are exported from India into Nepal.

6.2.13 The Seti Region

The Seti region is hemmed in by the Bheri and Karnali regions at the east and the Mahakali region at the west. It also borders the UP (India) on the south and Tibet on the north. About four-fifths area of the region is mountainous. Roughly 4 per cent of total population of the country dwells in the region.

The trade of the region was mostly carried through Dhangarhi trade centre and was directed towards India. Doti was another major trade centre in the interior of the region. The centre was further connected with the traditional route that leads to India through Dandeldhura in the Mahakali region.

In this region, paddy predominates in exports from Nepal. Mustard seeds and pulse also contributed to the large volume of region's export from Nepal. Cotton textiles, cigarettes were the main items of the regions exports from India into Nepal.

6.2.14 The Mahakali Region

The Mahakali is the western-most region of Nepal. It borders the Seti region on the east; Tibet on the north and UP (India) on the south and western border. Roughly three-fourths area of the region is mountainous where approximately 92 per cent of the regions population dwells. The region contains only 2 per cent of the total population of the country.

The trade of the region is carried mainly through the trade centres of Mahendra Nagar, Baitadi and Drachula and is directed towards India. A traditional trade route runs from Baitadi to Silgarhi through Dandeldhura while another runs from Darchula to the trade centres of Bajary and Bajang in Seti region.

Ghee predominates in the region's export from Nepal. Paddy, pulse, and mustard seeds were the important commodities that were exported from Nepal into India. Cotton textiles and salt were exported from India into Nepal.

Notes and References

1. P.C. Rawat, *Indo–Nepal Economic Relations,* National Publishing House, Delhi, 1974. p. 59.
2. On May 1897, approximately 325 maunds of cardamom had been purchasd at a total cost of Rs. 11,848. In addition approximately 1.25 maunds of cardamom were acquired in lieu of duty (Chungi), while 1/4 maunds were confiscated from smugglers. Unsold stocks from the previous years totalled 1.5 maunds worth Rs. 4949. From June to December 1896, eight maunds of wax were purchased at a total cost of Rs. 217-12, and approximately 1.25 maunds were collected as duty or confiscated from smugglers Cited from Mahesha Chandra Regmi, "State Trading at Brahmadeo Mandi," *Regmi Research Series,* Kathmandu, 1 October 1981. p. 145.
3. Debi Chandra Shrestha, "Brahmadeo-Mandi". *Nepal Economist* (Arthik Nepali) Vol. I, No. 3, June 1983, p. 25.
4. Nepal Residency Record. File No. 1972 of 1833. Abstract translation of Memorandum from the officiating Prime Minister and Commander in-Chief of Nepal to the British President in Nepal, dated 18 April 1884 (Baisakh, Samvat 1941) Record No. D 45 III.
5. *Ibid.* No. 843 of 1885. The Commissioner, Kumaun Division to British Resident in Nepal, dated 21 May 1884.
6. Revenue A. August, 1877, No. 15 p.
7. *Ibid.*
8. Foreign Department A. December 1877. No. 2. E. Buck, Director of Agriculture and Commerce, North Western Provinces to C. Robertson, Secretary to the Government of North Western Provinces, dated 1 November, 1877. No. T-187.
9. M.C. Regmi, Development Activities in the *Naya Muluk,* Regmi Research Series, Year 13, No.5; May 1981, p. 73.
10. Foreign Department, Revenue A. August 1877 No. 15. The Deputy Commissioner of Bahraich to The Deputy Commissioner of Faizabad, 13 December 1875. (N.A.I.).

11. *Ibid.*
12. Revenue A. August 1877. No. 22.
13. The principal ingredient in the soap was a light grey kind of earth called Kharimitti.
14. *Indian Trade Journal,* 2 May 1907, p. 234.
15. Revenue A. August 1877, No 22.
16. M.C. Regmi, "Impact of Railway", *op. cit.*
17. *Ibid.*, "Birgunj Bazar Adda". *Regmi Research Series,* Kathmandu, Year 13, No. 9, September 1,1981, p. 135.
18. *Ibid.* pp. 36-37.
19. Revenue A. August 1877, No. 22.
20. M.C. Regmi, 'The Calcutta Buying Agency'. *Regmi Research Series,* Kathmandu, Year 13, No. 8,1 August 1981, p. 126.
21. *Ibid,* Cardamom Farming in Nepal, p. 54.
22. Surendra Gopal, '*Patna in the 19th Century (A Socio-cultural Profile),* Naya Prokash, Calcutta, 1983, p. 42.
23. M.C. Regmi, "Appointment of Forwarding Agent in India". *Regmi Researcn Series.* Kathmandu, Year 13, No. 7, 1 July 1981, p. 128.
24. P.C. Rawat, *Indo–Nepal Economic Relations, op.cit.* p. 60.
25. Revenue A. August 1877, No. 22.
26. *Ibid.*
27. L.S.S.O' Malley, *Bengal District Gazetteers. Muzaffarpur.* Calcutta, 1907, p. 156.
28. *Ibid.* p. 138.
29. Revenue A. August 1877, No. 22.
30. P. C. Roy. Chaudhury, *Inside Bihar, Bookland Pvt. Ltd.,* Calcutta, July 1962, p. 169.
31. M.C. Regmi, 'The Golas of Eastern Nepal', *Regmi Research Series.* Kathmandu, Year 12, No. 5,1 May 1980, p. 78.
32. W.W. Hunter, *The Indian Empire, Its peoples, History and Products,* London, 1892, Reprint, Concept Publishing Co., Delhi 1973, p. 691.
33. Foreign Department Foreign Consultations, 26 August 1859, No. 211.
34. Francis Egerton, *Journal of Winter Tours in India with a visit to the Court of Nepal.* Two Volumes. Vol. I, London, 1852, p. 233.
35. Foreign consultations, 26 August 1859, No. 211.
36. *Ibid.*
37. Revenue A. August 1877, No. 16. Deputy Commissioner, Gonda to the Commissioner of Fyzabad Division. No. 964 dated 15 April 1876.
38. Revenue A. August 1877, No. 16. Deputy Commissioner, Bahraich to the Commissioner, Fyzabad Division. No.1877 dated 13 Dec. 1875.
39. Revenue A. August 1877, No. 14. Deputy Commissioner, Kheri to the Commissioner, Sitapur Division. No. 681 dated 6 April 1876.
40. Revenue A. August 1877, No. 15 P.

41. P.C. Rawat, *Indo –Nepal Economic Relations*, op.cit p. 59.
42. Vikas Zilla ekbum Anchal Bibhajan Samiti Ko Report (In Nepali), Kathmandu, Department of Publicity and Broadcasting, Nepal, 1962, pp. 1-5.

7

Impact of Indo-Nepal Trade

7.1 Impact of Indo-Nepal Trade

The trade was the major activity for interaction between the two countries. It affected every aspect of life of the people especially in the domain of politics, culture and economy. In fact, Nepalese trade with British India was a two way traffic. It was based on mutual gains. The Britishers always thought that as along as Nepalese engaged themselves in trade, there was nothing to worry about and it provided also them a shield against any aggression from the north during the reign of Ranas.

Trade and commerce had been important in the Nepalese ecomony. For several hundred years before the beginning of the present century, Indo-Tibetan trade was conducted through Nepal and the Kingdom enjoyed the status of an entrepot which contributed to its prosperity, though its own share in that trade (by way of giving or taking from it) was marginal only.[1]

The Britishers observed the pattern of interaction and behaviour of the people. The people were very little concerned with politics and they did not bother about whether there was reign of Thapas or Ranas. In this context the observation of Hodgson seems appropriate – the more Nepalese people became trade minded, less would be the possibility of a war between India and Nepal. After rise of Rana family, people got themselves engaged more in trade. After 1857, the situation changed, as it was the period of revolt in India. The Nepalese government watched the situation closely and studied all the steps of the Britishers in surfing power in India by their nepharious designs.

The Nepalese Government instructed the local authorities not to tolerate any attempt to loot or kill people of Nepal by English and Chinese troops. It also instructed to take appropriate steps to defend the Nepalese territories.[2]

It was also necessitated to take prompt actions for defending the territory and inform the higher authority about the reasons and actions. The order also made it mandatory to repulse the enemy.[3] But after 10 years, the authority became more centralised and told the lower authorities to wait for the Kathmandu's final approval.[4] Such type of tendency shows that Nepal did not anticipate any threat to national security. The Government of Nepal then started reorganising the district administration and settlement in the Terai region. There was no fear of external aggression.

As a result of Indo-Nepal trade several new treaties and engagements were signed as it was necessary for both the Governments to maintain law and order for the promotion of trade. In 1855 an extradition treaty was signed and as per terms of the treaty, each Government had to extradite criminals guilty of murder, attempt to murder, rape, maiming, thuggee, dacoity highway robbery, poisoning, burglary in each other's territory.[5] However, the officials of both the countries were prohibited to intrude into each other's territories in pursuit of criminals.[6] A treaty was also signed in 1923 to safeguard the commercial interests of both the countries. About 95 per cent of Nepal's foreign trade was with India but till 1923, the formal agreements between these two countries remained unfulfilled. It was by convention that India used to provide certain trade and transit facilities to Nepal which was an unmatched example of good relations in the international scene.

India and Nepal had been the co-sufferers in foreign trade due to the similarity in the composition of their export trade and unrestricted movement of goods between them.[7]

Articles VI of the treaty of 1923 made it mandatory for the British Government not to levy any duty on the goods imported on behalf of the Nepal Government, provided the officials of Nepal to furnish certificate to that effect. These articles were for the consumption of the people of Nepal and property of the Nepal Government and sent under the orders of the Nepal Government.[8]

The Government of British India also granted full exemption without any immediate payment made. The rebates might be claimed on the authority of a certificate signed by the said authority that the goods had arrived at Kathmandu with the customs seals unbroken and otherwise untampered with.[9]

Internal administration of the country had been affected and it was guided by the Indo-Nepal trade. It paved the way for opening new offices and new posts for it. First of all, Jang Bahadur opened, a new office for the general administration of the country named Maluki adda.[10] Rana Administration had to perform the two main functions, the collection of revenues and the maintenance of law and order.[11]

Internal administration saw the new set up under Jang Bahadur. 'Mosh Tahvil' was introduced to look after all the revenues. Malaki Khama was opened as the Government treasury. A forest office was opened. 'Kumari Chawk', was started by Prithvinaraan Shah. It was an accounts and audit offices, and it was also retained by Jang Bahadur. A Tesakhana, as the disbursement was retained from the previous regimes. Also, the same Munshi Khana, the foreign office was retained. This foreign office was started by Bhim Sen Thapa.

Later, the Ryotwari system was established for an efficient system for the collection of national revenue and audit of public accounts by Ranodip Singh.[12] Chandra-Shamsher also brought about many changes in the administrative set up of the country. He reorganised the old Kumari Chowk office with more sections in order to have stricter control over audit and accounts.[13] An office to investigate and report on different sources of revenue and to dispose of monopolies, called Rakam Bandobast was opened immediately. The administration of forest was paid better attention. The office of Banfanch Goswara and a number of chowkis of forest guards were opened for this purpose.[14]

The main function of Muluka Adda was to collect reports from the districts regarding law and order, revenues, woods, forest, rate of timber, customs etc.

The Kath Mahal Niksari was used for sale of timber, forest product, their management and administration and exercised general control over Kathmahal hakins in the Terai.[15] Several centres were opened to carry on Indo-Nepal trade effectively for example, Bazar Adda, Bhansar Adda, Taksal Adda, Lagat Adda etc.. The officer in charge of collecting customs was known as Bazar Hakim. The Bazar Adda was responsible for collection of customs. The Bazars were opened in Terai districts. The Bazar Adda looked after both bazars and customs for the Terai during the entire Rana period. Taksal Adda was opened after the days of Prithvi-Narayan Shah. More staff was added by Bir Shamsher and Chandra Shamsher. The Lagat Adda maintained more staff to it. The main function of this Adda was the maintainance of list of goods and articles and checked their estimates, prices etc., and this was under the control of Kumari Chowk and commander in chief of Nepal.[16]

All these offices were under the control of the Prime Ministers as they were established in proximity of the Government officials.[17]

Establishment of many agencies and institutions in Nepal was another feature of the impact of Indo-Nepal trade. These agencies were also spread to Indian tycoons in the vicinity of Nepal—Singha Darbar, Jinsi Adda in Nepal[18] and Calcutta buying agency[19] and Patna Illaychi Kothi in India were the prominent among them.

The articles purchased from Calcutta and England were stored into Jinsi Adda. Ilaychi Kothi was situated near Jalasis fort in Patna on the bank of the Ganga. It imported Illaychi (cardamom) from Nepal to Patna during the Rana regime.[20] This Illaychi Bhawan performed the founction of Nepalese consulate office and dealt with the East India company. It also kept liaisons between Kathmandu, Patna and Calcutta.

Migration from Nepal to India and vice versa was the other feature of the Indo-Nepal trade. Benefited from large cost difference in their comparative analysis, large number of people migrated from Nepal to India and vice-versa. Opponents of Rana also encouraged the people of hill area in Nepal to settle down in the Terai region with the intention of developing the resources as well as the region. The Terai region was not suitable for living due to hot and malarious conditions and people preferred to inhabit India, Sikkim and Bhutan. A large number of Indians started migrating to the Terai region after incentives were provided by Rana rulers to settle people. The number of traders was larger among them.[21] The people of India adopted the Nepalese living pattern and made matrimonial relationships with the Nepalese.

The large scale migration of people in Nepal led to the emergence of economic difficulties, such as unemployment , social disorder . Government was not efficient to solve these problems. It caused irritation in the officials. Majur, the president of *Rashtriya Samaj Sudhar Sangathan* (National Social Reform Forum of India) condemned the Indian Government for the massive influx of Indians into Nepal. He said, "If you want to take over Nepal, march your army in, but for God's sake do not march your population."[22] In the same way, migration from Nepal to India also created large problems for India . It grew to such an extent that in 1900 ,a quarter of a million people who migrated into India were of Nepalese origin. This number had increased by over 30,000 in the period 1900 to 1911. But at the same time there was no recruitment in the Indian Army. About one Nepalese-born person in twenty was living in India by early 1930's.[23]

Nepalese traders had to face great difficulty during transportation of goods from one place to another. They had to face hardships of the nature and torrid climate of Tibet because they had to cross dense forests and malarious region of Nepal. Some of the traders could not cope with the hardships and they died. The dense forests often caused malarious conditions.

Indo-Nepal trade was the monopoly of the specific castes such as , Newars, Thakalis and Sherpas among the Nepalese and Gosains, Iraquis, Musalmans, Baniyas and Marwaris from India. They played vital role in Indo-Nepal trade.

The Newar traders were prominent in trade between India in the south and Tibet in the North.[24] They had been carrying on trade from the earliest times.[25] The Newars, the efficient traders, were the indigenous traders of the Kathmandu Valley. They were spread throughout Nepal since the 15th century A.D. They settled in the remote corners of the hill for the sake of trade.[26] These Newars affected physical as well as economic growth of a number of settlements. Tansen, Pokhara, Butwal and Bandipur grew as a result of the emigration of Newars from Kathmandu to these places. The size of Bandipur town increased along with its importance due to growing commercial interest since 1870. They also acted as intermediaries on the north-south trade route from Tibet to India. Since then the volume and size of trade between Nepal and India increased rapidly.[27] During the latter part of the nineteenth century, Butwal, Tansen and Bandipur increased much in size and they became the major trading centres of west-central Nepal. Traders from these towns approached upto Lucknow and other Indian towns to purchase their commodities.[28] These merchants had little to export and they always carried cash with them to purchase things. Some of the merchants were lifted with their cash and were escorted by army for the safety. They purchased manufactured goods from the Indian towns.[29]

The Newars enjoyed political clout and monopoly in trade. In Kathmandu, they had much influence among the general mass. They were supported by Rana Government for the growth of trade and commerce. These merchants were supposed to be role models in business acumen in the areas close to Kathmandu. A Newar named Subba Dhurb Narayan was a close associate of Jang Bahadur Rana. He had commercial links with some of the Indian towns.[30] In local dialect Newars were termed as Bharu for their profession as traders.[31] They also had clout in the administration of Kathmandu.

Before the merchants appeared in the Kathmandu valley, the Newars were the sole agents for entrepot trade.[32] One of the features of Newars was that they did not settle at any place permanently. They could test the water only for five to six years and afterwards they took exile for prolonged period.[33] There were about 3,000 Nepalese and Nepalese Vakil (consul or resident) in Lhasa in 1877. They carried iron, oil, tobacco, confectionery and other articles of domestic consumption to Tibet.[34] They were experts in Nepal-Tibet trade. They had established several shops in Tibet.[35]

The Newars were affluent due to successful business and were leading a better life than the rest of the tribes. They built beautiful multi-storeyed buildings reflecting their architectural acumen. They also founded new pattern of cities and villages in the Kathmandu valley. The streets were paved with bricks and the settlement was divided into '*toles*' each of which were inhabited bymembers of a single caste traditionally. The towns were arranged in circles and in ripples. The high caste people as well as the traders lived in the centre, the low caste lived in the next outer ring. The untouchables were used to settle outside the boundaries of the town.[36]

The Newar businessmen made farmhouses far from their trading establishment. They usually had large number of the family members, some of them ran the business while the others carried the business. The rest of the members looked after the home affairs with the help of the hired labours.[37]

The women of the traders led a rich life and were richly ornamented. *Percy Brown*, a thinker of the period described the women as follows. "In marked contrast to the somewhat common place garb of men was the particularly striking costume of the women. This attire included a brilliantly coloured jacket, opened so as to display another gaily-dyed garment underneath. But it was the voluminous cut of the lower portion of the costume which made the Nepalese ladies presence so unusual".[38]

Thakalis, resident of north western frontier district of Nepal, were an important trading community and played a dominant role in the trans-Himalyan trade. These merchants were given the customs contracts by the Nepalese Government and thus, they were in control of the import trade in salt from Tibet. For the geographical reason, the Thakalis had to store goods because it was difficult to carry goods during monsoon and winter season.[39]

The salt and grain, the main articles of trade of the Thakalis, were exchanged through Thak Khola in Musting district adjoining Tibet in the North. The salt was collected from the lakes of Tibet and it was exchanged for the grain. The salt collected from Tibet was stored at the village of Tucke in the heart of Thak Khola. If it was not possible to exchange the grains for salt, the Thakalis themselves transported the salts up to Baglung and Pokhara. There were several articles which were exchanged—sugar, tea, spices, tobacco, cigarettes, paper, cotton and cloth for the Tibetan wool, sheep and goats. The wool was sold in the immediate Indian market while the sheep and goats were taken to the middle hills or occasionally as far as the Terai. In Tibet, the Thakalis sold the goods of Nepalese and Indian origin.[40]

The Nepalese government did not levy any custom duty before 1860 but after that the custom duty was auctioned in case of salt of Thak Khola. First customs contractor paid an annual royalty of Rs. 44,500. The period between 1860 to 1932 was subjected to keen competition for contracts between Thakali merchants and a few outsiders.[41]

The Subbas and the Thakalis made Bhairahwa a business centre which was a small settlement as described by London in the late 1920. This Bhairahwa was comparable to a small village Bethri. He described as to the south, a few miles nearer India, was the unprogressive little village Bethri.[42] Here there was a brick court-house, a gaol, and a few other official buildings. It was the residence of Bada Hakim, with two subas under him. A few sentries were detailed from Butwal to guard the Nepalese Government treasury there. Bethri was a fair example of many smaller towns in the district situated along the northern side of the terai and in the danger zone, they acted as centers of commerce without at the same time having any considerable number of inhabitants. During the summer, the place was almost empty. Markets were held twice a year to which many villagers came in from a far and wide area. They brougt in large quantities of rice, pulses, vegetables and fruits, and bartered them for the produce of the hills and Tibet. The place was almost encircled by extensive jungles and a few mangoroves close to the Kachari, or court-house, rendering the town picturesque. Still, as was once said of a famous bridge at Cambridge. Bathri was eminently a place of transit and not of lounge, and the small colony of permanent inhabitants in the reed houses which paid a heavy toll in human life for trading profits. It was one of the places like Hetaura, of which the permanent existence, despite climatic defects, was secured by its position on the high road just where the under features of Himalayas burst up through the Terai."[43] After coming of the Thakali and other merchants from India and the Nepalese hills, the situation changed drastically. The reed houses were replaced by brick buildings and seasonal markets changed into a permanent big town.

The Chinese policy in Tibet saw a turn around after 1959 and it affected the trade of Thakali and then onwards the business activity started shifting in the lower regions of Nepal. The Thakalis started to settle down in the Pokhara valley and adjoining areas. The lower regions of Nepal were mostly inhabited by the Thakalis.[44] The opening of the motorable road joining Indian border (Bhairahawa) to Pokhara (hill) caused the reduction of price of the salt. This also caused a drift into business of salt. The Thakalis of Bhairahwa were the descendants of the Subbas who were awarded trading contracts by the Nepalese Government in the late nineteenth and early twentieth centuries.

Sherpas as trademen were completely different from other tribes in the mid-hilly region. Furer- Haimendorf once observed, "The sherpas" favourable position as middlemen in the trade between the Tibet and lower-lying regions of Nepal enabled them to obtain a standard of living far above that of most other Nepalese hill people, and in particular that of their southern neighbours, who were mainly agriculturallists. The Sherpas also started leading an affluent life as they possessed much luxurious life. But Rais were relatively low income people and their cultural achievement could not match the sherpas. They did not know how to cope with cold in highlands of Khumbu.[45]

Sherpas were very brave and they were the next Nepalese traders after Thakali who were engaged in Indo-Nepal and Trans-Himalayan trade. Their pattern of trade was the same as Thakalis. The differences found were only geographical location viz one in the east[46] and the other in the west. Similarly Sherpas brought salt, wool sheep and sent foodgrains and other commodities. For land in Tibet was not suitable for the cultivation of the crops, so Tibet did not grow enough foodgrains for their consumption. It produced only abundant quantities of salt and wool. The situation in hills were different. The sherpas traditionally functioned as middlemen in exchange of the foodgrains of the hill and Terai region for Tibetan salt and wool.

After Chinese Government closed the Tibet border, the Sherpas economy came to standstill and they had to develop other profession. The mountaineering became their chief occupation. The Sherpas became very popular when Tenzing Norgay reached the summit of Mount Everest with Sir Edmund Hillary[47] in 1953. The basis of their mountaineering was found in their habit to climb the high mountains for carrying on economic activities.

Apart from these, some of them also took part in Indo-Nepal trade. The Dokhas and Banjaras were active in entreport trade.

The Marwaris[48], Iraquis[49] and Muslims[50] were the most notable among the Indian traders who were engaged in Indo-Nepal trades. The Muslims shifted from Kashmir[51] and other parts of India but they used to sell the bangles and were called Churauti in the hill.[52] Some Iraqui Muslims had set up their shops in Kathmandu.

The Marwaris[53] of Indian origin also started their business in Nepal.[54] The Nepalese Government acquired a considerable amount of revenue by imposing taxes on these merchants.[55] The Iraqui shops were very popular among the Nepalese women living in the Kathmandu valley. The Raqi Bazar and Raqi Sadak were named after the Iraquis. A special class of merchants called 'Bathis Kothi' had favoured tax regime in Nepal. The full knowledge about these 'Bathis Kothi' merchants is not available to anybody.[56] The Collector of Bhagalpur once wrote that British subjects who had shops in Nepalese towns were never charged import duty on goods brought into Nepal for their sale at their shops. They had to pay only for the ground not for these shops.[57] The Deputy Commissioner of Kheri had also remarked that there were two descriptions of traders from British territories-those who rented shops from the authorities and resided in the Nepal marts for the entire trading season from January to May and those who merely lived long enough to make their sales and purchases. The former was alone permitted to trade with the hill men. They were traders as well as the brokers. The parbatia (hill men) like the itinerant dealers from Nepal. They stayed only long enough to buy and sell the articles of their wish or desire.[58] The merchants could be categorised as those concerned primarily with the purchase and exports of Nepalese goods and others who were primarily concerned with importing Indian goods. The Indian merchants were able to restrict competition from potential, Nepalese merchants. They used to attend village and Haat Bazars and purchase the grains. They also advanced loans to farmers against the value of crops. Thus they trapped the products of merchant as the farmers were found to sell their products.[59] This practice continues till today in Nepal[60] Indian merchants spread over the whole of Nepal in large numbers and this was not in interest of the local merchants. Even though the Government of Nepal collected large revenues, there was local resentment about the Indian merchants being engaged in various economic activities and monopolizing the trade. According to estimates of the president of National Social Reform Forum of India, 80 per cent of Nepal's economy was controlled by the Indian business community.[61] He expressed fear of the fall out of the Indian merchants migrating into Nepal and overpowering the resources, if the rate of migration continued this was a matter of concern.[62]

The Nepalese Government had to establish several police posts (chowkis) from east to west for the security of the traders and merchants.

There were police *chowkis* at the distance of three to six *kos* (approximately 2 miles). As per the report of the British Resident on 27 May, 1893, the Government had to open district courts[63] to hear the frequent cases of litigation arising out of the skirmishes. The British Residents also cited that the establishment of courts along the Indian districts reflected the growing trade-related litigation and also supplied a long list of the courts[64] adjoining Indian districts.

The Nepalese elite always preferred the British articles as they were of better quality. The rich people near Kathmandu always preferred European cloth. The Nepalese traders to capitalize on this demand imported the European cloths in large quantity for catering to the elites and also exported the articles for re-export to Tibet.

The elite army and all the higher officials had a conclave in Kathmandu and therefore the demand was the highest in Kathmandu. Thus, all shops and malls were situated near Nepal's capital.[65] In course of time, their demands also went on increasing.[66] In the second half of the 19th century the Nepalese nobility and the Rana family came in contact with the European culture and acquired a taste for upper class western style of affluent living symbolized by beautiful palaces without glass. Several articles were purchased either by India or by Europe. Hence, the Indian currency was in large demand in Nepal and Nepalese tapped a number of sources to obtain the Indian coins for these transaction.[67] Several arrangements were made but the most productive sources were revenue from land and commerce.

The trade also gave way for the extensive postal network into Nepal. Government felt the need for employing more porters for the transportation of mail. Two types of porterage services were employed in Nepal. Kagatehulak for transportation of official mail and *thaple-hulak* for the transportation of arms and ammunition, gifts and presents to the royal palace and such other goods as may be specified from time to time under the signature of the Prime Minister.

The slave system of 'Jhara' and 'Rakam' started becoming more acute. These were the labour taxes imposed on the porters. The porters working under Jhara system had no choice but to provide services without wages.[68] But the porters working in the 'Rakam' system enjoyed some facilities and privileges during the early years of the Nineteenth century. They were exempted from the payment of homestead taxes and levies. They also got the security of occupancy rights on their rice lands. The Brahmans of both Jaise and Upadhyaya had privilege for the transportation of mail. There was no forced enrolment of the lowest castes people for this purpose. The slaves were largely taken from the lowest castes and thus the caste discrimination existed for the labour taxation. Consequently the burden of such obligation fell heavily on the non-Brahman sections of the mass population.[69] Now the Government requirements were met by unpaid and forced labour. But forced slave in the private affairs was prescribed as per the declaration of Nepalese Government in June 1809. The prescription of the Government further said that labour should be paid a wage at the rate of 2 annas only. But the wage paid by the Government for the porterage services from the inhabitants of homesteads and villages were partly-10 paise daily. The government tried to improve the lot of the people of the slave origin. In 1888, permission was allowed by which the wage to the forced labour was paid depending upon the mutual consent.[70] The exploitation of the labourers by wealthy merchants and outers forced them to migrate to Bengal, Assam, Burma and elsewhere. There was great demand of the skilled labour in the coal-mines of Bihar and Bengal. These forced labour were brought from Nepal and employed in these areas in coal-mines, rubber planting, tea gardens. This migration helped the Indian economy as it got the active labour force at low cost. Major Northey observed "Another and not less important factor was the unauthorized recruitment, very often on a very large scale, of Nepalese coal-mines, rubber planting and worked generally under conditions that could but be reverse of beneficial to the hill men. Prompt measures were needed to prevent such immigration becoming a real menace to the future welfand prosperity of the nation."[71] These labourers also contributed to the opening up of new areas for redemption and settlement in India.[72]

The Rana Prime Ministers opened educational institutions on a restricted scale. A English High school was established for the first time in Kathmandu for the Rana Family and the nobility. Chandra Shamsher established an intermediate college in his name in Kathmandu in 1919.[73] The arrangements for the scholarships to enable Nepalese students to study medicine was also granted for their study in India and abroad.[74]

Towns were planned and the system of drainage was started. Kathmandu got its first sewer in 1899. The pipe lines were laid in 1892 for the supply of drinking water in Kathmandu.[75]

All this development work was started when the revenue of the country increased as a result of improvement in trade and commerce. The Government of Nepal also started moderansation of army. It was possible only when the British Indian Government allowed Nepal to import arms and ammunitions in accordance with Article V of the Anglo-Nepal treaty of 1923.[76]

For long, this supply was maintained by the Indian Government. In 1853, the revenue receipts of the state totalled to Rs. 961, 875 in different Indian rupee, worth Rs. 1,182, 491 in Nepalese currency at the official exchange rate of 100:123.[77] In the latter period collection of amount increased substantially but Rana rulers appropriated the whole money in the personal possession-into the accounts of wives and children.[78]

The growth of trade and commerce also gave way for the modernisation. The western science and technology were adopted. A telephone line of 74 miles was opened in 1915 between Kathmandu and Birganj.[79] Electric supply plant was set up near Kathmandu under the direction of an English engineer.

The attention was also paid on the export promotion measures as the government started to explore the material resources of the country and it planned for the maximum export of commodities to India and elsewhere.

An Indian mineralogist was in charge of geological exploration and forestry department was also established with the Indian co-operation. The river irrigation projects were started with the help of the British and Indian engineers. Chandra Shamsher established the chain of hospitals for the first time and in 1850 a hospital was opened with fourteen dispensaries. An X-ray unit and bacteriological laboratory was also set up. Initially only Bengalese doctors and nurses were recruited but in the course of time they were replaced with the Nepalese doctors. These doctors were trained in Indian medical colleges.

The public money got spent in the form of several palatial buildings constructed in the Ratgunabdee valley. These buildings were based on the model of western architecture. The residence of the Prime Minister Jang Bahadur at Thapathali in Kathmandu had four or five storeyes. It had large, lofty and ornamental public rooms containing pictures and carvings and other curios of Nepalese, Chinese and English manufacture.[80] The rooms were filled with murals, ceilings and glass windows, pictures etc. The floors were covered with Brussels carpets, ornamental articles and English and French furniture. Besides that, the buildings were furnished with steel fire places with marble mantelpieces, sofas, couches, easy chairs billiard tables and four-posted beds, candel bars, pianos, organs, glassware, vases etc.[81]

At least thirty palaces in Kathmandu were made the royal palaces and all were built in European fashion.[82] The Narayanhiti seto Darbar of Prime Minister Bir Shamsher was the first building in such style.

Kishore Narsingh and Kumar Narsingh were the architects of the later Rana palaces which belong to Rana family .

Kaiser Mahal, Bahadur Bhawan and Sital Niwas were built after the first world war. The architectures of Singha Darbar, the biggest palace were built by the French architects. This building had 7 inner courtyards and some 1,600 rooms.[83] This building was built in 1903 for the residence of Chandra Shamsher.

The Rana family had motor cars in Kathmandu since, 1920s as the porters carried the cars from Indo-Nepal borders. There was no road connection from India to Nepal over high mountains. The porters also carried statues of Prime Minister, mirrors, chandeliers, town clocks, sofas, bathtubs, grand pianos, central heating apparatus, and so on. The Rana family had furniture which was unknown during ancient and medieval times in Nepal. The gardens were decorated with ponds and trees.[84] When the construction of these palaces stimulated a demand for building materials and services of masons, carpenters and labourers.[85]

A significant portion of the income derived from commerce and land revenue was spent on imported luxuries.[86]

But one of the drawbacks of the development under the Rana regime was neglect of the growth of industry. The Ranas did not encourage the establishment of new industrial enterprises in order to keep the country isolated from external liberal influences. The industrialisation could have changed the value system and aspirations of the common man which would have been dangerous for the survival of these officials. They were very cunning in assessing of the situation arising with the new system of social organisation and growing awareness of the people of Nepal. The rulers were often afraid of slipping the political power from their hand to the common men. This approach could not help in furthering the goal of industrialisation. The treaty of 1923 allowed for practically unrestricted import of British goods to Nepal. Thus, it caused lessening the industrial base in Nepal[87] and made Nepal dependant upon the foreign goods. Since long there was no structural changes into the export of Nepal and the exports consisted only of raw materials.

However on the southern part of Nepal where there were flourishing industries on the Indo-Nepal borders, the trade was flourishing and exports boomed.[88]

After maintaining a strong administrative machinery ,the Rana regime worked in Nepal for personal gains and hence they exploited the natural resources for this purpose. The ruling offices also helped in personal aggrandizement of the wealth of the Rana family. These offices were sufficiently reimbursed for working and sustaining the monopoly of their Prime Ministers. But some of the Ranas were deprived of these benefits.[89] These offices took active part in the revolution against the Rana Government. The general people, intellectuals and ordinary merchants were also against the Rana rule. These section of people took active part in the revolution against the Rana Government and campaigned intensely against the Rana Regime.

As a consequence of these uprisings,the Prime Minister had to resign and Rana Government failed in 1951.

Notes and References

1. K.N. Singh, 'Small Neighbours of Big Powers', *India Attitude Towards Nepal,* Capital Publishing House, Delhi,1988, p. 80.
2. Shreeram Prasad Upadhyaya, *Indo-Nepal Trade Relations 1992*, Nirala Publication, Jaipur, p. 250.
3. M.C. Regmi, Thatched Huts and Stucco Palaces, *Peasants and Landlords in the Nineteenth Century Nepal,* Manjusri Publishing House, New Delhi, 1979, pp. 18-19.
4. *Ibid.*
5. Ramakant, *Indo -Nepalese Relations, 1816 to 1877.* S. Chand & Co., New Delhi, 1968, pp. 373-74.
6. M.C. Regmi, *op. cit.*

7. P.C. Rawat, *Indo –Nepal Economic Relations*, National Publishing House, Delhi, 1974, pp. 63-64.
8. A.S. Bhasin, *Documents on Nepal's Relations with India and China 1949-66.* Academic Book Ltd. Bombay, 1970, p. 11.
9. *Ibid.*
10. Hem Narayan Agrawal, *The Administrative System of Nepali from Tradition to Modernity,* Vikas Publishers, New Delhi, 1976, p. 11.
11. Blaikie Piers, John Cameron, David Seddon, *Nepal in Crisis Growth and Stagnation at Periphery,* Oxford University Press, New Delhi, 1980, p. 32.
12. Francis Tuker, *Gorkha : The Story of the Gurkhas of Nepal,* Constable and Co., London, 1957, p. 168.
13. Hem Narayan Agrawal, *op. cit.* pp. 19-20.
14. *Ibid.* p. 21.
15. *Ibid,* pp. 39-40.
16. *Ibid,* pp. 62-64.
17. Hem Narayan Agrawal, *op. cit.* p. 12.
18. *Ibid.* p. 65.
19. M.C. Regmi, "The Calcutta Buying Agency". *Regmi Research Series,* Year 13, No. 68. August 1, 1981. p. 126.
20. M.C. Regmi, 'Sale of Wax in Patna". *Regmi Research Series,* Year 15, No. 3, 1 March 1983, p. 37.
21. Ramakant and B.C. Upreti, "India Community in Nepal : A Study of the Indian Migrants". *Indian in South Asia* (ed.) I. J. Bahadur Singh.South Asian Publisher, Delhi, 1984, p. 23.
22. *Ibid,* p. 5.
23. Piers Blaikie, *op. cit.,* p. 37.
24. G.H.D. Gimlette, *Nepal and the Nepalese,* H.F. & G. Witherby, London, 1928, p. 79.
25. The Newars were the oldest living group not only in Nepal but in the whole of India. Their civilization goes back to a period older than Mohanjodaro. Their contribution to art and commerce is famous all over Asia. The main occupation of all the Newars except Jyapus (farmer) was commerce and craft and industry. They had covered the whole country as traders. All the mechanics of the country were Newars, except a few workmen from the plains of India, employed by the Government in the public workshops and arsenals. See. Daniel Wright, *op. cit.* p. 46: D.R. Regmi, *op. cit.* pp. 11-19.
26. *Ibid.* pp. 172-73.
27. Piers Blaikie, *op. cit.* p. 124.
28. M.C. Regmi, *A Study in Nepali Economic History, 1768-1845.* Manjusri Publishing House, New Delhi, 1971.
29. Piers Blaikie, *op. cit.* p. 125.
30. Political A. August 1864, No. 51.
31. Bhaju means trader and is appended to the name of every Newar, See, D.R. Regmi. *op. cit.* p. 19.

32. M.C .Regmi, *op. cit.* p. 24.
33. Alastair Lamb, *Britain & Chinese Central Asia: The Road to Lhasa 1767-1905. Routledge & Kegan Paul* London, 1960, p. 346.
34. G.H.D. Gimlette. *op. cit.* p. 80.
35. Danial Wright, *op. cit.* p. 46.
36. Seemann Heinrich, *Nepal: 2031 Till Yesterday, A Forbidden Country,* 1973, Reprint Delhi, 1978, p. 17.
37. Percy Brown, *Nepal Gurkha and Newars of Himalayan Valley* J. A. Hammarton, (ed). *Tribes, Races & Culture of India and Neighbouring Countries.* 1856, reprinted Delhi 1984, p. 322.
38. Piers Blaikie, *op. cit.* p. 245.
39. *Ibid. p.* 151.
40. *Ibid.*
41. Furer- Haimendorf, Chistoph Von *Himalayan Traders: Life in Highland Nepal,* London, 1975, p. 188.
42. Piers Blaikie, op. *cit.* pp. 151-52.
43. Bhairahwa was called Bethri at that time. See Piers Blaikie, *op. cit.* p. 125.
44. *Perceval* Landon *op. cit.* p. 363.
45. The Tibetan word Sher means East and Sherpa accordingly means "an easterner". The word is commonly used to denote the Bhotiyas of North Eastern Nepal, but the real homeland of these people is Solu Khambu, near Tibeto—Nepalese frontier, See, C. J. Morris, *The Gurkhas: An.Ethnology,* 1933, reprint B.R. Publishing Co.Delhi 1985, p. 125.
46. Furer Haimendorf. *op. cit.* p. 60.
47. Hillary took initiative for the development of the region inhabited by the Sherpas. With his efforts one hospital, a school, a number of bridges and a landing strip for planes were built at about 9,000 ft height. Heinrich Seeman *op. cit., p.* 18.
48. During the Mughal period of Indian history (1529-1707) several Marwaris began to move outside their homeland (in Rajasthan). They participated in the long range trade and high finance of North India. See, Thomas A. Timberg, *The Marwaris ; From Traders to Industrialists.* Vikas Publishers , New Delhi, 1978, p. 41.
49. Kashmiri and Iraqi were the principal traders in article of European manufacture. See, Danial Wright, *op. cit.,* p. 46.
50. The first Musalmans to arrive in Kathmandu were Kashmiri traders who came from Tibet during the rule of Ratna Malla in the late 15th and early 16th centuries. They were traders of rays, carpets, shawls and other woolen goods. They travelled back and forth from Kashmir to Lhasa via Ladakh. It is believed that a few of them were invited to Kathmandu by an envoy of Ratna Malla in Lhasa. Soon after that some more Musalmans entered into the western hills. During the 17th or 18th century other Musalmans were brought from India to Nepal in the service of some of the Chaubise rajas of Nepal to train soldiers in

the use of firearms. Later on large numbers of Musalmans migrated from India into the Terai area as agricultural labourers and into the hill as sellers of bangles, glass beads and leather goods during or after the Indian Mutiny of 1857. See, Dor Bahadur Bista. *People of Nepal.* Ratna Pustak Bhandar, Kathmandu, 1980, p. 150.

51. The Kashmiri merchants migrated to Tibet when the trade with their own land was not extensive. They were very important in the economy of Tibet. The native of Kashmir might be compared with the Jews in Europe or Armenians in the Turkish Empire, for their far flung commercial enterprises through the eastern Kingdoms of Asia. They carried on an extensive traffic between the distant parts of East Asia and Tibet. They had also agents in South east India and in Nepal. See, Schuler, *op. cit.* p. 61.
52. Dor Bahadur Bista, *op. cit.,* p. 150.
53. The Indian Marwaris and Baniyas were given right to settle down permanently in Kathmandu for trade after 1740 A.D. See, Jain, *op. cit.* p. 9.
54. Most of the industries in Nepal, were set up by them. They have shares in all the commercial activities of Nepal even today.
55. Piers Blaikie, *op. cit.* p. 149.
56. Report on the External trade of Bengal with Nepal, Sikkim and Bhutan for 1880-81.
57. *Ibid* for 1882-82.
58. Revenue A. August 1877, No. 14.
59. Report on the External Trade of Bengal with Nepal, Tibet etc.
60. Dor Bahadur Bista, *op. cit.* p. 130.
61. Upadhyaya Shreeram Prasad , Indo-Nepal Trade Relations. *op.cit.*, p. 261.
62. Ramakant and B.C. Upreti, *op. cit.*
63. General, E. June 1893, No. 35 Pros. Lieutenant Colonel H. Wylie, the officiating British Resident in Nepal to the Secretary to the Government of India, dated 27 May 1893, (N.A.I.).
64. All the Departments of the Government were run on military lines. All the civil and judicial functionaries bad military titles. District judges were given the title of Lieutenant. See, C.G. Bruce & W. Book Northey. "Nepal". *The Geographic Journal.* Vol. LXV. No. 4, April 1925, p. 289.
65. N. K. Sinha. (ed.) *The History of Bengal (1757-1905).* Calcutta, 1967, p. 363.
66. Piers Blaikie, *op. cit.*
67. Gaige, *op. cit.* p. 43.
68. For example, orders were issued in 1803 to the headmen of several villages in Sindhupal Chok district in the hill region east of the Kathmandu valley to round up labourers and assemble them in Chitwan for an elephant hunt. It was a normal practice throughout the nineteenth century. Most of the material for the construction of palaces was brought by the porters under Jhara system. See. M.C. Regmi, *The State & Economic Surplus.* footnote 56, p. 109.

69. M.C. Regmi, *op. cit.* pp. 96-97.
70. *Ibid.*, p. 100.
71. Bruce and Northey, *op. cit.* p. 298..
72. M.C. Regmi, *op. cit.* pp. 134-35.
73. B.P. Majumdar, *op. cit.* p. 9.
74. Manindra Bhushan Bhaduri, "Bagchi-Levi in Nepal, A Glimpse of Rana Rule in the Early Twenties". *Calcutta Review.* Vol. CLXIV. p. 32.
75. Shriman Narayan, *India and Nepal: An Exercise in Open Diplomacy.* Popular Prakashan Bombay, 1971, p. 62.
76. See Appendix VI, Article V.
77. M.C. Regmi, *The State and Economic Surplus,* p. 135.
78. Hem Narayan Agrawal, *op. cit.* pp. 127-28.
79. B. P. Majumdar, *op. cit.* p. 9.
80. Daniel Wright described the palace as a "curiosity of Nepalese, Chinese and English manufacture, from a baby's frock to a reflecting telescope or an Erad's Piano;" See, Wright, *op. cit.* p. 18.
81. H. Ambrose Oldfield, *op. cit.* p. 107.
82. Heinrich Seeman, *op. cit.* p. 68.
83. It was the biggest of all the palaces in Asia. From 1951 until the night of 9 July 1973, when a huge fire destroyed the whole complex within 48 hours, the palace served the Nepalese Government as its Secretariat. Only the front wing which was used for state receptions survived. See, *Ibid.*
84. *Ibid.*
85. Regmi, M.C. Thatched Huts and Stucco Palaces, *Peasants and Land-Lords in 19th centuary Nepal, op. cit.* p. 156.
86. *Ibid,* p. 157.
87. Lohini, P.C. "Industrial Policy : The Problem Child of History and Planning in Nepal". *Nepal in Perspective.* (eds) Pashupati Shamsher J.B. Rana and Kamal P. Malla, Centre for Economic Development and Administration, Kathmandu 1973. p. 2.
88. The location of industries in Bihar adjoining the Nepal border was based on agricultural raw materials. Up to the mid 19th century, Bihar enjoyed a fair share in India's trade and manufacture in hydro power, salt-petre, textile, opium, jute, rice, etc. Indian jute mills were mostly located in West Bengal, Bihar, Assam and Orissa. In 1910, there were 220 industries in U.P. adjoining western Nepal. See, S.C. Kuchhal, *The Industrial Economy of India.* Allahabad, 1965, p. 71, also see, T.N. Kapoor, *Industrial Development in the States of India.* Sterling Publishers India p, Delhi 1967, pp. 93-95, 102.
89. Chandra Shamsher divided the Rana family into A , B and C groups A class Ranas were born of wives who were of the similar castes as their husbands. B class were born of wives entitled by caste to every form of association with their husbands except eating of rice together and C class were wives of such caste status as were not permitted marriage. Only A class Ranas were worthy

to be a Prime Minister. Chandra Shamsher put Jang's sons and grandsons in B class. The condition of C class Rana was worst. In 1934 all C class Ranas were exiled to India. Among them Subarna Shamsher and Mahavir Shamsher were the two most important persons who played very active part in the revolution of 1950-51

Conclusion

India and Nepal have since times immemorial been closely connected with each other geographically, historically, politically, culturally and commercially. Nepal served as the link area in transmitting the religio-cultural heritage of India to Tibet and Central Asia. Many ruling dynasties of Nepal had actually emigrated from India to find secluded peace and meditation and also channels for trade and commerce. The Himalayas have nourished their bonds of religion with all fraternity and deep sympathy for each other. Besides numerous similarities with respect to culture, caste and customs, many mythological and legendary events of India are associated with Nepal and both shared each other's weal and woe. Due to seclusion of Nepal from the rest of the world for long, many valuable ancient scriptures have been preserved by this ancient homeland of sages and ascetics. This priceless treasure and trust, therefore, has to be preserved, protected and enriched with care to inspire the citizens of both the countries for times to come.

Foreign trade has been playing an increasingly important role in a country's economic development. All the South Asian countries are developing countries. Among the South Asian countries, Nepal presents fascinating case study of a small underdeveloped country, which is almost entirely dependent on India for its trade and transit facilities because it is a landlocked country surrounded by India from three sides and inaccessible mountains on northern frontier with Tibet.

Among all the countries with which India carried overland trade, Nepal occupied a leading position. Nepal's share in foreign overland trade of Bengal was about 92 per cent. Unlike other neighbouring South– East Asian countries, India's trade relations with Nepal were confined to the movement of goods only and did not involve the movement of other factors of production like labour, capital and enterprise.

The Indo-Nepal trade witnessed significant expansion and ramifications and it served as a pivot around which political, cultural and other relations between Nepal and the British India revolved. The British Government in India adopted free trade policy with Nepal. Neither import nor export duties were imposed by the Government of India. As far as Nepal is concerned, in some cases taxes were framed, in others these were *khas.*

The non-commercial factors frequently affected its nature and extent, altering its pattern and the commodities involved in transactions between the two countries. The fluctuations were often linked with the changing policies and attitudes of the Government of the two countries. The noticeable changes into the policies adopted by the successive Prime Ministers of Nepal reflect continuity which was often dictated by the motives of the personal gains and occasionally by their whims and fancies. One similarity is noticeable in the behaviours of these Prime Ministers i,e. they harboured deep suspicions about British motives.They were aware of the Nepalese proverb, "the tradesman brings the Bible, the Bible brings the bayonet." They were extremely reluctant to allow free access to British Indian traders into Nepal. They were aware of the tactics played by the Britishers on Indians. These clever tricks played by the British people led to the trap of the conquest of the Indian territory. This realisation prevented the Nepalese Government from allowing free access to British Government's capital into their territory. Hence, the Nepalese Government never permitted penetration of British capital and enterprise into Nepal. The Prime Ministers limited the commercial activities to the bilateral agreements made from time to time. They kept their relations with the British Government limited to workable relations. Even they did not severe ties with the Britishers either. The Nepalese Government followed a policy of monopolies in respect of certain specified commodities, particularly timber which accounted for a sizeable percentage of Nepalese exports. The policy of monopoly trade was also favoured because of the high profit derived from the lucrative Indo-Nepal trade in which senior civil and military officials were engaged. The rulers sold monopoly rights to merchants who remitted a share of their profit to Prime Ministers. This system also helped the Sardars, officials, and intellectuals in concentrating more on commerce than politics. It brought them handsome profits.

Fearful of political and territorial designs characteristic of British imperialism, the rulers of Nepal refused to surrender to the prospects of material prosperity dangled before them by the British. They preferred freedom of the country to enslavement and colonization as had happened in India. Influenced by the free trade movement in England,theBritish Government in India eagerly wanted to induce the Nepal Durbar to adopt free trade policy with India.However the British attempts to induce Nepal to accept the free trade policy were allowed to die in atrophy.

The policy followed by the rulers demonstrates that the restrictions imposed on Indo-Nepal trade were partly dictated by the vested interests of the Nepalese ruling class. Their position was strong in economically socially and politically backward Nepal, which they sought to perpetuate.

During the rule of Jang Bahadur Rana, the Indo-Nepal trade saw new heights. The British during the revolt of 1857 received valuable help from him. B During his rule, the Indo-Nepal trade flourished.

The trade flourished for the entire period of the Rana's rule. The period between 1858 and 1950 may be regarded as the Golden age in Nepal's commercial annals, for it enjoyed a favourable balance of trade by virtue of her exports which far exceeded imports. The successive regime in Nepal always followed the same policy of isolation and never gave an upper hand to the Britishers. Thus, the commercial policy never made a sharp break with the traditional policy of isolation and opposition to free trade and unrestricted British economic and commercial penetration into Nepal. Sometimes the Ranas took the support of the British people only to strengthen their position, which had political ramifications in Nepal. There was some flexibility scene during the time of Ranodip Singh and Bir Shamsher. But even this was tempered by genuine anxiety that too intimate connection with the British would be detrimental to the interests of the country. Hence their persistent policy was to keep the British at safe distance.

During the time of Chandra Shamsher, the British and Nepalese relations were very close because of the suspected France-Russian designs on Himalayan region. The British Government started recruiting the Gorkha soldiers whose loyalty was beyond doubt. It was during this time that the nationalist movement in India was growing and Indian people in the Armed forces could not be trusted as before. Thus, warm relations on the political front brought two countries closer and expansion of trade and commerce followed as a matter of course.

The Indo-Nepal trade also helped in expansion of the wide network of transport and communication. It is true that the means of transport and communication also gave impetus to the development of Indo-Nepal trade. A major factor in this growth was the opening of the Indian railways in the districts bordering Nepal. In fact, the expansion of railways and its branch lines in the border areas gave the timber trade an unprecedented boom. The Railways provided a vital link between a numbers of towns on the Indo-Nepal border situated along important centres of trade in Nepal. The railways provided a link to markets and this helped the growth of towns. Thus, Nepalganj, Birganj, and Biratnagar owe their growth to this factor. Newar traders and Muslim merchants set up their shops in these new emerging towns. The waterways along river and rivulets provided cheap source of transportation. The water- ways helped connecting Purnea, Bhagalpur, Darbhanga Muzaffarpur, Champaran, Gorakhpur, Basti and Pilibhit. Both railways and waterways ran parallel to each other.

The Road Policy of Nepalese Government always prevented the Britishers from establishing a road link between India and Nepal. The

Government of Nepal followed a very tricky policy to keep the Britishers at bay. They decided to remain in their fortifications. Hence, the policy of Nepalese Government did not seriously hamper Indo-Nepal trade.

The Nepal Government however did not give freeway to allow trade with Tibet through Nepal. Jang Bahadur and all his successors were extremely jealous of British attempts to open up Tibet for trade, fearing damage to Nepalese commercial interests in that country.

The trade with Tibet was much more profitable for the Indians than that with Nepal. The British were keenly interested in developing this entreport trade and this was the main source of difference between British and Nepalese Government. Thus, Jang Bahadur and all his successors were extremely jealous of British attempts to open up Tibet for trade. Nepal had favourable trade balance with her large export base.

The Indo-Nepal trade included hundreds of items of amazing variety. But trade in timber, food grains, opium, arms and ammunition and slaves acquired new dimension on account of its wider ramifications. Initially the forest products dominated the scene but with the growth of cultivation in the Terai region and large scale deforestation, the forest product gave the way to the rice towards the end of 19th century.

In the 20th century,Timber and food grains constituted the principal items of export from Nepal. Imports to Nepal consisted mainly of salt, sugar, tobacco and cloth. The luxury goods were imported to substantial quantities.

Several measures of instability and fluctuations in Nepal export proceeds don't show an exceptionally high degree of instability by international standard. This is not with understanding the high degree of a commodity and geographical concentration and the dominance of agricultural product in Nepal's export .

Our empirical study on concentration and instability has shown that the Nepalese exports were highly volatile. The three main items of Nepal's exports were rice, jute and ghee (melted butter). ghee was a less fluctuating commodity .On the whole, however, the Nepalese exports were highly fluctuating both quantitywise and valuewise and the degree of concentration of important commodities in Nepal's exports and imports was considerable.

Opium trade earned historical importance in Indo -Nepal trade relations. The Nepal opium was smuggled to Assam, Punjab, Chandernagore and Calcutta. From Chandernagore and Calcutta, opium was smuggled to China and other countries.

The slave trade was legalised in Nepal because of the socio-economic condition of the people. The ultra poor mass used to sell their sons and daughters for their survival. But there is evidence that when this slave trade was banned, people resorted to smuggling to evade detection and punishment. The slave trade was a socio-economic malady. The actual amount of this trade is not clear from the records. The sellers of slaves were povertystricken people of Bihar and North-Western Provinces and Oudh. In spite of the efforts, the Government of Nepal did not get success in abolishing the slavery. However, it was abolished in Nepal in 1924.

The commercial taxation and custom duties also caused friction between the Nepalese and the British Government. The British officials always pulled down the Nepalese authorities for imposing heavy taxation. This move was based on nefarious designs of the government. This was the reason why British could not influence the policy of the Nepal Government about the reduction of the duty. On the western frontier of Nepal, the British had no reason for complaint. The Nepalese Government imposed high export duties on Nepalese traders and very light import duties on Indian traders there. The main motive of the policy was the promotion of Indian goods and to compel the Nepalese traders to sell their goods in the Nepalese markets. The Indian merchants were attracted to the sparsely populated region of Nepal.Among the principal conclusions we may note that Nepal's co-efficient of commodity concentration in export had throughout been high. However, a decline in this concentration is noticeable.

The National Trading Company of Nepal and the State Trading Corporation of India should work together to expand the volume of the Indo-Nepalese trade, to handle nationally the supply of Indian raw materials, to secure better prices, to check the artificial price inflation, to implement barter agreements effectively and to secure a better revenue to both the governments. Since India has large stake in economic development of Nepal, sustained efforts should be made by the private merchants to maximise the bilateral commodity traffic.

Money and currency were introduced in the later period, initially the barter trade was the main mode of transaction between India and Nepal. The Rana family circulated the greatest amount of currency in order to buy luxurious foreign goods from India. The Rana family wanted more currency to circulate for purchasing largest luxurious foreign goods from India.

The monetary relations between India and Nepal too have been intimate and Nepalese and Indian coins have been circulating together in the adjoining (border) areas of both the countries in internal and foreign transactions. This 'Dual Currency System' prevailed as the people and the Nepal Bank preferred Indian currency because of its relative stability. The Indian rupee has been interwoven with the Nepalese fiscal arrangements, creating many monetary complications for them. In fact, Nepal was divided into two currency areas: Terai area where Indian currency was preferred and hilly tracts where Nepalese currency was preferred. The exchange rate of these two currencies varied from region to region according to the geographical situations and varied socio-economic factors. The frequent risky rate variation marred investments and savings in Nepal and many manipulators took its undue advantage. Prior to 1932, Nepalese Shroffs and a few Indian merchants transacted foreign exchange business in open market and the Government treasury supplied credit against gold and silver. The exchange stability was maintained due to limited Nepalese import requirements. The Shroffs were deeply interested in Nepalese currency for its greater metallic value. Tijarath was abolished in 1937 and its work was entrusted to the newly created Nepal Bank. Due to prohibition of free exchange facilities and discriminatory policy of the bank in supplying Indian currency, secret dealings in foreign exchange emerged. With the outbreak of the second World war in 1939, Indian-rupee lost its intrinsic value and the Nepalese currency began to be appreciated and it was also melted down and exported. The home return of the Gurkhas from the war created a heavy demand for Indian goods and Indian currency. Nepalese Government could not cope up with the growing demand as the value of Indian rupee sharply rose. Nepalese currency further fell in value in 1950 due to internal political instability and deficit financing. Consequently, various cross rates prevailed in different parts of the country. This chaotic condition lured people to hoard Indian currency which had a greater relative value.

The administrative set up was induced by the necessity of the Indo-Nepal trade. New offices were opened, old ones were re-organised and streamlined and new ports were created to cope with the ever-expanding commercial activities in the country. This also gave way for cultural exchange and matrimonial relationship between the people of the two countries. Palatial buildings were built by rich traders and their living standards improved markedly. The modern science and technology was familiarised by the Nepalese Government and it helped modernisation of those who were associated with trade and commerce.

Rana regime collected huge amounts of revenues but did not spend much on the development of the economy. This revenue went directly into the private sectors. The rulers also deposited money into the foreign banks. The beneficial shortsighted policy of the rulers kept Nepal an exporter of raw materials and importer of finished products from the foreign countries throughout the period under review. But the country remained economically and socially backward in spite of the growth of its commerce.

Nepal provided the route through which Indo-Tibetan trade was conducted. Before the opening of 20th century, entreport trade of Nepal with India was quite significant.

The world had so far been witnessing a developed country coming forward to assist one which is underdeveloped. But Indo-Nepalese economic relationship is a unique example of two underdeveloped economies which are trying to prove economically useful to each other. Apart from political relations, cordial economic relations between the two brought tremendous possibilities of future development for both. It does not need to point out that India enjoy comparatively better economic standing than Nepal and

Indian authorities have repeatedly expressed their benevolence to provide all possible assistance to the neighbouring countries, in general and Nepal in particular. Naturally, it is in the interest of Nepal to repose unflinching faith in India's bonafides to improve her economy. It is high time for her to realize that her interests are safe in the helping hands of a friendly country like India. On the other hand, India must express the same attitude towards Nepal.

Foreign aid is undoubtedly a significant facet of international economic co-operation. It helps in the creation of social overheads, diverts resources from war to peace which is vital for international solidarity, to eliminate poverty and to materialise revolutionary expectations of rising countries. The volume of foreign aid given by any nation is determined on the basis of humanitarian, economic and political considerations. Nepal, having suffered from internal political and economic chaos, has to look forward to it especially from India because she happens to be her neighbour and with whom she has close ties. India too was willing to extend all sorts of help to create a congenial atmosphere in Nepal. She lent a helping hand with cash and kind and trained Nepalese personnel. However, India has always kept in view the high ideals of neighbourly fraternity, liberty and world peace. There is an opinion that Nepal, being internally feeble cannot preserve her independence under pressure from aggressive countries.

Our analysis has also highlighted the heavy geographical concentration in Nepal's foreign trade with India. This is largely explained by its geographical position as a small land -locked country virtually flanked by India. It can also be suggested that the natural resources so abundant in this sub-continent should be tapped through joint efforts for mutual benefit.

Thus, there is a case for putting all effort to bring India and Nepal economically closer which is not only essential for the development of these two countries but also necessary for providing a model for other developing countries.

To enable India and Nepal should evolve measures for their mutual economic cooperation and integration. This can be done by establishing a free trade area, a customs union, or even a common market with complete factor mobility .

To sum up, it can be said that Indo-Nepal trade relations had a continuous and steady progress throughout the entire period under review.

The cumulative effect of Nepal's geographical situation, historical and cultural links with India is clearly reflected in trade relations between these two countries. India remains and probably will continue to remain the major trade partner of Nepal.

We hope that the present study will provide a useful base for further work on Indo-Nepal trade relations, as and when more adequate information becomes available.

Appendix-I

Treaty of Commerce With Nepaul, 1st March 1792

Treaty authenticated under the seal of Maha Rajah Run Behauder Shah Behauder Shumshcre Jung ; being according to the Treaty transmitted by Mr. Jonathan Duncan, the Resident at Benares, on the part of thc Right Honourable Charles, Earl Cornwallis, KG, Governor-General in Council, and empowered by the said authority to conclude a Treaty of Commerce with the said Maha Raja, and to settle and fix the duties payable by the subjects of the respective States of the Honourable English Company and those of Nepaul, the said gentleman charging himself with whatever relates to the duties thus to be payable by the subjects of the Nepaul government to that of the Company ; in like manner as hath the aforesaid Maha Rajah, with whatever regards the duties thus to be payable by the subjects of the company's government to that of Nepaul; and the said Treaty having been delivered to me (the said Maha Rajah) by Mowlavy Abdool Kadir Khan, the aforesaid gentleman's vakeel, or agent ; this counterpart there-of having been written by the Nepaul government hath been committed to the said Khan, as hereunder detailed:

Article 1. inasmuch as an attention to the general welfarc, and to the eas' and satisfaction of the merchants and traders; tends equally to the reputation of the administrators of both the governments of the Company and of Nepaul; it is therefore agreed and stipulated that 2.5 per cent shall reciprocally be taken, as duty, on the imports from both countries; such duties to be levied on the amount of the invoices of the goods which the merchants snail have along with them; and to deter the said traders from exhibiting false invoice, the seal of the custom houses of both countries shall be impressed on the back of the said Invoices, and a copy thereof being kept, the original shall be restored to the merchants; and in cases where the merchant shall not have along with him his original invoice, the custom house officers shall, in such instance, by the duty of *2.5* per cent on a valuation according to the market price.

Article 2. The opposite stations hereunder specified, with-in the Frontiers of each country, are fixed for the duties to be levied, at which place the traders are to pay the same; and after having once paid duties and receiving a rowannah there-on, no other or further duty shall be payable throughout each country or dominion respectively.

Article 3: -Whoever among the officers on either side shall exceed in his demands for, or exaction of duty, the rate here specified, shall be exemplarily punished by the government to which he belongs, so as effectually to deter others from the like offences.

Article 4: -In the case of theft or robberies happening on the goods of the merchants, the Foujedar, or officer of the place, shall, advising his superiors or government thereof speedily, cause the zemindars and proprietors of the spot to make good the value, which is in all cases, without fail, to be so made good to the merchants.

Article 5: -In cases wherein either country any oppression or violence be committed on any merchant, the officers of the country wherein this may happen, shall, without delay, hear and inquire into the complaints of the persons thus aggrieved, and doing them justice, bring the offenders to punishment.

Article 6: -When the merchants of either country, having paid the established duty, shall have transported their goods into the dominion of one or the other State, if such goods be sold within such State, it is well: but if such goods not meeting with sale, and that the said merchants be desirous to transport their said goods to any other country beyond the limits of either of the respective States included in the Treaty, the subjects and officers of these latter shall not take thereon any other or further duty than the fixed one levied at the first entry ; and are not to exact double duties, but are to allow such goods to depart in all safety without opposition.

Article 7: -This Treaty shall be of full force and validity in respect to the present and future rulers of both governments, and being considered on both sides as a Commercial Treaty and a basis of concord between the two States, is to be, at all times, observed and acted upon in times to come, for the public advantage and the increase of friendship.

On the 5th of Rejeb, 1206, of the Hegira, and 1199 of the Fussellee style, agreeing with the 1st of March 1792 of the Christian, and with the 22nd of Phagun, 1848, of the Sunbut Aera, two Treaties, to one tenor, were written for both the contracting parties, who have mutually engaged that from the third Bysack 1849 of the Sunbut Aera, the officers of both States shall, in pursuance of the strictest orders of both governments, immediately carry into effect and observe the stipulations aforesaid, and not wait for any further or new direction.

(True copy and translation)

(Signed) J. Duncan
Resident
Revenue Department.
(A true copy)

(Signed) G. H. Barlow
Sub-Secretary

(Source: Aitchison, C. U. *A Collection of Treaties, Engagements, and Sunnuds, Relating to India and Neighbouring Countries.* Vol. II, pp. 195-198. Calcutta: Printed by G. A. Savielle and P. M. Cranenburgh, Bengal Printing Company Limited 1863.)

Appendix—II

TREATY OF 1815
(The Treaty of Sugauli)

Treaty of Peace between the Honorable East India Company and Maharajah Bikram Sah. Rajah of Nipal, settled between Lieut Colonel Bradshaw on the part of the Honorable Company, in virtue of the full powers vested in him by His Excellency the Right Honorable Francis, Earl of Moira, Knight of the Most Noble Order of the Greater, one of His Majesty's Most Honorable Privy Council, appointed by the Court of Directors of the said Honorable Company to direct and control all the affairs in the East Indies, and by Sree Gooroo Gujraj Misser and Chunder Seekur Opedeea on the part of Maharajah Girmaun Jode Bikram Sah Behauder Shum-sheer Jung, in virtue of the powers to that effect vested in them by the said Rajah of Nipal.

Whereas war has arisen between the Honorable East India Company and the Rajah of Nipal, and whereas the parties are mutually disposed to restore the relations of peace and amity which, previously to the occurrence of the late differences, had long subsisted between the two States, the following terms of peace have been agreed upon:-

Article 1st: -There shall be perpetual peace and friendship between the Honorable East India Company and the Rajah of Nipal.

Article 2nd :-The Rajah of Nipal renounces all claim to the lands which were the subject of discussion between the two States before the war ; and acknowledges the right of the Honorable Company to the sovereignty of those lands.

Article 3rd :-The Rajah of Nipal hereby cedes to the Honorable the East India Company in perpetuity all the under-mentioned territories, viz.

First—The whole of the low lands between the Rivers Kali and Rapti.

Secondly—The whole of the low lands (with the exception of Bootwul Khass) lying between the Rapti and the Gunduck.

Thirdly—The whole of the low lands between the Gunduck and Coosah, in which the authority of the British Government has been introduced, or is in actual course of introduction.

Fourthly—All the low lands between the rivers Mitchee and the Teestah.

Fifthly—All the territories within the hills eastward of the River Mitchee, including the fort and lands of Nagree and the Pass of Nagarcote, leading from Morung into the hills, together with the territory lying between that Pass and Nagree. The aforesaid territory shall be evacuated by the Goorkha troops within forty days from this date.

Article 4th:- With a view to indemnify the Chiefs and Barahdars of the State of Nipal, whose interests will suffer by the alienation of the lands ceded by the foregoing Article, the British Government agrees to settle pensions to the aggregate amount of two lakhs of Rupees per annum on such Chiefs as may be selected by the Rajah of Nipal, and in the proportions which the Rajah may fix. As soon as the selection is made, Sunnuds shall be granted under the seal and signature of the Governor-General for the pensions respectively.

Article 5th :-The Rajah of Nipal renounces for himself, his heirs, and successors, all claim to or connexion with the countries lying to the west of the River Kali, and engages never to have any concern with those countries or the inhabitants thereof.

Article 6th:- The Rajah of Nipal engages never to molest or disturb the Rajah of Sikkim in the possession of his territories ; but agrees, if any differences shall arise between the State of Nipal and the Rajah of Sikkim, or the subjects of either, that such differences shall be referred to the arbitration of the British Government, by whose award the Rajah of Nipal engages to abide.

Article 7th :-The Rajah of Nipal hereby engages never to take or retain in his service any British subject, nor the subject of any European or American State, without the consent of the British Government.

Article 8th:- In order to secure and improve the relations of amity and peace hereby established between the two States, it is agreed that accredited Ministers from each shall reside at the Court of the other.

Article 9th:- This Treaty, consisting of the Articles, shall be ratified by the Rajah of Nipal within fifteen days from this date, and the ratification shall be delivered to Lieut-Colonel Bradshaw, who engages to obtain and deliver to the Rajah the ratification of the Governor-General within twenty days, or sooner, if practicable.

Done at Segowlee, on the 2nd day of December 1815.

Paris Bradshaw, *Lt. Col. P.A.*

Seal.

Received this Treaty from Chunder Seekur Opedeea, Agent on the part of the Rajah of Nipal, in the Valley of Muck-waunpoor, at half-past two o'clock P.M., on the 4th of March 1816 and delivered to him the Counterpart Treaty on behalf on the British Government.

(Signed) DD. Ochterlony,

Agent, Governor-General

Memorandum for the approval and acceptance of the Rajah of Nipal. presented on the 8th December 1816.

1. Adverting to the amity and confidence subsisting with the Rajah of Nipal. the British Government proposes to suppress, as much as is possible, the execution of certain Articles in the Treaty of Segowlee, which bear hard upon the Rajah, as follows:
2. With a view to gratify the Rajah in a point which he has much at heart, the British Government is willing to restore the Terai ceded to it by the Rajah in the Treaty, to win, the whole Terai lands lying between the Rivers Coosa and Gunduk, such as appertained to the Rajah before the late disagreement; excepting the disputed lands in the Zillahs of Tirhoot and Sarun, and excepting such portions of territory as may occur on both sides for the purpose of settling a frontier, upon investigation by the respective Commissioners; and excepting such lands as may have been given in possession to any one by the British Government upon accertainment of his rights subsequent to the cession of Terai to that Government. In case the Rajah is desirous of retaining the lands of such ascertained proprietors, they may be exchanged for others, and let it be clearly understood that, notwithstanding the considerable extent of the lands in the Zillah of Tirhoot, which have for a long time been a subject of dispute, the settlement made in the year 1812 of Christ, corresponding with the year 1869 of Bikramajeet, shall be taken, and everything else relinquished, that is to say, that the settlement and negotiations such as occurred at that period, shall in the present case hold good and be established.
3. The British Government is willing likewise to restore the Terai lying between the Rivers Gunduk and Rapti, that is to say from the River Gunduk to the western limits of the Zillah of Goruckpore, together with Bootwul and Sheoraj, such as appertained to Nipal previous to the disagreements, complete, with the exception of the disputed places in the Terai, and such quantity of ground as may be considered mutually to be requisite for the new boundary.

4. As it is impossible to establish desirable limits between the two States without survey, it will be expedient that Commissioners be appointed on both sides for the purpose of arranging in concert a well defined boundary on the basis of the preceding terms, and of establishing a straight line of frontier, with a view to the distinct separation of the respective territories of the British Government to the south and of Nipal to the north ; and in case any indentations occur to destroy the even tenor of the line, the Commissioners should effect an exchange of lands so interfering on principles of clear reciprocity.

5. And should it occur that the proprietors of lands situated on the mutual frontier, as it may be rectified, whether holding of the British Government or of the Rajah of Nipal, should be placed in the condition of subjects to both Governments, with a view to prevent continual dispute and discussion between the two Governments, the respective Commissioners should effect in mutual concurrence and co-operation the exchange of such lands, so as to render them subject to one dominion alone.

6. Whensoever the Terai shall be restored, the Rajah of Nipal will cease to require the sum of two lakhs of Rupees per annum, which the British Government agreed to advance for the maintenance of certain Barahdars of his Government.

7. Moreover, the Rajah of Nipal agrees to refrain from prosecuting any inhabitants of the Terai, after its revertance to his rule, on account of having favored the cause of the British Government during the war, and should any of those persons, excepting the cultivators of the soil, be desirous of quitting their estates, and of retiring within the Company's territories, he shall not be liable to hindrance.

8. In the event of the Rajah's approving the forcgoing terms, the proposed arrangement for the survey and establishment of boundary marks shall be carried into execution, and after the determination in concert of the boundary line, Sunnuds conformable to the foregoing stipulations, drawn out and sealed by the two States, shall be delivered and accepted on both sides.

(Signed) Edward Gardner,

Seal.

Resident

(A true translation)

(Signed) G.

Wellcsley,
Assistant.

SUBSTANCE of a LETTER under the Seal of the RAJAH OF NIPAL, received on the 11th December 1816

After compliments;

I have comprehended the document under date the 8th of the December 1816, or 4th of Poos 1873 Sumbut, which you transmitted relative to the restoration, with a view to my friendship and satisfaction, of the Terai between the Rivers Coosa and Rapti to the southern boundary complete, such as appertained to my estate previous to the war. It mentioned that, in the event of my accepting the terms contained in that document, the southern boundary of the Terai should be established as it was held by this Government. I have accordingly agreed to the terms laid down by you, and herewith enclose an instrument of agreement, which may be satisfactory to you. Morever, it was written in the document transmitted by you, that it would be restored, with the exception of the disputed lands and such portion of land as should, in the opinion of the Commissioners on both sides, occur for the purpose of settling a boundary ; and excepting the lands which, after the cessions of the Terai to the Honorable Company, may have been transferred by it to the ascertained proprietors. My friend, all these matters rest with you, and since it was also written that a view was had to my friendship and satisfaction with respect to certain Articles of the Treaty of Segowlee, which bore hard upon me, and which could be remitted, I am well assured that you have at heart the removal of whatever may tend to my distress, and that you will act in a manner corresponding to the advantage of this State and the increase of the friendly relations subsisting between the two Governments,

Moreover, I have to acknowledge the receipt of the orders under the red seal of this State, addressed to the officers of Terai between the Rivers Gunduk and Rapti for the surrender of that Terai, and their retiring from thence, which was given to you at Thankote, according to your request, and which you have now returned for my satisfaction.

(A true translation)

Seal. (Signed) G. WELLESLEY,

Assistant.

SUBSTANCE of a DOCUMENT under the Red Seal, received from the DURBAR on the 11th December 1816

Doorga *Bowanee.*

With a regard to friendship and amity, the Government of "Nipal agrees to the tenor of the document under date the 18th of December 1816 or 4th Poos 1873 Sumbut, which was received by the Durbar from the Honorable Edward Gardner on the part of the Honorable Company, respecting the revertance of the Terai between the Rivers Coosa and Rapti to the former southern boundary, such as appertained to Nepal previous to the war, with exception of the disputed lands.

Dated the 7th of Poos 1873 Sumbut.

(A true translation)

(Signed) G. WELLESLEY,

Assistant.

(Source: Aitchison, C. U. *A Collection of Treaties, Engagements, and Sunnuds, Relating to India and Neighbouring Countries.* Vol. II, pp. 205-11. Calcutta: Printed by G. A. Savielle and P.M. Cranenburgh, Bengal Printing Company Limited, 1863.)

Appendix—III

TREATY OF 1860
(November 1, 1860)

During the disturbances which followed the mutiny of the Native Army of Bengal in 1857, the Maharajah of Nipal not only faithfully maintained the relations of peace and friendship established between the British Government and the State of Nipal by the Treaty of Segowlee, but freely placed troops at the disposal of the British authorities for the preservation of order in the frontier districts, and subsequently sent a force to co-operate with the British Army in the recapture of Lucknow and the final defeat of the rebels. On the conclusion of these operations, the Viceroy and Governor General, in recognition of the eminent services rendered to the British Government by the State of Nipal, declared his intention to restore to the Maharajah the whole of the lowlands lying between the River Kali and the District of Goruckpore, which belonged to the State of Nipal in 1815, and were ceded to the British Government in that year by the aforesaid Treaty. These lands have now been identified by Commissioners appointed for the purpose by the British Government, in the presence of Commissioners deputed by the Nipal Durbar ; masonry pillars have been erected to mark the future boundary of the two States and the territory has been formally delivered over to the Nipalese Authorities. In order to secure more firmly the State of Nipal in the perpetual possession of this territory, and. to mark in a solemn way the occasion of its restoration, the following Treaty has been concluded between the two States:

Article 1: -All Treaties and Engagements now in force between the British Government and the Maharajah of Nipal, except in so far as they may be altered by this Treaty, are hereby confirmed.

Article 2 :-The British Government hereby bestows on the Maharajah of Nipal in full sovereignty, the whole of the low-lands between the Rivers Kali and Rapti, and the whole of the lowlands lying between the River Rapti and the District of Goruckpore, which were in the possession of the Nipal state in the year 1815, and were ceded to the British Government by Article III of the Treaty concluded at Segowlee on the 2nd December in that year.

Article 3 :-The boundary line surveyed by the British Commissioners appointed for the purpose, extending eastward from the River Kali or Sardah to the foot of the hills north of Bagowra Tal, and marked by pillars, shall henceforth be the boundary between the British Province of Oudh and the Territories of the Maharajah of Nipal.

This Treaty, signed by Lieutenant-Colonel George Ramsay, on the part of His Excellency the Right Honourable Charles John Earl Canning, G.C.B., Viceroy and Governor General of India, and by Maharajah Jung Bahadur Rana, G.G.B., on the part of Maharajah Dhera Soorinder Vikram Sah Bahadoor Shumshere Jung, shall be ratified, and the ratifications shall be exchanged at Khatmandooj within thirty days of the date of signature.

Signed and sealed at Khatmandoo, this First day of November, a.d. one Thousand Eight Hundred and Sixty, corresponding to the Third day of Kartick Budee, Sumbut Nineteen Hundred and Seventeen.

Sd/- G. Ramsay, Lieut-Colonel
Resident at Nepal

(Seal)
Sd/- Canning

Viceroy and Governor General

This Treaty was ratified by His Excellency the Governor-General, at Calcutta, on the 15th of November 1860.

Sd/- A R Young
Deputy Secretary to the Government of India

(***Source***: Sanwal, B.D. *Nepal and the East India Company*. Asia Publishing House, Bombay, 1965, appendix 15. pp. 340-41).

Appendix- IV

EXTRADITION MEMORANDUM OF 1866

Memorandum dated the 23rd of July 1866, supplemental to the Treaty with the State of Nepal of the 10th of February 1855, for the mutual surrender of heinous criminals, adding to the 4th Article of the said Treaty the offences of cattle stealing, of embezzlement by public officers, and serious theft.

It is hereby settled and concluded by Colonel George Ramsay, Resident at the Court of Nipal, by virtue of full powers vested in him by His Excellency the Right Hon'ble Sir John Laird Nair Lawrence, Baronet, G.C.B. and K.C.S.L, Her Majesty's Viceroy nnd Governor Genera! of British India, and Maharajah Jung Bahadoor, Rana, G.C.B., Prime Minister and Commander-in-Chief of Nipal, in virtue of powers to that effect granted to him by his Sovereign the Maharajah Dheraj of Nipal.

That, subject to all the other conditions of the Treaty which was executed at Khatmandoo by the same parties on the tenth day of February one thousand eight hundred and fifty-five, corresponding to the eighth day of Fagoon, Sumbut nineteen hundred and eleven ; and with the view to the prevention of frontier disputes, and the more speedy and effectual repression of crime upon the border, the offences of cattle-stealing, of embezzlement by public officers, and of serious theft, that is to say, cases of theft in which the amount stolen may be considerable, or personal violence may have been used, shall be included in the list of crimes for which surrenders shall be demanded by either Government. In fact, they are hereby formally added to the list of crimes specified in the 4th Article of the said Treaty.

Executed at Khatmandoo this twenty-third day of July a.d. one thousand eight hundred and sixty-six, corresponding to the twenty-sixth day of Asarh, Sumbut nineteen hundred and twenty-three.

Sd/- G. Ramsay, Colonel.
Resident at Nepal
(Seal)

Sd/- John Lawrence,

Governor General

This Treaty was ratified by His Excellency the Governor General at Simla on the 9th of August 1866.

W. Muir,
Secretary to Government of India

Source: Sanwal, B. D. *Nepal and the East India Company.* Asia Publishing House, Bombay, 1965, appendix 14, p. 339.

Appendix—V

EXTRADITION MEMORANDUM OF 1881

Memorandum dated the 24th of June 1881, Supplemental to the Treaty with the State of Nepal, dated the 10th February 1855, a.d., corresponding to the 8th Phagun, Sumbut 1911, and the Memorandum with the State of Nepal, dated 23rd July 1866, a.d., corresponding to the 26th Asarh, Sumbut 1923, for mutual surrender of criminals—24th June 1881.

It is hereby agreed by Charles Edward Ridgeway Girdlestone. Esq., of the Bengal Civil Service, Resident at the Court of Nepal, by virtue of full powers vested in him by His Excellency the Most Honourable the Marquis of Ripon, K.G., GMSI, GM1E, Her Imperial Majesty's Viceroy and Governor-General of India, and by Maharaja Sir Runoodeep Singh, Rana Bahadur, KCSI, Thonglin Pimma Kokang Vyang Syang, Prime Minister and Commander-in-Chief of Nepal, by virtue of full powers vested in him by His Highness the Maharaja Adhiraj of Nepal.

That the offence of escaping from custody whilst undergoing punishment after conviction of any of the offences specified in the fourth Article of the aforesaid Treaty, or in the aforesaid Memorandum, shall be deemed to be added to the list of offences specified in the fourth Article of the aforesaid Treaty.

Executed at Katmandoo, this twentyfourth day of June, a.d. one thousand eight hundred eighty-one, corresponding to the thirteenth day of Asarh, Sumbut one thousand nine hundred thirty-eight.

Charles Edward Ridgeway Girdlestone

Resident in Nepal

Ripon,

Viceroy and Governor-General of India

This treaty was ratified by His Excellency the Viceroy and Governor-General of India, at Simla, on the eleventh day of August, one thousand eight hundred and eighty-one.

A.C. Lyall

Secretary to the Government of India

Foreign Department

Source: Aitchison, C.U. *A Collection of Treaties, Engagements and Sanads Relating to India and Neighbouring Countries,* Vol. XIV, Calcutta, Government of India, Central Publication Branch, 1929, No. XII, pp. 74-5.

Appendix -VI

Treaty of 1923

TREATY of FRIENDSHIP between Great Britain and Nepal signed at KATMANDU, 21st December 1923, and Not bearing the same date respecting the importation of Arms and Ammunition into NEPAL—1923

(Exchange of ratifications took place at Katmandu on the 8th April 1925)

TREATY

Whereas peace and friendship have now existed between the British Government and the Government of Nepal since the signing of the Treaty of Segowlie on the 2nd day of December 1815, and whereas since that date the Government of Nepal has ever displayed its true friendship for the British Government and the British Government has as constantly shown its good-will towards the Government of Nepal; and whereas the Governments of both the countries are now desirous of still further strengthening and cementing the good relations and friendship which have subsisted between them for more than a century; the two High Contracting Parties having resolved to conclude a new Treaty of Friendship have agreed upon the following Articles:

Article I:- There shall be perpetual peace and friendship between the Governments of Great Britain and Nepal, and the two Governments agree mutually to acknowledge and respect each other's independence, both internal and external.

Article II:- All previous treaties, agreements and engagements, since and including the Treaty of Segowlie of 1815, which have been concluded between the two Governments are hereby confirmed, except so far as they may be altered by the present Treaty.

Article III:- As the preservation of peace and friendly relations with the neighbouring States whose territories adjoin their common frontiers is to the mutual interests of both the High Contracting Parties, they hereby agree to inform each other of any serious friction or misunderstanding with those States likely to rupture such friendly relations, and each to exert its good offices as far as may be possible to remove such friction and misunderstanding.

Article IV:- Each of the High Contracting Parties will use all such measures as it may deem practicable to prevent its territories being used for purposes inimical to the security of the other.

Article V:-In view of the longstanding friendship that has subsisted between the British Government and the Government of Nepal and for the sake of cordial neighbourly relations between them, the British Government agrees that the Nepal Government shall be free to import from or through British India into Nepal whatever arms, ammunition, machinery, warlike material or stores that may be required or desired for the strength and welfare of Nepal, and that this arrangement shall hold good for all time as long as the British Government is satisfied that the intentions of the Nepal Government are friendly and that there is no immediate danger to India from such importations. The Nepal Government, on the other hand, agrees that there shall be no export of such arms, ammunition, etc., ' across the frontier of Nepal either by the Nepal Government or by private individuals.

If, however, any Convention for the regulation of the Arms Traffic, to which the British Government may be a party, shall come into force, the right of importation of arms and ammunition by the Nepal Government shall be subject to the proviso that the Nepal Government shall first become a party to that Convention, and that such importation shall only be made in accordance with the provisions of that Convention.

Article VI:- No Customs duty shall be levied at British Indian ports on goods imported on behalf of the Nepal Government for immediate transport to that country provided that a certificate from such authority as may from time to time be determined by the two Governments shall be presented at the time of importation to the Chief Customs Officer at the port of import setting forth that the goods are the property of the Nepal Government, are required for the public services of the Nepal Government, are not for the purpose of any State monopoly or State trade, and are being sent to Nepal under orders of the Nepal Government.

The British Government also agrees to the grant in respect of all trade goods, imported at British Indian ports for immediate transmission to Katmandu without breaking bulk *en route,* of a rebate of the full duty paid, provided that in accordance with arrangements already agreed to, between the two Governments, such goods may break bulk for repacking at the port of entry under Customs supervision in accordance with such rules as may from time to time be laid down in this behalf. The rebate may be claimed on the authority of a certificate signed by the said authority that the goods have arrived at Katmandu with the Customs seals unbroken and otherwise untampered with.

Article VII:- This Treaty signed on the part of the British Government by Lieutenant-Colonel W. F. T. O'Connor, C.I.E., C.V.O., British Envoy at the Court of Nepal, and on the part of the Nepal Government by General His Highness Maharaja Sir Chandra Shumshere Jung Bahadur Rana, G.C.B., G.C.S.I., G.C.M.H., G.C.V.O., D.C.I., Thong-lin Pimma—Kokang-Wang-Syan, Prime Minister and Marshal of Nepal, shall be ratified and the ratification shall be exchanged at Katmandu as soon as practicable.

Signed and sealed at Katmandu this the twenty-first day of December in the year one thousand nine hundred and twenty-three *Anno Domini* corresponding with the sixth Paush, Sambat Era one thousand nine hundred and eighty.

W. F. T. O'Connor, *Lt.-Col.* (Under Vernacular translation of Treaty.)
British Envoy at the CHANDRA
SHAMSHERE, *Court of Nepal* *Prime Minister and Marshal of Nepal.*

NOTE

From the Prime Minister of Nepal, to the British Envoy at the Court of Nepal

Nepal, December 21, 1923.

My dear Colonel O'Connor,

Regarding the purchase of arms and munitions which the Government of Nepal buys from time to time for the strength and welfare of Nepal, and imports to its own territory from and through British India in accordance with Article V of the Treaty between the two Governments, the Government of Nepal hereby agrees that it will, from time to time before the importation of arms and munitions at British Indian Ports, furnish detailed lists of such arms and munitions to the British Envoy at the Court of Nepal in order that the British Government may be in a position to issue instructions to the port authorities to afford the necessary facilities for their importation in accordance with Article VI of this Treaty.

I am, etc.,
CHANDRA

To

Lieutenant-Colonel W. F. T. O'Connor, C.I.E., C.V.O., British Envoy at the Court of Nepal.

(***Source:*** Aitchison, C. U. *A Collection of Treaties, Engagements and Sunnuds Relating to India and Neighbouring Countries.* Vol. XIV, pp. 75-77. Calcutta: Government of India Central Publication Branch. Revised edition, 1929.)

Appendix - VII

Treaty of Peace and Friendship Between The Government of India and The Government of Nepal (1950)

The Government of India and the Government of Nepal, recognising the ancient ties which have happily existed between the two countries for centuries;

Desiring still further to strengthen and develop these ties and to perpetuate peace between the two countries;

Have resolved therefore to enter into a Treaty of Peace and Friendship with each other, and have for this purpose, appointed as their plenipotentials the following persons, namely:

THE GOVERNMENT OF INDIA

HIS EXCELLENCY SHRI CHANDRESHWAR PRASAD NARAIN SINGH Ambassador of India to Nepal.

THE GOVERNMENT OF NEPAL

MOHUN SHAMSHER JANG BAHADUR RANA, MAHARAJA,

Prime Minister and Supreme Commander-in-Chief of Nepal.

Article I:- There shall be everlasting peace' and friendship between the Government of India and the Government of Nepal. The two Governments agree mutually to acknowledge and respect the complete sovereignty, territorial integrity and independence of each other.

Article II:- The two Governments hereby undertake-to inform each of any serious friction or misunderstanding with any neighbouring State likely to cause any breach in the friendly relations subsisting between the two Governments.

Article III:- In order to establish and maintain the relations referred to in Article I the two Governments agree to continue diplomatic relations with each other by means of representatives with such staff as is necessary for the due performance of their functions.

The representatives and such of their staff as may be agreed upon shall enjoy such diplomatic privileges and immunity as are customarily granted by international law on a reciprocative basis; provided that in no case shall these be less than those granted to persons of a similar status of any other State having diplomatic relations with either Government.

Article IV:- The two Governments agree to appoint Consuls-General, Consuls, Vice-Consuls and other Consular agents, who shall reside in towns, ports and other places in each other's territory as may be agreed to.

Consuls-General, Consuls, Vice-Consuls and Consular agents shall be provided with exequature or other valid authorisation of their appointment. Such exequature or authorisation is liable to be withdrawn by the country which issued it, if considered necessary. The reasons for the withdrawal shall be indicated wherever possible.

The persons mentioned above shall enjoy on a reciprocal basis all the rights, privileges, exemptions and immunities that are accorded to persons of corresponding status of any other State.

Article V:- The Government of Nepal shall be free to import, from or through the territory of India, arms, ammunition or war-like materials and equipment necessary for the security of Nepal. The procedure forgiving effect to this arrangement shall be worked out by the two Governments acting in consultation.

Article VI:- Each Government undertakes, in token of the neighbourly friendship between India and Nepal, to give the nationals of the other, in its territory, national treatment with regard to participation in industrial and economic development of such territory and to the grant of concession and contracts relating to such development.

Article VII :-The Government of India and Nepal agree to grant, on a reciprocal basis, to the nationals of one country in the territories of the other same privileges in the matter of residence, ownership of property, participation in trade and commerce, movement and other privileges of a similar nature.

Article VIII :-So far as matters dealt with herein are concerned, the Treaty cancels all previous treaties, agreements, and engagements entered into on behalf of India between the British Government and the Government of Nepal.

Article IX :-This Treaty shall come into force from the date of signature of both Governments.

Article X:- This Treaty shall remain in force until it is terminated by either party by giving one year's notice,.

Done in duplicate at Kathmandu this 31st day of July, 1950.

Sd/- Chandreshwar Prasad Sd/- Mohun Shamsher Jang Naraln Singh Bahadur Rana

For the Government of India For the Government of Nepal

No. II
Nepal's Zone of Peace Proposal

Distinguished Friends,

1. Ceremonies have occupied much of my time, and I have not even had the opportunity to tell you how deeply we appreciate your friendly gesture coming to Nepal to participate in our Coronation. We celebrate this occasion as an event symbolising our national unity and historical continuity. Your distinguished presence has no doubt, deeply gratified us. It is an added evidence of the good-will and friendship that you have for my people and country.
2. May I take this opportunity to assure you tnat this nation gratefully remembers and warmly reciprocates your feeling of friendship and cooperation, so generously extended to us in our time of rejoicing as well as in our time of need.
3. Nepal is a small country placed among the highest mountain-chains in the world. Our land covers tracts that are both tropical and temperate. Most of our people are engaged in agriculture as a·way of life. Some of our countrymen still lead a pastoral life while others in the cities and towns are beginning to take to an industrial age. For its size Nepal presents an extremely varied picture of people and topography.
4. Tenacity, courage and simplicity, together with an inborn sense of independence that we have since the beginning of our history, characterize our way of life. However varied the face of land, we are a united people with a common historical experience, confidently looking to the future with hope and determination. Our land provides the visitor with a continual surprisē of change and contrast, of richness and beauty. Its panoramic beauty has, since time immemorial, attracted sages and seers as it does attract modern explorers and tourists. The nature of our land has enabled us, the Nepalese, to weave an enduring fabric of life this is based on peace, concord and harmony.
5. Since 1951—which provides a watershed in our history—we made experiments with different forms of government. We discovered that, however good a polity be, it cannot take root without some germinal seed in the tradition of a native culture. Nepal has been independent

throughout history. It has never been a colony of any country and it has little experience of adopting a system alien to it. Naturally, therefore, when we tried to imbibe a system, root and branch, imported from abroad it was difficult to harmonize the need for order with the need for change. As a result, we faced a crisis of identity. It was this transitional feature as well as geopolitical compulsions which led us finally to the road of the partyless Panchayat system of government. It is not only indigenous and democratic, but also the Nepalese variant of a people-based system of government. Its evolution is dictated as much by our historical experience as by our culture and geography. Under the system, Nepal is socially and politically awake and is moving into an era of equal opportunities for all with a readiness to embrace suitable reforms.

6. In our system the day-to-day administration of the country is entrusted to a Council of Ministers headed by the Prime Minister. We have a national legislature known as the Rashtriya Panchayat which consists of people's representatives elected from all districts of the Kingdom. We have also an independent judiciary. Public participation in our policy can be measured by the fact that in Nepal there are about four thousand village councils which locally manage their own affairs. At the national level, we have a Planning Commission which, together with the National Development Council, devises development strategies and evaluates programmes.

7. If the creation of a modern infrastructure, political as well as administrative, has taken some years, we have never lost sight of our goal of creating a viable economic order in the country together with the need for distributive justice and social reforms. My august father enunciated a New Legal Code which has enabled every Nepalese to see the light of social norms infused with human dignity. The land reforms carried out under the Panchayat system have brought tiller participation in rural development closer to reality. A New Education Plan seeks to combine the acquisition of skills, attitudes and ideas with actual application. The plan also tries to elevate the quality of teachers and taught alike, and seeks to improve the living standards of our people in general.

8. In the past twenty-five years, we have built more roads and bridges, generated more electricity and constructed more schools, factories and buildings than ever before in our history. For investing our resources more equitably, we have established four development zones on a geographic basis. We are slowly but surely, moving out of a purely agricultural economy to an economy of self-sufficiency based on small-scale industries and diversified trade. Nevertheless, we are far behind in the global endeavour for economic advancement, which in the last quarter of the twentieth century represents the focus of national

endeavour of every country in the world. For us development has thus an urgency and a compulsion not felt elsewhere. Our strategy is to bring about development largely through the mobilization of our own resources, supplemented where necessary by international co-operation. These tasks call for a condition of peace.

9. As heirs to one of the most ancient civilizations in Asia, our natural concern is to preserve our independence—a legacy handed down to us by history. The absence of peace will delay, make more difficult and even deform our development, just as a world without peace will jeopardize our traditional independence. As we are a peace-loving people, we seek to work for peace, not in isolation from the rest of the world, but in collaboration with the whole world. I can assure you that Nepal harbours no ill-will or any unfriendly feeling towards any country in the world. We take pride in the fact that we have close and cordial ties of understanding with our neighbours. If our relations with India have been deep and extensive, our relations with China have been equally close and friendly, consistenly marked by understanding of each other's problems and aspirations.

10. We adhere to the policy of non-alignment because we believe that it brightens the prospects of peace. We need peace for our security, we need peace for our independence, and we need peace for development. As a matter of fact, Nepal in the past had signed formal peace and friendship treaties with both our friendly neighbours. And if today, peace is an overriding concern with us it is only because our people genuinely desire peace in our country, in our region and everywhere in the world. It is with this earnest desire to institutionalise peace that I stand to make proposition—a proposition that my country, Nepal be declared a zone of peace.

11. We believe that only under a condition of peace will we be able to create a politically stable Nepal with a sound economy which will in no way be detrimental to any country. I also wish to declare that in making a proposition for the zone of peace we are not prompted out of fear or threat from any country or quarter, As heirs to a country that has always lived in independence, we wish to see that our freedom and independence shall not be thwarted by the changing flux of time when understanding is replaced by misunderstading, when conciliation is replaced by belligerency and war. It is with such a perspective view of the future that with the help of our friends we seek peace.

12. Distinguished friends, if I have taken the opportunity of your presence here to relate something of what we in Nepal are doing and intend to do in the future, I hope you will understand us as, friends. Your visit to Nepal has furthered the bonds of our friendship. I am conscious of the fact that, during your brief stay, we have not been able to provide you

with such comforts and facilities as we would have liked to. When you return home, we would like to carry back with you memories of our friendly feelings towards your country and people. My wife joins me in extending thanks to you and on behalf of both of us as well as on behalf of government and the people of Nepal, we request you to convey to your government and people a message of peace, greetings and goodwill.

Thank you.

Note: This is a speech from His Majesty King Birendra Bir Bikram Shah Dev at the Farewell Reception hosted at the conclusion of His Majesty's auspicious coronation at Narayanhity Royal Palace on 25th February 1975. Here HM King Birendra declared the proposition that Nepal be declared a zone of peace.

(Source: *Foreign Affairs Journal* (Kathmandu), January-April 1976. pp.63-66.)

Appendix VIII

FOREST DEPOTS IN NEPAL

Depot	District
Mahakali	Kanchanpore, New Territory, Ceded in 1860
Gwari Karnali	New Territory
Bewace(Babace)	Nepal ganj, bordering on Baraich
Dadha Gadhi (DarhaGarhi)	
Rapti, Nepalganj	
Ban Gunga	Butwal, bordering on Gorakhpur.
Mohna	Kailari, New Territory
Tribeni	Between Chitwan and Butwal at the point where the Gandak leaves the hills on the right bank.
Riomadi (Riomari)	On the little Rapti in the Chitwan valley.
Thori (Bikna) Between	Chitwan and Ramnagar at the point where the Pundai stream flows between the Someswar and Chiriaghata range to the north of the Inderwa (Indian police outpost).
Chhapkaiya	Bara. A few miles north of the Raxaul (Indian police outpost on the road leading from Sugauli to Kathmandu.
Jamni (Jamooni)	Bara. On the stream named Jamni, which flows to the west of Semorounghur and is an affluent of the Bara.
Gandak	
Bagmati	Rotahut. On the main stream named Bagmati
Kamla	Mohotri. On the stream: bordering on named Kamla
Darbhanga	
Bhamarpoora	Mahotri
Pachwari (Kosi Ko)	Saptari On the west bank of the Kosi, Bordering on Bhagalpur and Purnea.

Purwari (Kosi Ko)	Morung on the east bank of the Kosi
Lohindra, Athmouza	Morung, Bordering on Purnea
	Bakraha and Kankai

(***Source:*** Sen ,Jahar, *Essays in Indo- Nepal Trade, A Nineteenth Century Study,* K.P. Bagchi & Company, Calcutta, 1991.)

Appendix IX

KINGS OF NEPAL
(Shah Dynasty)

1.	Prithvi Narayan Shah	Sep 25, 1768 - Jan 11, 1775
2.	Pratap Singh Shah	Jan 11, 1775 - Nov 17, 1777
3.	Rana Bahadur Shah	Nov 17, 1777 - Mar 23, 1799
4.	Girvan Yudha Vikram Shah	Mar 23, 1799 - Nov 20, 1816
5.	Rajendra Bir Vikram Shah	Nov 20, 1816 - May 12, 1847
6.	Surendra Bir Vikram Shah	May 12, 1847 - May 17, 1881
7.	Prithvi Bir Vikram Shah	May 17, 1881 - Dec 11, 1911
8.	Trivuan Bir Vikram Shah	Dec 11, 1911 - Nov 7, 1950
9.	Gyanendra Bir Vikram Shah Dev	Nov 7, 1950 - Jan 7, 1951
10.	Tribhvan Bir Vikram Shah (IInd time)	Jan 7, 1951 - Mar 13, 1953
11.	Mahendra Bir Vikram Shah	Mar 14, 1955 - Jan 31, 1972
12.	Birendra Bir Vikram Shah	Jan 31, 1972 - June 1, 2001
13.	Dipendra Bir Vikram Shah	June 01, 2001 - June 4, 2001
14.	Gyanendra Bir Vikram Shah	June 4, 2001 - May 28, 2001

President of the Fedral Democratic Republic of Nepal
(2008-present)

15.	Ram Baran Yadav	July 23, 2008 - Incumbent

(*Source*: Nepal Home page, Govt. of Nepal. www.netfornepal.com.)

PRIME MINISTERS OF NEPAL
Prime Minster during the Absolute Manarch (1799-1990)

	From	To
Damodar Pande	1799	1804
Bhimsen Thapa	1805	1837
Rana Jung Pandey	1837	1843
Mathawar Singh Thapa	1843	1846

Jang Bahadur Kunwor/Rana	1846	1856
Bam Bhahadur Rana	1856	1857
Jang Bahadur Kunwor/Rana	1857	1877
Rana Udip Singh Bahadur Rana	1877	1885
Bir Shumsher Jang Bahadur Rana	1885	1901
Dev Shumsher Jang Bahadur Rana	1901	
Chandra Shumsher Jang Bahadur Rana	1901	1929
Bhim Shumsher Jang Bahadur Rana	1929	1932
Juddha Shamsher Jang Bahadur Rana	1932	Nov. 29, 1945
Padma Shamsher Jang Bahadur Rana	Nov. 29, 1945	April 30, 1948
Mohan Shamsher Jang Bahadur Rana	April 30, 1948	Nov. 16, 1951
Matrika Prasad Koirala(1/2)	Nov. 16, 1951	Aug. 14, 1952
Direct rule by King Tribhuvan Bir Bikram Shah	Aug. 14, 1952	June 15, 1953
Matrika Prasad Koirala	June 15,1953	April 14,1955
Direct rule by King Mahendra Bir Bikram Shah	April 14, 1955	Jan. 27, 1956
Tanka Prasad Acharya	Jan. 27, 1956	July 26, 1957
Kunwar Indrajit Singh	July 26, 1957	May 15, 1958
Subarna Shamshir Jang Bahadur Rana	May 15, 1958	May 27, 1959
Bishweshwar Prasad Koirala *(First elected PM of Nepal)*	May 27, 1959	Dec 26, 1960
Tulsi Giri (1/3)	Dec 26, 1960	Dec 23,1963
Surya Bahadur Thapa (1/5)	Dec 23, 1963	Feb 26, 1964
Tulsi Giri (2/3)	Feb 26, 1964	Jan. 26, 1965
Surya Bahadur Thapa (2/5)	Jan. 26, 1965	April 7, 1969
Kirti Nidhi Bista (1/3)	April 7, 1969	April 7, 1970
Gehendra Bahadur Rajbhandary	April 13, 1970	April 14, 1971
Kirti Nidhi Bista (2/3)	April 14, 1971	July 16, 1973
Nagendra Prasad Rijal (1/2)	July 16, 1973	Dec 1,1975
Tulsi Giri (3/3)	Dec 1, 1975	Sept 12,1977
Kirti Nidhi Bista (3/3)	Sept 12, 1977	May 30, 1979
Surya Bahadur Thapa (3/5)	May 30, 1979	July 12, 1983
Lokendra Bahadur Chand (1/4)	July 12, 1983	March 21, 1986
Nagendra Prasad Rijal 1(2/2)	March 21, 1986	June 15, 1986
Marich Man Singh Shrestha	June 15, 1986	April 6, 1990
Lokendra Bahadur Chand	April 6,1990	April 19,1990

PRIME MINISTER DURING CONSTITUTIONAL MONARCHY (1990-2008)

Krishna Prasad Bhattarai (1/2)	April 19, 1990	May 26, 1991
Girija Prasad Koirala (1/4)	May 26, 1991	Nov 30,1994
Man Mohan Adhikari	Nov 30, 1994	Sept 12, 1995

Sher Bahadur Deuba (1/3)	Sept 12, 1995	March 12, 1997
Lokendra Bahadur Chand (3/4)	March 12, 1997	Oct 7, 1997
Surya Bahadur Thapa (4/5)	Oct 7, 1997	April 15, 1998
Girija Prasad Koirala (2/4)	April 15, 1998	May 31, 1999
Krishna Prasad Bhattarai (2/2)	May 31, 1999	March 22, 2000
Girija Prasad Koirala (3/4)	March 22, 2000	July 26, 2001
Sher Bahadur Deuba (2/3)	July 26, 2001	Oct 4, 2002
Direct rule by King Gyanendra Bir Bikram Shah Dev	Oct 4, 2002	Oct 11,2002
Lokendra Bahadur Chand (4/4)	Oct 11, 2002	June 5, 2003
Surya Bahadur Thapa (5/5)	June 5, 2003	June 3, 2004
Sher Bahadur Deuba (3/3)	June 3, 2004	Feb 1, 2005
Direct rule by King Gyanendra Bir Bikram Shah Dev	Feb1, 2005	April 25, 2006
Girija Prasad Koirala (4/4)	April 25, 2006	May 28, 2008

(***Source:*** Nepal Home page ,Govt. of Nepal. www.netfornepal.com.)

PRIME MINISTER OF THE FEDERAL DEMOCRATIC REPUBLIC OF NEPAL (2008 - PRESENT)

1.	Girija Prasad Koirala	May 28, 2008 - Aug 18, 2008
2.	Prachanda	Aug 18, 2008 - May 25, 2009
3.	Madhav Kumar Nepal	May 25, 2009-February 6, 2011
4.	Jhala Nath Khanal	February 6, 2011 - Aug 29, 2011
5.	Bahuram Bhattarai	August 29, 2011-Incumbent

THE BRITISH RESIDENTS IN NEPAL

1.	Captain Knox	1802 - 1803
2.	Lt. Boileu (Offg.)	1816
3.	E. Gardner	1816 - 29
4.	B.H.Hodgson (Offg.)	1829 - 31
5.	Sir H. Maddock	1831 - 33
6.	B.H. Hodgson	1833 - 43
7.	Major H. Lawrence	1843 - 46
8.	Lt. Col. C. Thoresby	1846-50
9.	J.C. Erskine	1850-52
10.	Lt. Col. G. Ramsay	1852-67
11.	Lt. Col. R.C. Lawrence	1865 - 72
12.	C.E.R. Girdlestone	1872 - 88
13.	F. Henvey	1877-88

14.	Lt. Col.E.C. Impey	1878
15.	Major F.A. Wilson	1883
16.	Col. I.C. Berkely	1885 - 86
17.	Major E.L. Durand	1888 - 91
18.	Major -Gen. H. Wylie	1891 - 99
19.	Lt. Col.W.H.C. Wylle	1898
20.	Lt. Col.A.M. Muir	1899
21.	Lt. Col.W. Loch	1899-01
22.	Lt. Col.T.C.Pears	1901-02
23.	Lt. Col.C.W Ravenshaw	1902-05
24.	Lt. Col. J.Manners Smith	1905-06
25.	Lt. Col. F.W.P.Macdonald	1908-09
26.	Lt. Col.H.L.Showers	1912-13
27.	Lt. Col.S. F. Baylay	1916-18.
28.	Lt. Col.W.F.T.O'Connor	1918-2
	Envoys	
29.	R. L. Kennion	1920-1921
30.	Lt. Col. W. F. T. O'Connor	1921-1924
31.	W. H. J. Wilkinson (officiating)	1924
32.	Lt. Col. W. F. T. O'Connor	1924-1925
33.	W. H. J. Wilkinson	1925-1929
34.	Col. Sir Clendon Daukes	1929-1934

(***Sources :*** Landon, Perceval, *Nepal.* Vol. II, Constable & Co. London, 1928 ; Mojumdar, Kanchanmoy, *Political Relations between India and Nepal.* Munshiram Manoharlal Publishers, (Delhi, 1973) ; British Embassy, Lainchour Kathmandu).

Regents

1.	Queen Rajendra Lakshmi Devi	1778-1785
2.	Bahadur Shah	1785-1795
3.	Queen Raj Rajeshwari Devi	1799-1800
4.	Queen Suvarna Prabha	1800-1803
5.	Queen Raj Rajeshwari Devi	1803-1804
6.	Queen Lalit Tripura Sundari	1806-1832

(***Source:*** Sen, Jahar, *Essays in Indo-Nepal Trade*, A Nineteenth Century study, K.P. Bagchi & Company, Calcutta, 1991.)

Bibliography

I. UNPUBLISHED MATERIALS

(A) Government Records, Documents, Secret Correspondence (English)

In the National Archives of India, New Delhi

Foreign Political Consultations, 1850-1935.
Foreign Political Proceedings, 1850-1935.
Foreign Secret Consultations, 1850-1935.
Foreign Secret Proceedings, 1850-1935.
Foreign Miscellaneous Proceedings, 1850-1935.
Foreign Department Proceedings, Revenue Branch, 1850-1935.
Foreign Department Proceedings, Revenue and Irrigation Branch, 1850-1935.
Foreign Department Proceedings, General Branch, 1850-1935.
Foreign Department Proceedings, External Branch, 1850-1935.
Foreign Department Proceedings, Secret E Branch.
Nepal Residency Records

In Uttar Pradesh State Archives, Allahabad

Pre-Mutiny Records of the Kumaun Collectorate, Letters Received and Issued; Political Letters Received and Issued.

In State Central Record Office, Patna

District Records of Champaran, Letters Received and Issued.
District Records of Purnea, Letters Received and Issued.
District Records of Bhagalpur.
District Records of Champaran.
English Records of the Patna Commissioner's Office.
Important Judicial Bundles, Alphabets N-P.

In West Bengal State Archives, Calcutta

Bengal Government Political Consultations.
Bengal Government Judicial (Criminal) Proceedings.
Bengal Government Mutiny Proceedings, 4 Vols.
India Office Copies of Political Proceedings, 3 Vols.
Letters to and from the Government of Bengal.

(B) Government Records, Documents, Secret Correspondence (Nepali)

Nepal Foreign Office Papers, Kathmandu
Nepal Government Records,Documents,Secret Correspondence from 1901-1947.

In the foreign office, Kathmandu

Letters from the Chinese Ambans in Tibet to the King of Nepal, V. S. 1872-73.

Secret Report from Major Raghubir Singh and Jamadar Mannu Singh to the King of Nepal, 1895, Sravan Sudi 15, Roj 1.

(C) Private Papers

Chelmsford Papers (Mss. Eur. E 264), Correspondence of Lord Chelmsford, Viceroy of India, 1916-21, with the Secretary of State, persons in India and England.

Cross Papers (Mss. Eur. E 243), Correspondence of Lord Cross, Secretary of State, 1886-92, with Lords Dufferin and Lansdowne.

Curzon Papers (Mss. Eur. Fill), Correspondence of Lord Curzon, Viceroy of India, 1899-1905, with the Secretary of State, persons in India and England.

Dufferin Papers (on Microfilm Nos. 510-18); Correspondence of Lord Dufferin, Viceroy of India, 1884-88 with the Secretary of State.

Durand Papers (uncatalogued until 1968), Correspondence of Sir Mortimer Durand, Secretary to Foreign Department, 1885-94, with Lords Dufferin and Lansdowne and with various other persons.

Elgin Papers (Mss. Eur. F 84), Correspondence of Lord Elgin II, Viceroy of India, 1894-99 with the Secretary of State.

Lansdowne Papers (Mss. Eur. D 558), Correspondence and Papers of Lord Lansdowne, Viceroy of India, 1888-94, with the Secretary of State; Selections rom his official. despatches, notes and minutes.

Lytton Papers (Mss. Eur. E 218), Correspondence and Papers of Lord Lytton, Viceroy of India, 1876-80, with the Secretary of State; notes and minutes.

Morley Papers (Mss. Eur. D 573), Correspondence of Lord Mor Ley, Secretary of State for India, 1905-10, with Lord Minto II, Viceroy of India.

White Papers (Mss. Eur. F 108), Correspondence and Papers of General Sir George White, Commander-in-Chief, India, 1893-98.

II. OFFICIAL PUBLICATIONS

(A) GOVERNMENT REPORTS

Annual Report on the Administration of the Bengal Presidency during 1860-1900.

Report on the Foreign Trade of North Western Provinces and Oudh During the Year 1877-78. N.W.R and Oudh Government, Allahabad, 1878.

Report on the Trade of the North Western Provinces and Oudh from 1879-85.

Annual Report on the Foreign Trade of the North Western Provinces and Oudh for the year ending 31 March 1880.

Report on the Administration of the North Western Provinces and Oudh for the year ending 31 March 1899, Allahabad, 1900.

Annual General Report on Nepal for the year 1906-07.

Administrative Report of the Patna Division for the year 1872-73.

The General/Administration Report of the Bhagalpur Division for the year 1881-82.

Annual General Report of the Patna Division for 1881-82.

Annual General Administration Report of the Patna Division for 1890-91.

Report on the External Trade of Bengal with Nepal, Sikkum, Bhutan and Tibet 1878-79 to 1913-14.

Baker, Henry D., Special Consular Report No.72, British India with Notes on Ceylon. Afganisthan, Tibet. Washington, 1915

(B) GOVERNMENT DOCUMENTS

Aitchison, C.U.: *A Collection of Treaties, Engagements and Sanads Relating to India and Neighbouring Countries,* 14 Vols., Central Publication Branch Calcutta, 1863, 1892, 1909, 1929, 1931.

Bhasin, A.S. (ed): *Documents on Nepal's Relations with India and China, 1949-66*, Academic Book Ltd., New Delhi, 1970.

British Ministry of Defence: Nepal and the Gurkha. London 1965.

Bose, E.C.: *Copies of Treaties between the East India Company and the Native Powers in Asia* (London 1812).

Ganguly, D.C.: *Select Documents of the British Period of Indian History* (In the Collection of the Victoria Memorial, Calcutta), (Calcutta, 1958).

Itihas Pattra Sangrah: Kathmandu. His Majesty's Government of Nepal, Ministry of Law and Justice: Sri 5 Surendra Bikram Shah Devakashasan Baneka Muluki Ain. (Legal Code enacted during the reign of King Surendra Bikram Shah Dev) Kathmandu 2022 V.S. (1965).

His Majesty's Government of Nepal and Asian Development Bank: *Nepal Agriculture Sector Strategy Study.* Vol. II. Kathmandu, December 1982.

Intelligence Branch Army Headquarters of India: *Frontier and Overseas Expedition from India.* (Volumes 7) reprint of 1857, ed. Delhi 1983.

Rajvamsi, Shankarman: Shamkalin Aitihasik Chittipatra Sangraha. (Collection of Documents of the Shah period) Vol. I. Department of Archaeology, Kathmandu, 2023 V.S. (1966).

(C) MEMORANDUM

Memorandum on some of the Results of Indian Administration: During the Fifty Years of British Rule in India. Calcutta 1911.

(D) GAZETTEERS, DICTIONARIES AND OTHER REFERENCE WORKS

Alexander, E. B. (ed.), *Gazetteer of the N. W. Provinces.* Vol. VI. Gorakhpur 1881.

Atkinson, E. T. (ed.), *Gazetteer of the N. W. Provinces,* Vol. VI. Allahabad 1881.

Bryne, J. (ed.), *Bengal District Gazetteer*. Bhagalpur, 1911.

Conybeare, H. C (ed.), *Gazetteer of the N. W. Provinces,* Vol. VI. 1881, Allahabad.

Dash, A. J., (ed.), *Bengal District Gazetteers,* Darjeeling, Alipur, 1947.

District Gazetteers of U.P., Gorakhpur Vol. XXXI.

Gazetteer of North Western Provinces 1881. Vol. VI.

Fisher, F. H. (ed.), *Gazetteer of N. W. Provinces,* Vol. XIII, 1883.

The Gazetter of India. Extraordinary, Part I, Section I, (Tuesday). August 17, 1971.

Gazetteer of the Provinces of Oudh, Lucknow 1877. Vol. I (A to G). Vol. II (H to M) 1877. Vol. III (N to Z) 1878.

Hamilton, Walter (ed.), *East India Gazetteer* London, 1815.

Hunter, W.W. (ed.), *A Statistical Account of Bengal, Tirhut and Champaran.* Vol. XIII, Trubner & Co., London, 1877.

Statistical Account of Bengal, Purnia Vol. XV., London, 1877.

Statistical Acçount of Bengal, Patna, and Saran. Vol. XI., London, 1877.

Imperial Gazetteer of India 1881, 1908

Statistical Account of Bengal, Bhagalpur. Vol. XV. Calcutta, 1877.

Imperial Gazetteer of India, Afghanistan and Nepal, Calcutta, 1908.

NevilL H.R. (ed.), *District Gazetteers of the United Provinces of Agra and Oudh.* Vol. VIII. Allahabad 1909.

District Gazetteers of the United Provinces, Basti. Vol. XXXII. Calcutta, 1907.

Northey W. Brook, *The Land of the Gurkhas*, John Lane, London, 1933.

O'Malley, L.S.S. (ed.), *Bengal District Gazetteers*, Champaran. Calcutta, 1907.

Bengal District Gazetteers, Muzaffarpur, Calcutta 1907.

Bihar and Orissa Gazetteers, District Champaran, Patna, Purnia, Darbhanga, Muzaffarpur, 1911, 1938.

Bengal, Bihar, Orissa and Sikkim, Delhi.

Rishley, H.H. (ed.), *The Gazetteers of Sikkim*, 1894.

Roy Chaudhury, P.C., *Bihar District Gazetteers,* Darbhanga, Patna 1964.

Bihar District Gazetteers, Champaran. Patna 1960.

III. BOOKS

ENGLISH

Abrol, Mridula, *British Relations with Frontier States* (1863-1873). S. Chand & Co., New Delhi 1974.

Acharya, Yagyanath, *An Outline History of Nèpal,* Ekta Book Narayan Prasad Upreti Publisher, Kathmandu (2039 V.S.) 1982.

Agrawal, Hem Narayan, *The Administrative System of Nepal, From Tradition to Modernity,* Vikas Publishers, New Delhi, 1976.

Alexander, McLiesh, *The Frontier People of India*, London 1931.

Banskota, N. P., *Indo-Nepal Trade and Economic Relations,* B.R. Publishing Co., Delhi, 1981.

Bhasin A.S. (ed), *Documents on Nepal's Relation with India and China* (1949-66). Academic Book Ltd. Bombay, 1970.

Bhattacharjee, G. P., *India and Politics of Modern Nepal*, Minerva Associates, Calcutta, 1970.

Bhattarai, Madan Kumar, *Diplomatic History of Nepal* (1901-1929), Royal Nepalese Embassy, New Delhi, 1990.

Bhoosan, B.S., *The Development Experience of Nepal,* Concept Publishing Co., New Delhi, 1979.

Bista, Dor Bahadur, *People of Nepal*, Ratna Pustak Bhandar, Kathmandu, 1980.

Blaikie, Piers; *Cameron, Nepal in Crisis: Growth and Stagnation* at John and Seddon, David Periphery, Oxford University Press, New Delhi, 1980.

Burathokey, J.B.S., "The Physical Aspects of the Kingdom of and Malla U.M. Nepal". Seminar Paper on the Ecology of the Tropical Highlands. Nepal National Commission for UNESCO, 1968.

Camman, Schuyler, *Trade Through the Himalaya, the Early British Attempt to open Tibet.* Princeton University Press, Princeton, New Jersey, 1951.

Campbell, A., *Notes on the Agriculture and Rural Economy of the Valley of Nepaul* Kathmandu, 1837.

Cavenagh, Orfeur, Rough Notes on the State of Nepal, Its Government, Army and Resources, W. Palmes, Calcutta, 1951.

The Nepalese Embassy, *Reminiscences of an Indian Official* W.H.Allen, London 1884.

Chakravarty, Haripada, *Trade and Commerce in Ancient India* C-100 B.C. to 650A.D., Calcutta,1966.

Chaudhary, K.C., *Anglo-Nepalese Relations from the Earliest Times of the British Rule in India till the Gorkha War,* Modern Book Agency Pvt. Ltd., Calcutta, 1960.

Coupland, R., *Britain and India,* 1600-1941, Longmans, Greens and Co.Ltd., London.

Dahal, Kishor, *Indo-Nepal Trade:Problems and Prospects,* Ratna Pustak Bhandar, Kathmandu, 1987.

Dhanalaxmi, Ravuri, *British Attitude to Nepal's Relations with Tibet and China 1814-1914.* Bahri Publications, New Delhi 1981.

Dharamdasani, *Indian Diplomacy in Nepal,* Aalekh Pub-Murlidhar lishing House, Jaipur, 1976.

Digby, William, 1857: *A Friend in Need, 1887, Friendship Forgotten. An episode in the Indian foreign office administration,* London, Indian Political Agency; 1890.

Diwakar, R.R., *Bihar Through the Ages,* Orient Murlidhar Longman, New Delhi, 1959.

Egerton Francis, *Journal of a Winter's Tour in India, with a visit to the court of Nepal,* Two Volumes, Vol. I, John Murray London, 1852.

Fairbank, J.K., *Trade and Diplomacy on the China Coast,* 2 Vols. Cambridge mass, 1953.

Furer-Haimendorf, Himalayan Traders : *Life in Highland Chistoph von* Nepal, London, 1975.

Gimalette, G.H.D., *Nepal and the Nepalese.* London, H.F. and G. Witherby, 1928.

Gopal, Surendra, *Patna in the 19th century* (A Socio-Cultural Profile), Naya Prokash, Calcutta, 1982.

Hamilton, C.J., *The Trade Relations between England and India (1600—1896),* Spink and Co., Calcutta, 1919 reprint Delhi. 1975.

Hamilton, Francis, *An Account of the Kingdom of Nepal,* and the territories annexed to the house of Gurkha, Archibold Constable & Co., Edinburgh, 1819.

Hammerton, J.A. (ed), *Tribes, Races and Culture of India & Neighbouring Countries.* 1856 reprint Delhi, 1984.

Hodgson, B.H., *Essay on the Languages, Literature and Religion of Nepal and Tibet,* philopress, Amsterdam, 1874, reprint Manjuri Publishing House, New Delhi, 1972.

Hunter, W.W., *Life of Brain Haughton Hodgson, British Resident at the Court of Nepal,* John Murray, London, 1896.

A Statistical Account of Bengal, Concept Publishing & Co., New Delhi, 1976.

The Indian Empire, Its People, History and Products. December 1892. reprint New Delhi, 1973.

Husain, Asad, *British India's Relations with the Kingdom of Nepal* 1857-1947. George Allen and Unwin Ltd., London 1970.

Indu Bala, *Compulsions of a Land-Locked State: A Study of Nepal-India Relations*. Batra Book Service, New Delhi, 2001.

Jain, Girilal, *India meets China in Nepal,* Asia Publishing House, Bombay, 1959.

Jain,M.S., *The Emergence of a New Aristocracy in Nepal* (1837-58), Sri Ram Mehra & Co., Agra, 1972.

Jha, B.K., *Indo –Nepalese Relations* (1951-1972), Vora Publisher, Bombay, 1973.

Jha, H.B., *Nepal-India Border Relations,* Centre for Economic and Technical Studies, 1995.

Jha, S.K., *Indo-Nepal Relations*, Archives Books, New Delhi, 1989.

Uneasy Partners: *India and Nepal in the Post Colonial Era*, Manas Publications New Delhi, 1975.

Kapoor, T.N., *Industrial Development in the States of India.* Sterling Publisher India, Delhi,1967.

Katti, Vijaya, *Indo-Nepal Trade: Post- WTO Dimension,* Kalinga Publications, Delhi, 2001.

Kirkpatrick, William, *An Account of the Kingdom of Nepaul* Being the substance of observations made during a mission to that country in the years 1793, Miller, London 1801, reprint Manjusri Publishers, New Delhi,1969.

Kuchhal, S.C, *The Industrial Economy of India,* Allahabad, 1965.

Kumar, Satish, *Rana Policy in Nepal : Origin and Growth*, Asia Publishing House, Bombay, 1967.

Lama, M.P., *The Economics of India -Nepalese Co-operation,* M. N. Publishers New Delhi, 1985.

Lamb, Alastiar, *Britain and Chinese Central Asia : The Road to Lhasa* 1767-1905. Routledge and Kegan Paul, London, 1960.

Landon, Perceval, *Nepal:* Vol. I & II.Constable & Co., London, 1928. Reprint Ratna Pustak Bhandar, Kathmandu, 1976.

Lohini, P.C., Industrial Policy : the Problem Child of History and Planning in Nepal, in Rana Pashupati Shamsher J.B. and Malla Kamal Prakash (eds), *Nepal in Perspective*. CEDA, Kathmandu, 1973.

Majumdar, B.P., *The Socio-Economic History of Northern India.* Calcutta, 1960.

Majumdar, Kanchanmoy, *Anglo-Nepalese Relations in the Nineteenth Century.* Firma K.L. Mukhopadhyay Calcutta, 1973.

Political Relations between India and Nepal. Munshiram Manoharlal Publishers Pvt. Ltd., New Delhi, 1973.

Majumdar, R.C, *The History and Culture of the Indian People*, Bhartiya Vidaya Bhawan, Bombay, 1962.

Markham R. Clement, *Narrative of the Mission of George Bogle to Tibet and of Journey of Thomas Manning in Tibet.* Trubner & Co. (2nd ed.), London, 1793.

Martin R. Montgomery, *The History, Antiquities, Topography and Statistic of Eastern India.* Vol. 2. reprint of 1838 ed. Cosmo Publications, Delhi, 1976.

Mehra. Parshotam, *The Younghusband Expedition,* Gyan Publishing House, Bombay, 2004.

Mihaly, E.B., *Foreign Aid and Politics in Nepal : A Case Study*, Oxford University Press, London, 1966.

Morris, C.J., *The Gurkhas : An Ethnology*, 1933. reprint B.R. Publishing Co, Delhi, 1985.

Muni, S.D., *India and Nepal, A Changing Relationship,* Konark Publishers, New Delhi, 1992.

Foreign Policy of Nepal, National Publishing House, Delhi, 1973.

Narayan, Shriman, *India and Nepal : An Exercise in Open Diplomacy,* Popular Prakashan, Bombay, 1970.

Nehru, Jawaharlal, *India's foreign policy, selected speeches,* September, 1946 -April, 1961. New Delhi : Publication Division, Government of India, 1961.

Speeches 1949-53, New Delhi: Publication Division, Government of India, Second Impression, 1957.

Oldfield, H. Ambrose, Sketchas from Nepal. Vol. II, London 1880, W.H. Allen & Co., reprint Delhi

O' malley, L.S.S (ed.), 1911, *Bengal District Gazatteer*, Purnea, 1974.

Pant, Y. P., *The Economics of Indo - Nepalese co-operation,* M.N. Publishers, Delhi,1985.

Pradhan, Radhey S., *Industrialization in Nepal,* NBO Publishers, Delhi,1984.

Premble, John, *The Invasion of Nepal*, Oxford, Oxford University Press 1971.

Ram Rahul, *Royal Nepal, A Political History,* Vikas Publishing House Pvt. Ltd. New Delhi, 1996.

Modern Nepal, Munshi Ram Manohar Lal Publishers Delhi.

Ramakant, *Indo-Nepalese Relations* 1816-1877. S. Chand & Co. New Delhi, 1968.

Nepal, China and India. Abhinav Publications, New Delhi, 1976.

Ramakant and Indian Community in Nepal, A Study of the, Upreti, B.C. Indian Migrants. in I.J. Bahadur (ed.) *Indians in South Asia*, South Asian Publishers, Delhi, 1984.

Ramakant and *Indo -Nepal relations*, Upreti, B.C. (ed) South Asian Publishers Pvt. Ltd, New Delhi, 1992.

Rana, Pashupatti, *Economic Development and Nepal in perspective.* J. B. and Shamsher Malla, Kamalin Prakash (eds) Centre for Administration, Kathmandu, 1972.

Rawat, P.C., *Indo-Nepal Economic Relations*. National Publishing House, New Delhi, 1974.

Regmi, D.R., *Ancient Nepal*, Firma, K.L. Mukhopadhyay (Third edition) Calcutta, 1969.

Ancient and Medieval Nepal. Prem Printing Press, Lucknow, 1952. Inscriptions of Ancient Nepal. New Delhi, 1983.

Modern Nepal. Firma K.L. Mukhopadhyay, Calcutta, 1960.

Regmi, M.C., *A Study in Nepalese Economic History* 1768-1846, Manjusri Publishing House, New Delhi, 1971.

Thatcted Huts and Stucco Palaces, *Peasants and Land-lords in19th Century* Nepal.Vikas Publisher; New Delhi, 1978.

The State and Economic Surplus; *Production, Trade, and Resource Mobilization in early 19th Century in Nepal.*Varanasi, 1984.

Reading in Nepal Economic History. Kishore Vidaya Niketan Varanasi, 1979.

Rose, Leo E., *Nepal Strategy for Survival.* Oxford University Press, Bombay, 1971.

Roy Choudhury, P.C., *Inside Bihar*, Bookland Private Limited, Calcutta, 1962.

Sanwal, B.D., *Nepal and the East India Company*, Asia Publishing House, Bombay, 1965.

Sarkar, Sutapa , *India-Nepal Relations,* (1960-91), Minerva Associates, Calcutta 1993.

Seemann, Heinrich, *Nepal, 2031-Till Yesterday, A Forbidden Country,* Arnold- Heinemann Publishers, Delhi, 1978.

Sen, Jahar, *Indo-Nepal Trade in the Nineteenth Century.* Firma KLM Pvt. Ltd., Calcutta, 977.

Essaysin Indo-Nepal Trade: A Nineteenth Century Study. K.P. Bagchi & Co., Calcutta, 1991.

Shah, Ali Ikbal, *Nepal: The Home of the Gods;* London, n.d.

Shah, K.T., *Trade, Tariffs and Transport in India.* National Books, Bombay, 1923.

Shaha, Rishikesh, *An Introduction to Nepal.* Ratna Pustak Bhandar Kathmandu, 1975.

Essay in the Practice of Government in Nepal. Manohar Publisher; Delhi 1982.

Sharan, P., *Government and Politics of Nepal,* Metropolitan Book Co. Pvt. Ltd., New Delhi, 1983.

Shrestha, B.P., *An Introduction to Nepalese Economy,* Ratna Pustak Bhandar, Kathmandu, 1974

Shrestha, Chandra B, Physical Setting and Natural Resources, and Sharma Availability and Prospect, *Nepals Economy -An Overview.* Centre for Economic Development and Administration, Tribhuvun University, Kirtipur. Kathmandu, Aptil 1980.

Shrestha, Devi, *Mabarg Niwaran* (Price Control Measure).

Chandra (ed), *Kathmandu* (V.S. 2030), 1973.

Shreshtha, Saranhari, *Modern Geography of Nepal*, Kathmandu 1972.

Shrestha, Sita, *Nepal and the United Nation's,* Sindhu Publications New Delhi, 1974.

Sinha, N.K. (ed), *The History of Bengal 1757-1908.* Calcutta University Press, Calcutta, 1967.

Economic History of Bengal, Vol. I Calcutta, Firma KLM Pvt. Ltd.,1965.

Singh, I.J. Bahadur (ed) , *Indians in South Asia*, South Asian Publishers, Delhi, 1984.

Singh, Kirtyanand, Small Neighbours of Big Powers : *India's Attitude Towards Nepal, (1946-1963)*, Capital Publishing House, Delhi, 1988.

Srivastava, S.N., *Harijans in India.* Lucknow, 1980.

Stiller, Ludwig F. S.J, *The Rise of the House of Gorkha : A Study in the Unification of Nepal 1768-1816,* Manjusri Publications New Delhi, 1973.

Ptithvinarayan Shah, in the Light of Dibya Updesh, Kathmandu, 1968.

Timberg, Thomas A., *The Marwaris: From Traders to Industralists,* Vikas Publishers, New Delhi, 1978.

Tuker, Sir Francis, Gorkha : The Story of the Gurkhas of Nepal, constable and Co, London, 1957.

Turner, Captain Samuel, *An Account of an Embassy to the Court of the Teshoo Lama in Tibet.* W. Bulmer amd Co. London, 1800. Reprint Manjusri Publication, Delhi, 1971.

Tyagi, Shushila, *Indo-Nepalese Relation 1858-1914.* D.K. Publishing House, Delhi, 1972.

Upadhyaya, Shreeram, Prasad, *Indo-Nepal Trade Relations: A Historical Analysis of Nepal's Trade with the British India*, Nirala Publication, Jaipur, 1992.

Uprety, Prem R., *Nepal Tibet Relations 1850-1930 : Year of Hopes, Challenges and Frustrations.* Commonwealth Publishers Kathmandu 1980.

Vansittart, Lt. Col. Eden., *The Gurkhas.* 1890 reprint, Delhi, 1980.

Vansittart, Eden, *Gurkhas,* Superitendent of Goverment printing 1915, Calcutta.

Walse, E.H., *The Coinage of Nepal,* Delhi, 1973.

Wright, D (ed), 1877, *History of Nepal*, Cambridge University Press, reprint, Calcutta, Ranjan Gupta, 1966.

Wright, Daniel , *Nepal : History of the Country and People,* Cambridge University Press, 1877, reprint, Delhi, 1983.

Hindi

Acharya Babu Ram, *Rajender Vikaram Shah ko Shasan*, Purnima Vol.27, Kathmandu, 1977.

Nepali Chittaranjan, *General Bhimsen Thapa Ka Tatkalin Nepal.* Kathmandu (2013 V.S.), 1956.

Sharma, Balchandra, *Nepal Ka Aitihasik Rup Rekha.* Banaras, 1976.

Singh, Shiv Bahadur, *Nepal Shasan Avam Rajniti,* Ganga Saran & Grand Sons, Varanasi, 2000.

Upadhya, Ramji , *Nepal ko Itihas arthat Digdarshan,* Subba Homnath Kedarnath, Banaras, 1950.

IV. Research Papers and Articles

Acharya, Baburam, *Rajendra Vikram Shah Ko Shasan* (Role of Rajendra Vikram Shah). Purnima. Vol. 27 Kathmandu, 1972.

Acharya Harihar, "Uttari Sima Vyapar" (Northern Frontier Trade). Gorkhapatra 5 May 1980.

Adhikari Krishana Kant, "A Brief Survey of Nepal's Trade with British India During the latter Half of the Nineteenth Century" *Contribution to Nepalese Studies.* Vol. 2, No. 1. February 1975.

Bhaduri, "Bagchi-Levi in Nepal: A Glimpse of Rana Rule in the Early Twenties" *Calcutta Review* Vol. CLXIV, 1 July 1962.

Gurung, Hark, "Geographic Foundations of Nepal" *The Himalayan Review.* Nepal Geographic Society, Kathmandu. 1968.

Hodgson, Brain H., "On the Native Method of Making the Paper, denominated in Hindusthan. Nipaleso". *Journal of Asiatic Society of Bengal.* Vol. I, No. 1. January 1832.

Jha, S.K., "British India's Policy towards Nepal." *Journal of Bihar-Research Society.* Vol. IV, Pts 1-4.

Kachikian, Levon., "The Ledger of the Merchant Hovhannes Joughyetri." *Journal of Asiatic Society.* Vol. VIII, No. 3, Calcutta 1966.

Katti, Vijay., "Commodity and Geographic concentration in Indo-Nepalese Trade", *Foreign Trade Review.* (18) October-December 1983.

Majumdar, Kanchanmoy.: "British Impact on Nepal" Bengal Past and Present. January-June. 1971.

Manandhar, Triratna, "Rana Kalin Parcha Estihar". Voice of History. *Journal of History Instruction Committee.* Vol. II, Kathmandu 1976.

Nepal, Gyanmani., "Nepal Ka Dhan Videshi Bank ma". (Nepal's wealth in Foreign Bank). Arthik Nepal (Ed.) Devi Chandra Shrestha. Kathmandu, November 1982.

Northey W. Brook, "Nepal". *The Geographical Journal* Vol. and Bruce C.G.LXV No. 4. April 1925.

Sen, Jahar, The Tune of Timber in Indo-Nepal Relations *Calcutta, Historical Journal* Vol. VII No. 1, July-December 1992.

"Slave Trade on the Indo-Nepal Border in the Nineteenth-Century" *Kailash,* Kathmandu, January-February, 1973.

Shamsher, Barun (ed), "From the Himalayan Height" *Nepal Guardian* Kathmandu, n.d.

Shrestha, "Brahmadeo-Mandi" *Arthik Nepal.* Vol. 1.

Devi Chandra (ed), No. 3, *Kathmandu,* June 1983.

Stiller, S.J Ludwig F., "A Note on Himalyan Trade" *Journal of Tribhuvan University*. Vol. VII, No.1.

November 1972., "Currency confusion" *Journal of Tribhuvan University,* Vol.VIII, No.1 November, 1973.

V. Unpublished Ph.D Theses

Adhikari K.K., "Nepal under Jang Bahadur 1846-1877" University of Nagpur, 1974.

Ansari M.H., "Nepal in World Affairs" Vikram University. Ujjain.1974.

Husain Asad, "British India's Relations with Kingdom of Nepal from1857 to 1947". University of Minnesota. 1965.

Kumar, Satish. "Political System of Nepal under the Ranas 1845-1901". New Delhi: Indian School of International Studies, 1961.

Majumdar, Kanchanmoy., "Indo-Nepalese Relations, 1837-1877." New Delhi: Indian School of International Studies, 1962.

Sharma, N., "Nepal Foreign Trade" University of Delhi, 1968.

Index

C

D

O

P

R

S